# THE PEELITES AND THE
# PARTY SYSTEM 1846–52

General Editor Michael Hurst

*Church Embattled: Religious Controversy in Mid-Victorian England* by M. A. Crowther

*The Politics of Government Growth: Early Victorian Attitudes Toward State Intervention 1833–1848* by William C. Lubenow

# THE PEELITES AND THE PARTY SYSTEM 1846–52

J. B. Conacher

DAVID & CHARLES
ARCHON BOOKS 1972

This edition first published in 1972 in Great Britain
by David & Charles (Publishers), Newton Abbot, Devon,
and in the United States
by Archon Books, Hamden, Connecticut 06514
ISBN 0 7153 5411 6
ISBN 0 208 01268 0

Set in eleven on twelve point Imprint
and printed in Great Britain
by Latimer Trend & Company Limited Plymouth

# Contents

# Preface

THE PEELITES are surely one of the most interesting and significant splinter groups in the history of British party politics. They represented the cream of the Conservative party that had been rebuilt so laboriously under Peel's leadership in the years following the debacle of 1832, and yet in the end most of the survivors were absorbed into the Liberal party. There were three stages in this process. This book deals with the first and most intriguing period from the resignation of Peel in June 1846 to the formation of the Aberdeen coalition in December 1852. During these years the Peelites constituted an independent force in British party politics, a force of great potential but hamstrung by Peel's refusal to give it any lead in the crucial years following 1846. The second stage was that of the coalition of 1852–5 (which I dealt with in my *Aberdeen Coalition*). The third stage (which I hope to treat in a later volume) covers the years from the break-up of the coalition in 1855 to its reformation under Palmerston in 1859. It is the most obscure, since in the years 1855–9 the Peelites were no longer the identifiable and effective political group that they were, at least potentially, in the years 1846–52. In this book I have tried to identify them more precisely than has previously been done and to show more clearly the influence they exerted on the political situation during the years of the Russell and Derby ministries.

There are many approaches to the writing of history and in my view the narrative approach, which I have followed in this volume, while less fashionable today than it used to be, is still a legitimate one. The task of the narrative historian is in large part the selection and presentation of the evidence. To a great extent the facts if properly presented can speak for themselves and if the historian belabours his point too much by way of explanation he underrates the reader's intelligence. I am not denying the his-

7

torian all right of comment, but I am suggesting that it is possible for him to write this sort of history and keep himself in the background, indicating his point of view by the discreet choice of adjectives and, where appropriate, some economic presentation of his conclusions. The narrative historian is concerned, as are all historians, with explaining what happened in the past, but he is also telling a story for its own intrinsic interest, just as the biographer, the novelist or the journalist does. The sophisticated reader wants to know why it happened as it did, but it is also legitimate to satisfy his curiosity as to how it happened.

J. B. Conacher

# Chapter 1 PEEL AND THE PEELITES
## Out of Office 1846-50

The Session of 1845 was the last of those that witnessed party connection in its normal state. Throughout the decade which preceded that year it had been in full and brilliant blossom. Since then we have had properly speaking no parties: that is none in the best sense of the term: none compact and organized after the ancient manner. . . .

On each side of the House of Commons was to be seen from 1835 onwards a large and unbroken phalanx, every man of which was united to his leaders and his comrades not only by the firmest political ties but in most cases by sentiments of personal respect and confidence. . . .

FEW HISTORIANS today are likely to find the above lines a convincing description of political parties in the decade preceding 1845, and yet they are taken from a paper written in 1855 by a prominent statesman who had been a member of the House of Commons for more than twenty years and a Cabinet Minister for more than four.[1] Gladstone was undoubtedly using the politician's licence to exaggerate in making his point, but even when the necessary reservations are made his statements are a useful warning to those who would extend the Namier view of party too far into the nineteenth century. Indeed to judge from the press opinion of the time there was nothing very surprising to contemporary ears in Gladstone's view of party; for some years papers such as *The Times*, the *Spectator* and *The Economist* had welcomed its decline. For instance the *Spectator* (28 February 1846) observed that no real issues divided the two main parties as in the days before 1832 and *The Economist* (9 January 1847) announced that parties were 'dissolved' and looked forward to the millennium when all statesmen 'without regard to personal and party views' acted 'only on the broad principles established by political science'. Gladstone had a better grasp of the significance of political parties and wrote to deplore not to welcome their decline. It is difficult to say when political parties in the modern sense first emerged. There were Whig and Tory traditions, but no such political entities as *the* Whig or *the* Tory party at the accession of George III; any man who seriously sought office called himself a Whig. Seventy years later, however, following the accession of William IV, an administration that was known as Tory and did not reject the name was replaced by one that was predominantly Whig. All the Whigs now crossed the floor to sit on the Government benches while most of the Tories crossed to the Opposition side. The Canningite Tories provided some talented members to the new government's front bench, but their numbers on the back benches were few. By this time the great majority of members appear to have accepted either the Government or the Opposition whips and to have called themselves either Whigs or Tories, or, before long, Liberals or Conservatives, names more acceptable to the new electorate. Some Radicals of course never accepted the name Whig, although accepting the Whig whips.

The Whigs, who were in office for the greater part of the 1830s were, however, scarcely the solid body that Gladstone recalled twenty years later. They survived the loss of Stanley and Graham, who failed to bring many followers with them, but they were always in difficulties with their long Radical tail, made up of Irish Repealers, Benthamite or Philosophical Radicals, and later the men of the Manchester School, not to mention other independent Radicals defying definition.

During the thirties the Tories, chastened by three electoral defeats in 1830, 1831 and 1832, each worse than the preceding one, were putting their house in order under the level-headed leadership of Peel, assisted by his indispensable party agent, Philip Bonham.[2] Not all Tories were pleased with the terms of the Tamworth Manifesto or the adoption of the name Conservative and there was some inevitable plotting against Peel's leadership, but probably no party leader had ever been in a stronger position than Sir Robert when he won the election of 1841. In the paper already quoted Gladstone attests to the remarkable unity both in the cabinet and in the party during Peel's great ministry, although there was some agitation occasioned by particular measures. He recognised that there was 'on the horizon a cloud, though one no bigger than a man's hand' in the person of Mr Benjamin Disraeli and 'some two or three members of the party who had emerged with just enough notoriety to attract to themselves the nickname of Young England', but in Gladstone's view 'they aimed their puny weapons at Sir R. Peel as Lilliputians might at Gulliver'. Indeed Gladstone goes so far as to say: 'the numerical and on the whole the moral strength of the party was still entire: it bore without a rent even the act for the better endowment of Maynooth: the Session of 1845 closed like the calmest of summer sunsets. . . .'[3]

Gladstone was a loyal and devoted follower of Peel and, despite some differences with him after 1845, his real political heir. He wrote these lines while still in active politics and probably with a view to their possible publication. He was perhaps incapable of seeing that the Protectionist party's aversion to Peel's policies, both fiscal and religious, had not come into being full grown but was germinating below the surface even in the years when Peel's leadership of the party seemed unchallenged. Explosions such as that which occurred in the Conservative party in 1846 do not come completely out of the blue.

On the other hand it must be realised that in a two-party system of government each party, although held together by some common traditions and principles, is bound to be something of a coalition of sub-groups and subject to various tensions. It is the responsibility of the party leadership to resolve these tensions before the explosion point is reached. The Conservative party of the eighteen-thirties and forties was actually a more homogeneous body than the Whig-Liberal party despite the signs of rifts that preceded the Corn Law crisis of 1846. Both parties were still dominated by leaders drawn from the landed classes, but in the half-century following the outbreak of the French Revolution the bulk of that class looked to the party of Pitt and Liverpool, to which Peel had fallen heir, as being the safer party of the two. Aristocratic Whig landowners were a little more adventuresome and thought they could combine slightly more advanced political views and an uneasy alliance with middle-class Radicals without endangering the position of their class. The more intelligent and enlightened members of the landed classes in both parties recognised some of the implications of the industrial revolution, in particular the desirability of promoting the interests of the manufacturing and commercial classes if the nation was to thrive. No one realised this more than Peel and his close colleagues in the great budgets of 1842 and 1845. Indeed from Pitt through Liverpool and Huskisson the Tory party had done more for the economic prosperity of the country than the aristocratic Whigs.

Gladstone undoubtedly exaggerated the unity in the party prior to 1846, but the history of all parties is full of backbench discontent with party leadership. Peel clearly fanned the flames by his brusque and imperious manner towards the rank and file of his followers and to a certain extent invited the treatment that he got in 1846. In a statistical study of the Conservative party in the parliament of 1841–7 Professor W. O. Aydelotte has shown that the breach between Protectionists and Free Traders (whom he calls Peelites) can be foreseen in the earlier years of the parliament, but that it becomes much more pronounced after 1844. The most serious challenge, of course, came in 1845 when only 134 Conservatives supported the third reading of the Government's Maynooth Bill while it was opposed by 137 of whom 119 were future Protectionists. The difference between this and the rebellion of the following year, however, apart from numbers, lay in the lack of leadership. There was no break in the cabinet and Stanley loyally supported it in the Lords, as did Bentinck in the Commons. Disraeli contented himself with a long derisive speech and a negative vote aimed more against the ministers than the measure, which was only passed thanks to Liberal support. In short, the rebellion was simply on the particular measure—as was the case with the Canada Wheat Bill in 1843, against which 41 Conservatives voted (all of them future Protectionists), and the Ten Hour clause of 1844, when 87 Conservatives deserted the Government (62 of them future Protectionists)—and it was not sustained after the particular vote.[4]

The situation was quite different in 1846 when a Protectionist party rapidly came into being in the House of Commons after Peel's introduction of his Bill at the end of January, with Lord George Bentinck drafted as its reluctant but determined leader.[5] More than two thirds of the Conservative party sided with the rebels, but the passage of the Bill was ensured by the support of the Liberal Opposition. The Protectionist leadership, however, was determined to press the fight against Peel and turn him out of office. Opposition to an Irish Coercion Bill was not the most obvious measure on which to rally right-wing Conservatives, and only 74 of the 241 Protectionists actually voted against the Government while another 51 abstained, but this was sufficient to turn the balance in favour of the Liberal Opposition. The vote brought Peel's ministry to an end, but it also signalised the weakness of the Protectionists as a party when less than a third of their total number were prepared to participate in the final act of rebellion. As Professor Aydelotte has demonstrated conclusively, Disraeli's famous passage in his *Life of Lord George Bentinck* about the overwhelming repudiation of Peel by the great county families is largely a myth. Moreover there was no substantial difference between the proportion of landed and non-landed rebels; that is to say 69 per cent of the landed Conservatives were opposed to repeal and 60 per cent of the non-landed. The one obvious difference between the Protectionist and Free Trade Conservatives, as Professor Aydelotte has remarked, was the very much higher proportion of the latter with experience in office.[6]

The majority of the party were probably still anxious for reconciliation, but Peel was too proud to make any attempt to court the rebels and the Protectionist leaders in the Commons were determined on war to the knife. Two members of Peel's cabinet tried to effect a reunion, the one just before, the other shortly after the fall of the Government, but each suffered a severe rebuff. Lord Ellenborough, who had only come into the cabinet when it was reconstituted in December and who was probably one of the ministers least sympathetic to Peel, wrote to him on 29 May arguing that it was impossible for the Government to remain in office after the passage of the Corn Bill and the Tariff Bill and urging the necessity of a Conservative reunion. He deprecated 'the admission of the Whigs to office as a preliminary to such a reunion' and, citing the scarcely happy precedent of the Addington ministry, suggested that Peel should resign the day the two Bills passed with 'the declaration that every possible aid' would 'be afforded to the construction of a Conservative Government'.[7] Peel's reply was flattening and unequivocal. He said he did not believe in making any prior decision about resignation and went on:

> But I could not be a party to the course which you advise—consequent on Resignation.
>
> In the first place I think the Queen ought in the event you suppose to have a perfectly unfettered choice in respect to those whom she might be disposed to select for her confidence. . . .
>
> Secondly a Conservative Government to be formed on the retirement of the present Government, must be I presume a Government formed on the principle of Protection to domestic Industry—or some analogous principle.
>
> I certainly could *not advise* the Queen to form an administration on that principle.[8]

A few weeks later Lord Lyndhurst attempted to bring both wings of the Conservative party together against Russell's Sugar Bill, but got short shrift from both sides. Bentinck denounced this intrigue of 'the meddling ex-chancellor', while Peel coldly declined to be 'any party to the proceeding' and required Lyndhurst to read his letter of repudiation in the House of Lords.[9] It may be noted that Peel's attitude drove Ellenborough almost immediately and Lyndhurst eventually into the arms of Lord Stanley.[10]

The year 1846 forms a watershed in the political history of nineteenth-century Britain, second only to that of 1832, for no issue aroused greater political passions between the passing of the great Reform Act of 1832 and the defeat of the first Irish Home Rule Bill a little more than half a century later. The most enlightened element in the Conservative party was permanently separated from the main body and in the long run the Liberal party was to benefit from the fusion of the surviving Peelite Free Traders in its ranks. Gladstonian liberalism was to be the child of this marriage.

In 1846 all this, of course, was hidden from view. When Peel's ministry fell, probably the majority of his Free Trade followers expected eventual reconciliation in one way or another with the Protectionist Tories who had broken with them on the Corn Law issue. Many of them, however, were less ready to accept the leadership of the renegade trio of Stanley, Bentinck and Disraeli.

Nevertheless as the years went by the leadership of Stanley (who became Lord Derby in 1852) and Disraeli (who was left supreme in the Commons after the resignation and subsequent death of Bentinck in 1848) became entrenched and the likelihood of Peel's lieutenants accepting office under them remote. Thus a distinction may be made between those who had held office under Peel in company with a number of members who still instinctively looked to Peel and his lieutenants for leadership on the one hand, and the rest of the back-bench Conservative Free Traders on the other. The latter, who had given support to repeal mainly out of loyalty to Peel and the party, might gradually slip back into their old places on the assumption that Protection was dead, although making wry faces at the new leadership. Genuine Peelites, however, men imbued with his ideas of fiscal reform and administrative efficiency and personally devoted to Peel and his name, were less likely to retrace their steps. As long as they remained independent after 1846 the natural evolution of the parliamentary two-party system was thwarted.

Sir Robert Peel's official career had come to an end with his resignation in June 1846 and only four years of life remained to him; the party that he had once led from disastrous defeat to victory now lay shattered by his act in repudiating the Corn Laws. Yet throughout the years from 1846 to 1850 he dominated Parliament in a unique fashion for a man holding no official position and leading no recognised party. The future of both the major political parties and of his own followers, the so-called Peelites, depended in large measure on the course he chose to take. Indeed it may be said that during these years, and even from his grave after his death, he kept the party system in a state of suspended animation.[11] Our immediate task, therefore, must be to examine Peel's course during these twilight years of his life and in particular his relations with his former followers.

One hundred and seven Conservatives, including the two tellers, voted for the third reading of the Corn Law Bill on 15 May.[12] To these we may add ten others who missed the third reading, but supported one or more earlier readings, seven of whom were paired in favour of the third reading,[13] and two other avowed Free Traders elected later in 1846,[14] making a total of 119 Free Trade Conservatives. Four of these voted against the

Coercion Bill on 25 June, but it may be presumed that they voted on the merits of the case and not to support Bentinck against Peel, as was the case with most of the rebellious Protectionists.[15] There were therefore approximately 119 Free Trade Conservatives in 1846–7, who might have been organised into a party had their leader so chosen. It would be premature to call them all Peelites, however, for it remained to be seen how many of them would continue to follow his lead when he ceased to demand their allegiance as a party leader.

The strength and significance of this group lay in their quality rather than in their numbers. Of the fifteen members of Peel's reconstituted cabinet (including Lord Lincoln who left in February 1846 to become Irish Secretary), Lord Ellenborough was the only one ever again to take office in a Conservative administration. Five other peers, Buccleuch, Haddington, Lyndhurst, Ripon and Wellington, took no further political office, but Lyndhurst eventually allied himself with the Protectionists; the Duke of Wellington of course remained Commander-in-Chief until his death in 1852. Lord Granville Somerset, who was a member of the Commons, was re-elected in 1847, but died the year after. The eight members who remained actively involved in politics may be divided into two distinct groups, a generation apart in age: Lord Aberdeen (born 1784), Henry Goulburn (1784), Sir Robert Peel (1788) and Sir James Graham (1792) with their careers mainly behind them; W. E. Gladstone (1809), Sidney Herbert (1810), Lord Lincoln (1811) and Lord Dalhousie (1812) still men of promise for the future. To this younger group we may add John (shortly Sir John) Young (1807), Peel's chief whip, Lord Canning (1812) and Edward Cardwell (1813), who had held offices outside the cabinet. It is interesting to note that these seven younger Peelites, all destined to hold high office again at home or overseas, were born within a period of seven years and attended the same university, Oxford, and five[16] of them, indeed, the same college, Christ Church. Thus most of them knew each other before entering parliament and in some cases had already formed close friendships. Of the other officeholders outside the cabinet Lord St Germans, H. B. Baring, Sir George Clerk and J. A. S. Wortley remained active Peelites, but Sir Francis Thesiger and Sir Fitzroy Kelly, who had both held legal appointments under Peel, eventually accepted office from Lord Derby.[17]

These Peelite leaders were men who shared a number of characteristics in common. They were all men of proven, in some cases exceptional, ability, high moral integrity and a marked seriousness of purpose; most, if not all of them, were strongly committed members of the Church of England, three of them, Gladstone, Herbert and to a lesser extent Lincoln, ardent high churchmen. Then, too, they were all men who shared Peel's approach to government, who had no difficulty in subscribing to the principles of the Tamworth manifesto and who were proud of the achievement of Peel's government in which they had shared in the years 1841–6. Like Peel they had changed their minds about the Corn Laws as the result of events and were satisfied that in 1846 repeal was in the best interests of the nation. They deeply resented what they regarded as vicious attacks made on Peel by Bentinck and Disraeli to the obvious delight of many of the Protectionist rebels. The term Liberal Conservative described them accurately, since they were all natural conservatives taking for granted that the existing structure of society and the existing institutions were most desirable. They were intelligent enough, however, to see that the system must be made to work justly and efficiently if it was to be acceptable to the whole community. This outlook and these views were not shared by all the 119 Free Trade Conservatives, and the term Peelite is best reserved for those who did share them. Their number in 1846 was still indeterminate.

Such, then, were the men in whose loyalty Peel might well have taken pride, but his strongest feeling seems to have been one of chagrin and resentment against the hostile Protectionist majority of the Conservative party who had rebelled against him. When release finally came in the summer of 1846 the reaction was great and one can detect from his correspondence with close friends how glad he was to get away from the burden of office and the responsibility of party leadership and to enjoy the domestic pleasures of Drayton Manor. 'I do not know how other men are constituted,' he wrote to his friend Lord Aberdeen, 'but I can say with truth that I find the day too short—for my present occupations which chiefly consist of lounging in my library, directing

B

improvement, riding with two dogs and my daughter—and pitying Lord John and his colleagues.'[18]

Gladstone, in the unpublished paper already quoted, was critical of Peel for his initial over-confidence and for his later defeatism. 'And when', he wrote, 'in the midst of the struggle, he [Peel] came to feel its real intensity, he seems in his own mind to have substituted indifference about the destruction of the party which was so eminently HIS, for his previous excess of confidence in its being preserved.' He admitted that there had been great provocation, but, he asked, had Peel not also given it? 'Had he not, when he announced in February his change of opinion . . ., shown too much of the front of Pride?'[19]

'It might have been in his power to make some provision for the holding together, or for the reconstruction, of that great Party which he has reared,' Gladstone argued, '. . . But although that party was the great work of so many years of his matured life, his thought seemed simply to be "It has fallen; there let it be". A greater idea still had overshadowed it, the idea of his Country, *now* become the Stewardess of the inheritance of his fame.'[20] He criticised Peel's decision to stay in the House of Commons when he was resolved never to return to office, observing rather ponderously that 'Prime Ministers unattached are dangerous: as great rafts would be dangerous floating unmoored in a harbour; . . . the position of Sir Robert Peel for the last four years of his life', Gladstone harshly concluded, 'was a thoroughly false position'.[21]

During the few weeks in July and August in which the new government wound up the business of the session, there were certain decisions that Peel could not avoid making. First of all there was the matter of seating arrangements in the House of Commons, always a matter of significance in time of party flux. Here Peel could not avoid showing his hand. When the House reassembled in the summer of 1846 after the formation of the Russell government he resumed his old place on the front Opposition bench. Where else could the outgoing prime minister sit? But the party position in the House at this juncture was quite extraordinary. The final great achievement of the Peel ministry had been the result of a tacit alliance between Peel and Russell, and the defence of that achievement in the years to come would

require the continuance of that alliance. Yet Peel had been overthrown by joint action between the Protectionists and the
Liberals, and for some time many Peelites suspected a secret
understanding between the 'two noble lords' (John and George).
Some substance was given to this suspicion by Bentinck's decision to remain on the Government benches when the administration changed, with the ironical result that the Liberal tail,
Radicals, and Repealers, had to join the Peelites on the Opposition
benches. This was an anomalous situation, and at the beginning
of the session of 1847, after discussion between Bentinck and the
Treasury Bench, the Protectionists crossed to the Opposition
benches,[22] which they shared with the Free Trade Conservatives
for the next five years. Young described the result in a letter to
Peel who was temporarily absent from the House. 'The Country
Party', he wrote, 'take from the gangway up to the red box, and
we have hitherto occupied the remainder of the places along the
table up to the Speaker's chair.'[23] Lincoln added more detail:

> The Protectionist leaders have attempted no further encroach-
> ments, neither Lord G. Bentink nor Mr. D'Israeli having come
> above the red box though they are generally flanked on that wing
> by Mr. Bankes and Mr. Christopher or both. We have continued
> to occupy the places we took the first night, and the *buffers* of the
> two parties have been the not very thickly wadded forms of Mr.
> Goulburn and Mr. Bankes. Young, Cardwell, and G. Hope have
> however occasionally thrown out pickets into the enemy's camp
> and upon the whole I think our left wing is generally better
> defended than it was on Tuesday. Graham continues to sit under
> the post . . . and upon the whole tho' there is an obvious absurdity
> in it I should be sorry to see him *now* change it. He evidently had
> made up his mind to go there from the first and he is much too
> long headed not to have had a reason for the decision. I confess
> however I should be very sorry to see *you* anywhere but on the
> front bench and I do not think that you will find your seat there
> at all inconvenient—you can always have 3 or 4 friends to your
> left and the benches immediately behind are never occupied by
> the hostile forces.[24]

Gladstone took a very different view from that of his friend
Lincoln of Peel's occupancy of this place on the front bench.
'This was a mistake', he wrote; '. . . no man should under any

circumstances hold that seat to which he clung, while intending to give to the administration . . . systematic support.'[25]

With two exceptions, it may be noted, Peelites and Protectionists continued to rub shoulders at the Carlton Club. According to Cardwell some amusement was occasioned there by the fact that the only two members who saw fit to withdraw their names as a result of the events of 1846 were Sir James Graham and Colonel Sibthorp.[26]

During the last six weeks of the session of 1846 after the Russell ministry took office one Bill was introduced that caused Peel some embarrassment. The Whigs proposed to extend Free Trade by greatly reducing the prohibitory duty on slave-grown sugar, a measure which had the advantage of substantially reducing the price of sugar, one of the few luxuries of the poor, and increasing the revenue as a result of the increased importation of the commodity that would result. Had Peel remained in office he had intended merely to reduce the duty on free-grown sugar, which would not have produced any substantial increase in the amount made available. He now had to listen to the anti-slave-trade argument made by Lord George Bentinck, with which he claimed to sympathise, but he announced that he was going to support the Government, since he was not prepared to turn it out of office six weeks after it had been formed.[27] (The Liberals argued that the slavery argument was an insincere one since no one objected to the importation of slave-grown cotton.) Lord George Bentinck's amendment to Russell's motion was defeated, 265 to 135 with 39 pairs; forty-nine Free Trade Conservatives supported the Government (including nine members of Peel's administration who had seats in the Commons), but ten voted against it (while a dozen Protectionists deserted Bentinck and many more stayed away).[28] The issue of slave- versus free-grown sugar was to be a divisive one among the ranks of the Free Trade Conservatives for some years to come.

The Protectionists in the meantime remained disorganised and divided in counsel and consequently ineffective.[29] The ability of the historian to look back on the past, aware of what subsequently happened, has its disadvantages. We know that in time the Protectionists, or Derbyites, made good their claim to be the Conservative party and that the loyal friends of Peel eventually disappeared as a separate political entity. That this would happen was by no means clear, however, in 1847, despite Peel's refusal to give his followers a lead. The front-bench Protectionists, with the exception of Disraeli, cut a poor figure in the House and to many Conservatives Bentinck proved an embarrassment as a leader. This was well illustrated by Young's description of a curious scene that occurred in the House one evening early in the session when Peel happened to be away.

> Lord George Bentinck [he wrote] made a furious onslaught on the Government . . . his voice was raised to screaming pitch—his eye gleamed like a wild animal at feeding time, and his whole deportment was so excited that no man out of Bedlam ever came near it. The Government people laughed, and cried oh, oh—his own people, now a select band, sat silent and downcast—and Newdigate, his own secretary to the Treasury and chosen confidant—repudiated his sentiments and apologized for him. This will I think close his career as a party leader—at any rate he will have no party to lead.[30]

No Conservative felt Bentinck's incapacity for leadership more strongly than Lord Ellenborough, one of the few ministers keen on reunion, and he now tried to effect it by promoting Lord Lincoln as leader of a reunited party in the lower House. 'I have always thought', Ellenborough observed to Lyndhurst, 'that his position in Society, & his talents as a man of business, together with the real liberality of his views, not extreme upon any point, but rational and suited to the Times gave him advantages possessed by no other man who could be considered as a possible Leader in the House of Commons.'[31] He thought Lincoln would be greatly preferable to Sidney Herbert in the eyes of the Protectionists, because he had resigned his seat and thereby had given his constituents an opportunity to pronounce upon his conduct. Ellenborough wrote to Lincoln before the opening of the 1847 session, urging these points on him. 'I think it due to those who supported the late Government to the last,' he argued, 'that they should not be thrown adrift and left to find their way individually into the ranks of the Protectionists, to be received there as Penitents. . . .'[32]

Lincoln rejected the proposal categorically. He would not presume to lead more experienced and abler colleagues and he was sure that no member of the former cabinet other than Peel was more hated by the Protectionists than himself. He denied that there was any discredit to Herbert for failing to resign his seat and asserted that he only did so himself because of his acceptance of a new office. He agreed only with Ellenborough's desire to prevent supporters of the late government being left adrift and being put in the position of returning to the rest of the party as penitents and offered his services 'in conjunction with others' for that purpose.[33] After this failure Ellenborough turned again to Stanley.[34]

Bentinck's support of Jewish emancipation at the beginning of the next session was the occasion rather than the cause of the Protectionists' rejection of him as their leader, but they were not yet ready for Disraeli, the only man of real ability whom they had as yet in the House of Commons.

From beginning to end Bentinck remained bitterly anti-Peelite, but Stanley took a more moderate position, hoping to effect reconciliation with 'the least prominent of Peel's followers', and urging Croker to follow this line in the Quarterly Review.[35] In the September 1846 issue Croker did appeal to the 112 gentlemen who had stood by Peel out of misguided loyalty to repudiate him now and return to the fold, but his condemnation of Peel was so strong that it was scarcely calculated to win over many of Peel's supporters.[36]

In a letter to Croker, Stanley made a remarkably accurate forecast of Peel's future role in Parliament:

> . . . I am satisfied that he intends to attend regularly [he wrote], take a leading part in most great questions, and act, with a small body of adherents, the part of an arbiter between the Government and the Protectionists, a position productive of the greatest embarrassment to all parties, and one which, I fear, will perpetuate the present dissension, render the reconstruction of a Conservative party all but impossible, and smooth the way for those measures of gradual downward progress which Lord John Russell must introduce. . . .[37]

Stanley supposed that Peel had released his former followers in order to free himself to form any connection, but he wrongly assumed that Sir Robert intended to head a party. This, of course, was just what some of Peel's followers vainly wanted him to do.

Of his older colleagues Goulburn appears to have been the first to concern himself about Peel's future, if we except the maladroit effort at reunion on the part of Lord Lyndhurst in August 1846. In mid-December Goulburn told Aberdeen that those of their 'official men' then in London (in particular Lincoln, Cardwell, Young, Bonham and himself) had been discussing what steps should be taken to meet the great activity going on in the Protectionist camp. He continued:

If we take no measures for collecting our friends I think it certain that left altogether without a leader & especially if it be announced that Peel will not lead them the greater part will probably attach themselves to Stanley who was always popular with them. . . . I feel every day more and more convinced that whatever Peel's feelings may be as to resuming office he will ultimately be driven to it by the force of circumstances. . . . The call for his return to office must be spontaneous (and it will be so) and must arise from the wants of the country and not from his direct or indirect action.

It was finally decided that 'the least objectionable course to pursue was that Young should write the usual letter of summons' to those whom they considered their friends, and on the day on which the meeting of Parliament was announced he sent out 240 such circulars.[38]

Meanwhile Goulburn wrote a very carefully prepared letter to Peel, strongly urging him to give them a lead.

My own view [he continued] is that the position which we ought to take would be one of observation rather than of party opposition to the Government, showing ourselves constantly alive to the real interests of the Country, neither refusing to support the Government in opposing the mad projects of the Protectionists nor on the other hand withdrawing the hand of fellowship from those of the Protectionist party who . . . are prepared to abandon their extravagant notions and to unite for the restoration of the public peace and welfare.[39]

Such appeals were to no avail, for Peel had made up his mind. He had never been fond of party, although in the past he had

grudgingly recognised its necessity.[40] Now that he was free he was
anxious not again to become entrapped, as he explained in no
uncertain terms in a letter to Hardinge:

> I intend to keep aloof from party combinations. So far as a man
> can be justified in forming such a resolution, I am determined not
> again to take office. . . .
> I will take care too not again to burn my fingers by organizing
> a party. There is too much truth in the saying 'The head of a
> party must be directed by the tail.'[41]

In turn he made it very clear to Goulburn that after the treatment
he had suffered at the hands of the landed aristocracy he would
not again endure the fatigue of office:

> . . . I would take none other than that which I have twice held,
> and that office I do not think it would be for the public interest
> that I should resume . . . nor will I undertake to reorganize a
> party in opposition to the Government.
> A party of observation as you call it will not succeed. The
> adherents of a party must be stimulated by something more
> exciting than the desire to have a compact body throwing its
> weight into the scale in favour of national interests. Competition
> for power and the determination to take every legitimate advan-
> tage of your opponents in possession of it—are the indestructible
> cement of a compact growing party.

The thought of resuming power was 'perfectly odious' to him
and consequently he was not prepared to take the necessary steps
to reorganise a party. Therefore he refused to allow Young to use
his name 'in requesting attendance at the meeting of Parliament'.
He had 'not the slightest objection of a personal nature to the use
of any other name', but he thought that in the existing state of
parties the issue of any summons of attendance 'could be a
matter of no small difficulty':

> Is the summons to be limited to the 112 or 114 Conservative
> members who supported the policy of the late Government?
> Would not such an invitation be both invidious and unwise? . . . I
> could name persons who did not vote with the late Government
> on the Corn Bill of last Session, but whom (if I were to issue a
> request for attendance) I should feel great difficulty in omitting
> from the Summons. . . . And yet if the definite Rule, (the limita-

tion of the Summons to the 112) be not adhered to, who could undertake in the present state of parties, to determine on the extent to which it should be relaxed? . . .[42]

This was not very helpful. Indeed, if Gladstone's strictures reflect any general opinion it may be concluded that Peel's younger followers found his attitude most annoying, since his arguments were by no means conclusive. What great enterprise, they might have asked, had ever been undertaken without difficulties to overcome? Goulburn himself accepted the decision with misgivings. 'You will find it equally difficult if you express any opinion on public matters in Parliament', he warned Peel, 'to avoid being a leader of those whom we may keep together however much you may be determined never to resume office or never again to guide a party.' And what of these followers? 'What are we to do', he added plaintively, 'who cannot approve of the acts of the Government on the one hand nor of the acts and opinions of Lord G. Bentinck or D'Israeli on the other?'[43]

Not long afterwards Lincoln gave Peel a frank account of what had been done. He had consulted Goulburn, Dalhousie, Herbert, Cardwell, Young and the Duke of Buccleuch and it had been agreed that Young should send out a letter of the usual sort to 240 Conservative members informing them of the day on which Parliament was to meet and asking whether they would be in their places. Ninety answers had been received by 1 January, 'all of them in a friendly tone and many of them very cordial'. 'I hope you will not think the course we have taken either wrong in itself or disagreeable to you,' he added disingenuously. 'I am sure it will have made Lord G. Bentinck's game a more difficult one.'[44]

Graham alone agreed with Peel, to whom he wrote upon first hearing of the circular proposal:

I ventured to suggest to both of them [Lincoln and Goulburn] that inasmuch as it was avowedly your intention not to issue any such invitation on your own behalf a Note from Young, who had been your Secretary to the Treasury and the accustomed channel of such Communication to your Friends, was open to misconstruction; that it was an indirect and equivocal proceeding; that unexplained, it would be misinterpreted; that explained it would do more harm than good. I added that you intended to be present on the first day of the Session; and that the knowledge of the intention, which would soon circulate among your Friends, was ample notice to them, that they ought to be in their places. . . .[45]

After the 'affair of the circulars' was completed Young wrote about it to Peel half-apologetically, but at the same time he warned that Stanley meant business and that, if Peel continued to stand aloof, then the Conservatives who had adhered to him would gradually drop off 'all but a score' and give Stanley a majority; 'and then,' Young argued, seeking Peel's vulnerable point, 'tho he will not dare or attempt to subvert, or reverse your commercial policy, he and his men will cramp and confine it, and not let it have fair play'.[46] Occasionally some of Peel's former colleagues met him to discuss informally what approach they might take to particular questions as they arose, but the issue of Young's circular appears to have been the only overt act of organisation among the Peelites while Peel lived. There was one occasion when Peel showed signs of relenting. In December 1847 he remarked to Young 'that he thought it necessary there should be some attempt at organizing the scattered individuals who had either belonged to the late Government or had adhered to their policy to the last'. Young immediately discussed this with Lincoln and Gladstone and reported the upshot of their discussions to Peel, but nothing came of it. Peel broached the subject to Graham and there apparently it was dropped. 'It is singular', Gladstone commented, 'that Peel should have started such a subject without knowing his own mind upon it. . . .'[47]

Throughout the session of 1847 the Liberals, of course, remained in a minority dependent on some Conservative support. Consequently on those issues where the Protectionists took a party line against the Government the attitude of the Free Trade Conservatives could have been crucial. The first such test came early in the session when Lord George Bentinck introduced a Bill for large-scale government investment in Irish railways, which was opposed by Russell and Sir Charles Wood, his Chancellor of the Exchequer. Russell warned his followers, some of whom were sympathetic, that a government must retain control of public finance and that they must choose between him and the measure. Goulburn, the ex-chancellor, and Peel both came to

Russell's support with traditional economic arguments, made on Peel's part in emotional language that contrasted strangely with the cold logic of his case.[48] Seventy-one Free Trade Conservatives voted against Bentinck's motion, which was defeated by a vote of 332 to 118.[49]

Later in the session the Russell government introduced a more limited Bill, with Bentinck's support, proposing to loan a much smaller amount of money to two Irish railway companies already in existence. Peel and Goulburn with complete consistency used the same arguments as before to oppose this measure and twenty-four other Free Trade Conservatives joined them and some Radicals in voting against it. There was, however, no threat to the Government since Bentinck, Disraeli, and many of their followers entered the Government lobby.[50]

Another issue on which Peel and his friends were able to take an independent line safely was Fielden's Ten Hour Factory Bill, which was supported by the majority of the Liberals and the Protectionists. Once again many Peelites found themselves in company with the more doctrinaire *laissez-faire* Radicals in opposing the measure. Actually on the second reading of the Bill the Free Trade Conservatives were divided, as were the Liberals. Twenty-one supported the second reading and twenty-six voted against it, including Cardwell, Goulburn, Graham, Lincoln, Herbert and Peel himself.[51]

The attitude of Peel and Graham to the Ten Hour Bill inevitably followed the line they had taken against Ashley's attempted amendment to Graham's Factory Act in 1844. Their attitude to the Government's proposed vote of £100,000 for Education, was, however, more liberal and humane, for this was an area where they accepted the argument for government interference as Graham had demonstrated in his original Factory Bill of 1843. It may be remarked that Graham, Herbert and Peel all expressed regret at the failure to include Roman Catholics in the measure. Russell was not unsympathetic to this idea but he did not believe it would be possible to get a majority of support for their inclusion.[52]

The session of 1847 was on the whole a barren one and in the view of *The Times* (2 July) many more such sessions would ruin the Empire. It was in fact a period of marking time before the general election of that summer. The Government was weak and incapable of dealing effectively with the grave crisis of the Irish famine, but neither section of the Opposition was prepared to turn it out. 'Sir Robert Peel and his friends are also few and biding their time', *The Times* (11 June) observed in discussing the Government's weakness. 'The Protectionists are neither in a condition nor a humour just now, in face of famine prices, to renew their old "whine".' Lord Stanley was bitterly aware of his difficult position, 'watching rather than opposing' a government which he could not trust, but unable to go along with some of his wilder supporters in their attacks, for instance on the education grant. He blamed everything on Sir Robert Peel, whom he called 'the apostle of expediency, professing entire abstinence from party, yet perpetually closeted with his under-strappers, interfering with every borough in the kingdom, through his agents, and bent on keeping together a party whose bond of union shall be personal subservience to Sir Robert Peel'. This description caricatures the situation, but it does reveal the weakness of Stanley's position at that time as the professed leader of the Conservative party. 'Protection as a cry is dead', he told Croker, but he advised the editor of the *Quarterly* to write an article on the long-run adverse effects of Free Trade.[53]

The election campaign was well under way when Parliament was finally dissolved on 23 July and voting began on the 28th. There was a lack of any meaningful issues and high grain prices tended to turn the Protectionists from the Corn Laws to take up the Protestant cry. This had been fanned by the enlarged Maynooth grant and by the proposal to pay the Roman Catholic clergy in Ireland, which was endorsed by many Liberals and Peelites. Although the overall results were of national significance, general elections still remained predominantly local affairs, and in most constituencies the candidates depended on their local influence or that of their patrons. In his post-election *Parliamentary Companion* for 1847 Dod identified most Conservative members elected as either Protectionist or Free Trade, but the election reports in *The Times* rarely alluded to these differences or indicated whether a Conservative candidate considered himself a supporter of Peel or of Stanley. Clearly in most

cases the incumbent member had a built-in advantage, and in
only thirteen constituencies were there more Conservative candidates, Free Trade or Protectionist, than seats.[54] In six of these
constituencies the Protectionists were challenging former officeholders, who were especially objectionable to them. These were
Gladstone at Oxford, Goulburn at Cambridge, Cardwell at Liverpool, Granville Somerset in Monmouthshire, Henry Fitzroy at
Lewes and George Smythe at Canterbury. In twenty-one two-
member constituencies in England and Wales there was one Free
Trade and one Protectionist Conservative, but in some cases they
appeared to be opposed to each other, presumably where one of
the seats was ear-marked as Liberal.[55] Thus in Dover Sir George
Clerk, in Brighton, Lord Alfred Hervey and in Salisbury C. B.
Wall were all opposed on religious grounds by ultra-Protestant
Protectionists.[56] J. H. T. Manners Sutton in the borough of
Cambridge and W. H. Bodkin in Rochester initially withdrew in
face of Protectionist opposition, and later stood only to be defeated by Liberals.[57] In several cases there was initial competition
between Free Trade Conservatives for the same seat. Thus Gladstone and Cardwell both canvassed for the second seat at Oxford
University, but eventually Cardwell withdrew from an un-
promising situation to stand for Liverpool.[58] To Sir Robert Peel's
embarrassment, his brother W. Y. Peel contested the second seat
at Tamworth against Captain A'Court, who had supported Peel
in 1846 and who was forced to withdraw.[59]

Peel made one tacit gesture of leadership in the general election
by issuing an address of more than local significance that was
published as a pamphlet and reproduced in *The Times* of 17 July,
where it filled four and a half closely printed columns. It was
almost entirely concerned with defending the policies of his
government from 1841 to 1846, both foreign and domestic, and
in particular his policies of Free Trade and conciliation to Irish
Catholics. He expressed support for the present government's
educational grants but recommended that they should be extended to Roman Catholics. His plain speaking on religious issues
did not help some of his followers, who were opposed by ultra-
Protestant Protectionists. ' "Maynooth" ', Bonham told him, 'has
certainly destroyed several of our friends. "Free Trade" hardly
any.'[60] In sending him a copy of his address, Peel half-apologised

to Goulburn for any injury he might have done him. 'I most earnestly hope', he wrote, 'that there is nothing in the expression of *my opinion* which can be of any disservice to you at Cambridge, but I have done all I could to make it distinctly understood that the opinions expressed are my opinions exclusively—and that any other person is at full liberty to disclaim participation in them.'[61]

Of the 119 Free Trade Conservatives in the previous Parliament some 88 were again candidates, of whom 78 were re-elected, in some cases for different seats.[62] Of these, two (W. S. Lascelles and R. Monkton Milnes) now declared themselves Liberals and three others (John Attwood, O. E. Coope and Lord Arthur Lennox) were subsequently unseated, reducing the total to 73. There were in addition some 35 more Conservatives, newly elected, who had not been in Parliament in 1846–7, but who expressed support for Peel's Free Trade policies. These included Gladstone, who had resigned his seat on returning to office in December 1845, but who had been unable to get himself re-elected before the government fell, and four others[63] who had taken the Chiltern Hundreds in 1846, because they supported Peel despite the disapproval of their constituents. Of these 108 Free Trade Conservatives, seven[64] died, two (W. B. Baring and Lord Lincoln) went to the Lords, two (Lords Brackley and Northland) took the Chiltern Hundreds and one (H. Barkly) became a colonial governor during the life of the Parliament, but another seven[65] professed Free Trade or Liberal Conservatives entered at by-elections in the years 1848–50. In addition to the 108 Conservatives who were elected as Free Traders there were some five others[66] who, although they had voted against the repeal of the Corn Laws in 1846, often co-operated with Peel's friends in the new parliament, bringing the total of potential Free Trade or Liberal Conservatives to a possible 113.[67] It is, however, impossible to make any firm division at this point between Free Trade Conservatives and Protectionists. It remains to be seen how many of the 113 (120) potential Liberal Conservatives or Peelites actually followed Peel's lead in the new parliament and how many in time accepted the lead of Bentinck and Disraeli.

A nice example of the difficulty in using party tags such as Protectionist, Liberal Conservative and Peelite is to be seen in the case of Roundell Palmer whom I have included among the 35 new Free Trade Conservatives. He complained to a friend about being miscalled a Protectionist by the newspapers, although acknowledging that *The Times* had corrected the error; 'though', he added, 'I did not call myself a Peelite, either; and if I had done so I should scarcely have been elected, the irritation of the Conservative party against Sir R. Peel being extreme'. He said that he looked upon 'the elections in general as giving a very strong majority to Liberal Conservative *principles*'. If the Government took 'a decided Liberal-Conservative line (as they did in the last Parliament)' all would be well; he would support them until they did something to make him feel that the country was 'not safe in their hands'.[68]

Despite Peel's avowed abdication of leadership, Bonham, the old party agent of happier days, sent him almost daily reports of all developments affecting Peelite candidates, although handicapped by the lack of any assistance.[69] Mail also poured in on the leader who would not lead from old colleagues telling of their victories or the progress of their contests. Cardwell reported a hard fight in Liverpool, Young a walkover in county Cavan, Lincoln, a 'tremendous contest' in Falkirk in face of 'Protestant bigots', Sidney Herbert an easy win in Wiltshire, accompanied to the poll by 'four hundred horsemen, mostly *farmers*', Goulburn victory at Cambridge, despite stiff opposition.[70] Gladstone, who surmounted similar opposition at Oxford, thanked Peel for his vote (which he would not have received if Cardwell had stayed in the contest),[71] while Graham was returned unopposed at Ripon, thanks to the patronage of Lord de Grey, who offered him the seat for this election only.[72] C. B. Adderly, who reported lukewarmness from friends because of his support of Maynooth and Peel's education scheme, asked for Sir Robert's support for Lord Brackley and himself in North Staffordshire. Adderley had opposed the repeal of the Corn Laws, but Peel promised him his vote, while declining to support Lord Brackley, a new candidate who promised to give Free Trade a fair trial,[73] a nice warning to the historian regarding the danger of making rigid divisions where they do not exist.

The friends of Peel had undoubtedly done better than had been anticipated, although it remained to be seen to what effect.

Lord George Bentinck saw the Protectionist party as smashed for the length of the new parliament.[74] He gloomily counted 116–130 Conservatives who would be glad to see Peel in power again and said he was doubtful of the loyalty of his 240 nominal followers. He consoled himself, however, by attributing the Peelite success to Whig support, which he regarded as only temporary.[75] Stanley told Croker that the future of their party, which he put at 230 in the Commons, depended on the Whigs and the followers of Peel. He was shrewdly inclined to think that there was more support for the aristocratic against the democratic principle from the former than from the latter and suggested that in the *Quarterly* Croker should appeal to 'the real Conservatives whether nominal Tories or nominal Whigs'.[76]

From a more detached position Lord Brougham made some shrewd comments on the election results to his friend Lord Ellenborough. He calculated that there were 85 Peelites, '30 more than could have been expected'. 'But then what right have we to call them Peelites—except some dozen or so?' he asked. 'The others are only so reckoned because they are not known to be Protectionists & are known not to be Whigs.' (The force of this statement cannot be easily denied.) He admitted that 80 or 90 might follow Peel's leadership under certain circumstances:

> . . . yet as leadership & still more place is now out of the question with him there can be no *party* of Peelites and in that sense of men to take office by turning out the Govt Peel has nothing like a party—and yet in no other sense can any party be said to exist. Peel himself is resolved you may be assured to keep himself aloof from all connexion that could possibly hamper him in his perfect liberty of action. He will consult with two or three & no more & he will take his own line on each question—possibly looking to support out of doors & reckoning on the division between those called Peelite & the Protect[ionist]s to ensure him a considerable support indoors also, a support for which he will have to pay no price. . . .[77]

In Graham's view, estimates of relative numbers were fallacious. 'All the ordinary rules of management and of influence', he wrote to Peel, 'are inapplicable to a House of Commons elected under circumstances such as the present. . . .'[78] Peel professed to be disinterested.

Lord Brougham [he told Aberdeen] has made a calculation which
I have not taken the trouble to make, namely the number *of
Peelites* as they are called in the new House of Commons. I know
not whether there are 60 or 6 and rather hope they may be the
latter in preference to the former or a larger number. This feeling
is quite consistent with regret for the fate of any one who, having
agreed with me, and wishing to remain in Parliament, has lost
his seat.[79]

Nevertheless, while renouncing party, Peel had no intention of
abandoning his role in Parliament.

Peel's position is a very extraordinary one [Graham is alleged to
have told Greville] and he is determined to enjoy it. He has an
immense fortune, is in full possession of his faculties and vigour,
has great influence and consideration in Parliament and in the
country. . . . In this position he will not retire from public life to
please any man; he does not want to be head of a party, still less
to return to office, but he will continue to take that part in public
affairs which he considers best for the public service. . . .[80]

Whether or not Graham used such candid words, this is not an
inaccurate description of Peel's position in 1847. Sir Robert
attended the new parliament most assiduously for the next three
years, right up to the week of his death. Before considering the
course taken by Peel and his followers in this parliament it will
be useful to look at some of the approaches made to them by the
other parties and some of the informal relationships established
behind the scenes. It will be seen that these developments had
much significance in the history of the Peelites.

*Notes to this chapter are on pages* 180–4

C

# Chapter 2 PEEL AND THE PEELITES
## The Relationship with the Whig Ministry 1847-50

IF THE Peelites had a collective fault it was their superiority complex. In discussing the Whig ministers with each other they had all the condescension of the professional for the amateur, while their contempt for the Protectionist leaders (with the exception of Stanley) was unbounded. Nevertheless both the larger parties, conscious of their weakness in numbers and in leadership, sought to enlist support from this formidable band occupying the middle ground between them. Even before Peel's death in 1850 the Protectionists and the Whigs had each made half a dozen overtures to his followers. While Bentinck remained leader of the Protectionists in the Commons reconciliation was unlikely, but as soon as he was deposed Goulburn had an invitation to lead them from a Protectionist member 'speaking from authority'. Goulburn expressed sympathy with the idea of reunion but said that he thought the time was premature.[1] Commenting on this offer years later Gladstone remarked that Goulburn 'could have had no difficulty on the score of opinion. . . . For his Free Trade opinions had been derivative rather than original while the general tone and frame of his mind was eminently conservative, perhaps rather inclined to immobility'![2]

Lyndhurst and Ellenborough continued to discuss the desirability of reunion together[3] and later in the session Graham, Goulburn, Lincoln and Gladstone were invited to meet them to discuss a meeting with Lord Granby and Bankes, two Protectionist spokesmen, on the subject of their relative political positions. Graham and Lincoln declined outright, but Goulburn and Gladstone had no objection to a meeting provided it was made clear that no permanent union was possible until their stand on commercial policy was recognised. Consequently the proposals went no further.[4]

The next person to essay the role of peacemaker was Lord Londonderry, who, perhaps because of his age and relative inactivity as a politician, had managed to keep a foot in both camps, as he demonstrated by entertaining Graham and Disraeli as guests in his house at the same time. Graham condescended to treat Disraeli 'with distant civility', but carefully avoided any political conversation with him. Londonderry sounded Graham out on Conservative reunion and asked him whether he would 'undertake a prominent part in leading it', but Graham declined. Earlier Londonderry had approached Aberdeen, but with no result.[5] In 1849 and 1850 Londonderry made two further approaches to Graham that were equally fruitless.[6] Indeed early in 1850 Londonderry told Graham that Disraeli regarded Protection as dead and was ready to stand down if Graham would return to lead the Conservatives. Disraeli probably banked on Graham's refusal which was categorical. In 1849 Sir John Pakington, unaware of Londonderry's attempt, also approached Graham on the matter of reunion, but Graham told him plainly that the various steps taken by the Protectionist leadership 'were at variance with a conciliatory spirit' and that his differences with the Government were less than with the 'implacable Protectionists'. Pakington admitted 'that the differences, which divided the old Conservative Party, were becoming wider every day, and rendered a reunion, even if it were desired, quite impossible'.[7]

Overtures from the Government were as numerous and more significant. On the very formation of his ministry Russell, after sounding out Peel, invited Dalhousie, Lincoln and Herbert to join it, telling them in identical letters that he wished to include 'some of those who belonging to a different party brought forward measures of commercial freedom and received our zealous support'. 'I said it would be no offence to me,' Peel told Graham, 'but I thought the attempt unwise and that it would fail.'[8] He thought that Russell made the offer to remove from the Whigs 'the charge of exclusiveness' and not with the expectation that it would be accepted.[9] In fact all three declined, but Dalhousie's refusal was less abrupt and left the way open for a future approach.[10]

Lord John had more success in inducing two Peelites, Graham and Lincoln, to join a new council set up at the request of the Queen to administer the business of the Duchy of Lancaster. After some hesitation they did so with Peel's blessing, on the understanding that it was the Queen's wish and that the appointments would have no political significance.[11] Nevertheless some of their former colleagues, notably Goulburn, were highly critical until Peel explained the peculiar circumstances that lay behind the offer. The previous year, unwilling to offend his Chancellor of the Duchy and further aggravate an already precarious political situation, he had been able to resist a similar proposal from the Court, but Russell, on taking office, had been less successful. 'I considered Lord John the Protector of Lord Campbell's feelings . . .,' Peel observed drily. 'Seeing that Lord Campbell should write the biography of the Chancellors of the Duchy, the historical account of the new Council will be an awkward chapter.'[12]

Meanwhile Russell had not forgotten Dalhousie and in August of 1846 he offered him the presidency of the Railway Board. Dalhousie again expressed his appreciation, but felt that he could not accept unless he kept 'entire freedom of political action', a condition which Lord John was not prepared to grant in this case.[13] When the governor-generalship of India fell vacant in the following year Dalhousie found it easier to accept this much more important post and Russell had fewer qualms about granting political liberty to a peer who would be too far from the House of Lords to exercise it effectively.[14] Dalhousie had accepted the office only after it had been refused by Graham.[15] He wrote to Peel, not to consult but to inform his former leader that he had accepted:

> In making this proposal they left me entire independence of political action, and gave me full assurance that my acceptance of the office would be clearly understood not to imply any separation from the party with which I have acted or any adherence, present or prospective, to that of which they are the leaders. Under these circumstances I felt that I should not be justified, either on public or private grounds, in declining the appointment; and I have agreed to accept it.[16]

It was said that later the ministers were not pleased with some speeches he made in Edinburgh in which he publicly proclaimed 'that he adhered to his old party attachments'.[17] To Peel Graham remarked: 'It is strange that the Whigs cannot produce a man of their own to send to India.'[18] Doubtless many Whigs thought so too.[19]

A few months after this Russell invited Lord St Germans to be Chief Commissioner of the Poor Law, but he declined with Peel's approval.[20] 'Excellent and truly honorable as he is,' Peel commented to Aberdeen, 'I do not think he is the material of which you could construct a *Breakwater* between the Executive Government and an unpopular Poor Law.'[21]

Perhaps Russell rather envied Peel the liberal-minded young aristocrats whom he attracted around him as disciples. At any rate the combination of rank, zeal and administrative efficiency which they were reputed to possess made them most eligible in his eyes for a variety of high offices.

The election of a new parliament led Russell and some of his colleagues to reassess the Government's position. Sir Charles Wood, who was always ready to give advice, if something of a Cassandra, feared the worst. Although admitting that 'Peel's party as a party numerically speaking [was] gone', he feared that the Government might make mistakes and lose control of the House of Commons, thereby enabling the Peelites to say to 'the popular party' that they were the only people capable of doing business and that they were ready. 'They and we are the rivals for the lead of the great popular party,' Wood argued. '. . . This is what has always made me anxious to enlist some of his best men. We are safe enough if we can rally some of his quondam supporters and get the H. of C. into two parties.'[22] Russell replied that all along it had been his object 'to secure a majority of Liberals, without attaching undue importance to the possession of power by the Whigs'. He acknowledged Peel's popularity in the country, but he did not believe that Peel was 'prepared to go headlong with Hume and Ellice into the adoption of radical changes' and he was sure that Peel 'would not make any sacrifices for the resumption of power'.[23] Lord John was always sensitive to suggestions of Whig exclusiveness, even when they came from inside the family, but his observations about Peel were sound.

An opening arose at the beginning of January 1849 with the

sudden death of the First Lord of the Admiralty. Within twenty-four hours his colleague, Lord Carlisle, had put in a bid to fill the vacancy created by 'poor Aukland', saying he was fed up with 'Woods and Forests'.[24] This, however, was not the sort of solution Lord John had in mind. He discussed the matter with Palmerston and Lansdowne, saying that his own notion, 'without objecting to Clanricarde, or Carlisle, or F. Baring' (stock Whig nominations), was 'to enlarge the basis of the Gov. and ask Sidney Herbert to accept the office'. His reasons, as advanced to Palmerston, are interesting:

> 1. Whigs and Peelites ought to govern the country and not to quarrel about trifles.
> 2. When old gentlemen retire or are worn out we want some young men, gentlemen, men of business, and men who will look beyond the web of cotton which obscures the sight of Cobden and his followers—to take our places in the H. of Commons.[25]

The Whigs were remarkably devoid of talented men born after the turn of the century.

Palmerston approved the offer to Herbert, but did not expect it would be accepted. 'My impression as to Sidney Herbert', he added in a postscript, 'is that he and others of the Peel Party look to forming a Govt. of their own upon the ruins of yours; and that neither he nor any of the others will come out singly to be merged in your Cabinet.'[26] Lansdowne was all for strengthening the Government from outside and suggested Lord St Germans 'for his character, recent conduct and general sincerity of views'.[27] Comparing this assessment with Peel's quoted above, one may assume that Lansdowne preferred one of the more Whiggish rather than one of the best Peelite members of the late government.

Russell next wrote to his colleague, Charles Wood, saying that he would like to bring three Peelites into the cabinet, Herbert immediately at the Admiralty, and two others to follow to fill two offices he expected to be vacated shortly. Alternatively he would welcome Graham to the Admiralty if he were considered likely to accept. He asked Wood to convey these views to Peel, but did not want any answer from Sir Robert.[28] Since Peel had no chance of forming a government himself, why should not his colleagues be borrowed? But it was only good manners and perhaps politically wise to keep him informed.

In the end, on the advice of Clarendon, strongly supported by Lansdowne,[29] Russell decided to approach Sir James Graham, who had proved himself an efficient First Lord in Lord Grey's administration. Palmerston expressed agreement, presuming that Graham would support the work of the Africa Squadron in suppressing the slave trade, although he recalled that Graham had been too economy-minded in his previous spell at the Admiralty.[30] On the afternoon of 11 January Graham received Russell's offer with a request that he call to hear the circumstances under which it was made. He took the night train from the north, arriving in London at 5 am with a speed that would have been undreamed of a few years earlier, and had a long conversation with Russell later the same morning. The fact that he made such a long journey at short notice suggests that he gave the offer serious consideration, although afterwards he tried to play it down.

Graham's conversation with Russell was frank but amiable and ranged over the whole field of public affairs. Russell indicated that there would be other cabinet openings later and that an offer might be made to Lord St Germans, but Graham answered that if he accepted he would make no such condition. In the course of the conversation Graham was critical of the policy governing the Africa Squadron in view of the altered sugar duties and expressed his fear that Palmerston would require too much force there and in the River Plate. He also questioned the wisdom of Russell's declaration that 'his should not be the hand to loosen the tie of the British Colonies' in view of the impending repeal of the Navigation Laws. 'He took this in very good part', Graham told Peel subsequently, 'and justified the Declaration by the necessity in his position of counteracting the effect in the Colonies of the opposite Language, which might lead there to the conclusion that the Crown of England was no longer anxious to protect them, and that we were weary of the connection.'[31]

With Russell's permission Graham left to consult Peel, but on second thoughts decided to make up his mind without implicating Sir Robert. He returned to Russell's house the same evening after sending a cryptic note to say that he preferred to give the

reasons for his decision verbally rather than in writing. 'This set
us speculating which way his mind was made up', Lady John
commented in her diary, 'till he came and declined.'[32] He did so,
he told Peel, from lack of confidence in Palmerston's foreign
policy, dissatisfaction with the failure to plan 'large retrench-
ments', and suspicion that the Government's plans for Ireland
were unconstructive and improvident. Graham advised Russell
to send for Sir Francis Baring despite Russell's fears of an outcry
against his appointing one of the 'Governing Family'. Yet when.
this appointment was made Graham rather inconsistently expressed surprise at Baring's acceptance, since he said the incom-
ing minister made himself responsible for all the mistakes of the
government over which he had had no control.[33] Having convinced himself that it would be unwise to join a weak ministry,
he found it difficult to see how anyone else could make a different
decision.

Although the overture came to nothing, it narrowed the gap
between Russell and Graham and in this way perhaps helped to
bring the coalition of 1852 a step closer. Whether it brought the
Peelites as a whole closer to the Whigs, as Russell's biographer
suggests, is more doubtful. Aberdeen[34] and Lincoln[35] both expressed surprise at Graham's 'initial hesitation' and satisfaction
that Peel was not implicated. 'I am almost more astonished at his
not at once seeing the impropriety of his consulting *you* upon the
subject,' the latter wrote to Peel. In 1852 Newcastle was to be
more moderate in his approach to the idea of coalition.

Formal coalition between Liberals and Peelites only came
thirty months after Peel's death, but throughout the years 1847–
50 the Whig ministers were in frequent touch with him (and with
some of his former colleagues), none more so than Sir Charles
Wood, the Chancellor of the Exchequer. If Wood was not a
particularly successful Chancellor, it was not for want of application. His views on public finance were similar to those of the
Peelites, whose field it was *par excellence*. Wood seems to have
recognised this and to have been aware of the deficiency of his
own colleagues in that respect. His deferential attitude towards
Peel is in marked contrast with the rather peremptory tone he
took with Russell. Indeed, in a letter to Peel Young once reported
Wood as saying to him that 'Lord John Russell knows nothing of

trade or finance, and Labouchere nothing of any practical business'.[36]

The Chancellor of the Exchequer often sent Peel the latest official papers on banking, trade and public finance, usually with a short covering note expressing the warmth of his regard for the elder statesman. They also met on occasion to discuss financial problems. A few examples of this intercourse may serve to illustrate the closeness of the tie.

Wood was always concerned to follow a sound banking policy and this was the occasion of much of his correspondence with Peel. When Peel concurred with Wood's views on the subject of over-circulation in December 1846 the Chancellor expressed his gratification. 'I should be very sorry', he wrote, 'that in my hands you had ever reason to think that your measure [the Bank Act of 1844] was not fully carried out. I never gave a more hearty support to any measure since I have had a seat in Parlt & it is one quite apart from all political considerations.'[37] This exchange set the tone of the correspondence that followed.

Early in February 1847 Wood met Peel by appointment after church one Sunday to discuss the difficult fiscal situation which faced him. After listening to Wood's proposals Peel said that if it was the deliberate intention of the Government to meet a deficiency by increased taxation they might depend upon his 'inclination to give them cordial support', but he made it clear that he spoke for himself only, for he 'wished to keep aloof', he wrote, 'from the fetters of party connection'. He pointed out the political implications of the policy to Wood and urged him to consider all factors fully before making a decision.[38]

At the end of the summer Wood again sought Peel's opinion, this time on a proposal to amend the constitution of the Bank of England by providing for the appointment of a permanent governor. Peel in exchanging long letters with Goulburn on the matter observed drily that Wood touched 'on none of the real practical difficulties'. Graham was more caustic, commenting that the Government was too easily shaken by newspaper proposals. 'The Ch of the Exchequer instantly seizes on the suggestion and fishes with it for our opinion,' he wrote to Peel.[39]

Shortly afterwards, when the banking crisis of October 1847 threatened the Act of 1844, Wood hastened to consult its author, 'in full confidence', he told Peel, 'in what Ellice truly calls your constant cordiality and kindness for which I have so much reason to thank you'.[40] After some exchange of letters Wood called on Peel on the evening of 22 October and again on the 23rd, and warned him that it might be necessary to suspend the Bank Act temporarily. He did not ask Peel to commit himself to his future course of action, but he was anxious to discuss the method of suspending the Act and showed Peel a letter which he proposed to send to the Governor of the Bank justifying his action. Peel criticised the form of the letter on the grounds that it might prove embarrassing later and that not all the arguments were sound. He advised a shorter and simpler statement, a course that was subsequently adopted. He made it clear that he was giving his advice on the grounds of public welfare 'without reference to personal or party considerations'.[41]

Peel sent off a long account of the affair to Goulburn in which he wrote:

> I advised him to confer with those who really understood the question of currency, whose prepossessions were in favour of the principles on which the Bank act was founded—and in favour of the Bank act itself. He said this was what he had done—that Lord John and he had seen Rothschild, Masterman, Glyn and the leading men of the City—but that those with whom he conferred in private were the very persons I named of deserving of his confidence in the matter, Jones Lloyd, W. Cotton, Norman and the Governor of the Bank. . . .
>
> I advised him to postpone acting (if he saw interference to be inevitable) to the very last—to take every chance of a favourable turn (which might come on very suddenly), to continue his communications with the parties that he named, and attach great weight to their opinions.[42]

Wood continued to keep in touch with Peel while the crisis lasted, either directly or through Cardwell as an intermediary. Peel appears to have supported his view that an act of indemnity was unnecessary, since his letter authorising the Bank to use its currency reserve did not have to be used.[43]

When the crisis had passed the Chancellor thanked Peel warmly for his advice and for his subsequent support in the House.[44] Goulburn and Graham, both of whom Peel had kept fully informed, expressed their doubts. 'It is quite true', wrote Graham, 'that you have no personal or party advantage in the confidential communications which are forced on you by Ministers in critical Emergencies; but I have my doubts whether the public Good be not best promoted by leaving to responsible Advisers of the Crown an undivided responsibility, and by exercising in Parliament an unfettered judgement upon all their acts.'[45]

Nevertheless Peel continued to favour Wood with his advice, which was asked for more and more frequently. For instance in the following May we find the Chancellor sending him the sketch of a report on the Bank Act, which he thought was 'pretty nearly in conformity with the suggestions' Peel had made earlier in the day.[46]

In the late summer of 1848 the Protectionist Herries threatened to bring on a motion attacking the Bank Act at a time when many of its defenders were out of town. A stream of letters from Wood, Goulburn and Cardwell followed Peel down to Drayton, keeping him informed of the situation as it developed and urging him to come up at the crucial moment to help defeat the challenge.[47] Peel agreed readily and suggested a plan of action which Wood accepted. The first call was a false alarm; 'I am sorry that we summoned you for nothing,' wrote Wood, '. . . but it is best to be prepared on such occasions.' Finally on 22 August the long-heralded motion came off and Peel hastened to London. The sequel is briefly told in his subsequent letter to Graham:

> I have twice been to London since we parted to lend any aid which it was [in] my power to lend to the Government to defeat a foolish motion of Herries on the Currency question.
> It was concocted by Herries and Monteagle and worthy of their joint cunning.
> Monteagle was the single stranger under the Gallery watching the proceedings with great interest.
> I did what I could to make his visit an unpalatable one. I was rejoiced to find a pretty universal condemnation of Monteagle's nostrum. . . .[48]

The repeal of the Navigation Acts was the most important issue of consultation in 1849. Wood was particularly concerned about the passage of the legislation through the Lords and kept

Peel fully informed of the prospects as he counted and recounted the lists of peers likely to vote. For instance, one Sunday (6 May?) he sent Peel such a list and then followed it up in the evening with an anxious note: 'Cardwell's account', he wrote, 'after he had seen you rather alarmed me from what he said of your impression and I immediately went off to Lord Strafford and I have gone carefully over the list of Peers with him. Calculating very carefully the for, against, doubtful and absent I do not see how we can fail to win unless he has been grossly misinformed.'[49] A few days later he was still more precise, forecasting 178 for and 170 against. These numbers included 24 doubtful of whom he listed by name 8 favourable, 7 against, 5 absent and 4 uncertain.[50] In fact the Government's actual majority on the crucial second reading was 10.[51]

During the last year of Peel's life Wood was writing to him more frequently than to any of his old friends (22 letters, July 1849 to May 1850).[52] The tone becomes more familiar and the range of topics broader, factory inspectors' and Poor Law reports, the defence of Free Trade, Ireland, Scottish banks, drainage, pensions and the political prospects of the Government. The Prime Minister used him as a channel of communication, as on 19 December 1849 when he wrote: 'John Russell desired me to tell you that he had given up all notion of meddling with the franchise this year, on which you had some conversation with the D.[uke] of B.[edford].'[53] His final letter raising problems connected with the Bank of Ireland opens with this characteristic sentence: 'I do not like taking [a] step in banking and currency without your knowledge and concurrence and I therefore trouble you with this letter.'[54] Was there ever such a correspondence between statesmen occupying the front benches on opposite sides of the House?

Lord Clarendon was another Whig leader who kept in touch with Peel during this period. No problem lay heavier on Peel's mind during these last years than that of starving Ireland. It was a subject of much correspondence between him and several of his former colleagues, who were often more caustic about the failure of the Government's Irish measures or the lack of them. Peel was slow to come to any conclusion, torn between the statesman's anxiety to alleviate the disastrous situation and the political economist's belief that natural laws must be allowed to run their course. This is illustrated in a letter to Goulburn in August 1846 in which he rehearses the case against state intervention, especially for the second time, only to conclude:

> All this is very true but what is to be done when starvation of thousands stares you in the face? even the philosophers who agree to your arguments, will condemn you if you let people perish, and if they will condemn you what will be the outcry of those who are not philosophers?[55]

And a few weeks later he wrote in the same vein to Graham: 'In spite of philosophy and rigid principles of political economy some immediate and decisive effort must be again made for alleviating the danger of sudden scarcity in districts both in Ireland and in Scotland.'[56]

It was not until March 1849 in a major speech in the House of Commons[57] that Peel proposed a positive plan that involved the drainage and improvement of the land, the opening up of roads through inaccessible districts, the erection of piers, the promotion of emigration, and above all 'the transfer of land from insolvent to solvent proprieters' and the abandonment of 'the present injurious system of giving gratuitous relief'.[58] These proposals involved more government intervention than Wood liked[59]— the disciple had learned the lesson better than the master—but it led to an interview with the Lord Lieutenant who called on Peel at Whitehall Gardens.[60] Sir Robert urged Clarendon to appoint a commission to control the grant of public aid in Ireland, to re-establish the principles of the Irish Poor Law of 1838 and to devise means to permit the simple transfer of encumbered estates in order to induce English buyers with capital to invest. He also advocated an alliance with the Roman Catholic Church. 'To make the population contented and orderly,' he wrote in a long memorandum which he presented to Clarendon, 'I would call in the aid of the priest. I would repair or rebuild the chapel of each Parish . . . and attach a small glebe to it. . . . I would do all this not as a Cabinet measure but as the act of a landlord. . . .' He concluded his advice with a timely warning. 'But the first act of the Commission', he wrote, 'would be to notify all Ireland that there was not the faintest hope of *a job*. That the Commission

would not give a shilling for the relief of any bankrupt Land
lord. . . .'[61]

The only sequel was an amendment to Clarendon's Encumbered Estates Act of 1848, a sorry attempt to solve the labyrinthine problem of Irish land in the *laissez-faire* tradition.
Henceforth, however, Clarendon consulted Peel and Graham
constantly and kept them informed of the course of events in
Ireland in letters that reflected his flair for pithy and caustic
observation.[62]

A more indirect link between Peel and the Whigs was provided
by Russell's brother, the indolent but gregarious Duke of Bedford, and his old Tory crony and frequent visitor, Charles
Arbuthnot. The latter on one occasion in the summer of 1849
revealed some of the weaknesses in the Whig camp. Telling Peel
that Bedford was 'very uneasy about the Government and about
his brother's health', he wrote:

> He [Bedford] said that there was no man to take his place, [that]
> Sir G. Grey had become unpopular and that he had the fault of
> not taking the trouble to argue and debate. That the only man was
> Palmerston; but that he wd not do as it was with the Radicals
> alone that he was popular in the House. I mentioned Sir. C.
> Wood. . . . The Duke agreed [that he was a good speaker] and
> said that he might do, but that Sir C. Wood also was not liked,
> and that he was over quick with Deputations. . . .[63]

The Duke of Bedford himself told Peel that he was always glad
to hear and read Peel's sentiments on public affairs since they
always seemed to be in agreement.[64] In particular he sought to
reassure Peel with respect to the soundness of the Whigs in the
matter of Free Trade. To prove his point in December 1849 he
sent Peel in confidence an extract from a letter of Russell's, copied
especially for Peel by the Duchess. In this Lord John dismissed
the idea of a fixed duty on corn as an absurdity, but declared
himself equally 'averse to giving any continuance to the plans of
Hume and Cobden', which he thought 'destructive of Empire'.
He was so convinced that his views were right and accepted by
'every able statesman in Parliament (Lord Stanley excepted)'
that he preferred to risk a contest in the position on which he
then stood 'than leave that position either for the old fortress of
Tory prejudice or the high ground of the Mountain'.[65]

There was little here to displease the late Conservative Prime Minister.

Sir Robert Peel may have been satisfied with the course that he followed during these last years of his life, but the same cannot be said of all his friends. Ambition was no spur to the older leaders such as Aberdeen, Goulburn and Graham, who were content to let events take their course and to watch the game from the sidelines. Some of the younger men who still had a future and consequently more cause for concern were preoccupied to a greater or lesser extent by other matters. These were the years in which Gladstone was wrestling with the problems of Oak Farm and the Hawarden Estate,[66] poor Lincoln was faced with the tragedy of his wife's desertion of himself and their children,[67] and Sidney Herbert was promoting the emigration of sweated female needle workers—a project looked upon askance by most of his Peelite friends as offending the laws of political economy.[68]

Nevertheless as time went on the younger Peelites showed growing signs of a frustration that is well illustrated in a letter that Edward Cardwell addressed to Lord Lincoln in the autumn of 1849. Congratulating Lincoln on breaking away from the distressing ties of politics he wrote:

> . . . In the feelings of disappointment you so truly express it is impossible not to join. The wishes we cherished and the hopes we formed are scattered to the winds: and the party we thought so worthy of power and pre-eminence has fallen into forgetfulness of itself and is actually forgotten by the world. . . . That Sir Robert Peel's party saved England from confusion and has been rewarded by its own annihilation is the simple fact:—and with this we must reconcile ourselves as best we may.[69]

In 1848 Lincoln, Herbert, Cardwell and perhaps some others took one definite step to promote their views and the fortunes of the Peelites by the purchase of the *Morning Chronicle*, a paper that under the proprietorship of Sir John Easthope had been the champion of Lord Palmerston.[70] Abraham Hayward, a friend of Lincoln and other Peelites, was associated with the *Chronicle* during these years, and J. D. Cooke was its editor. In the early stages he consulted Lincoln closely about the editorial line that he should take, making it clear that once Lincoln had given him 'the proper tone' he would have no difficulty in keeping it up.[71] It is interesting to note the gradual change in the editorial tone of the *Morning Chronicle* in the spring of 1848. On 11 April it was still criticising Lord Lincoln; on 27 April it mildly rebuked Lord Palmerston for his notorious despatch to Bulwer; but by 10 May it was making a full-fledged attack on the Foreign Secretary and upholding the views of Lord Aberdeen. The tone of the paper over the next few years was distinctly more hostile to the Whigs than were Peel and Graham, reflecting the greater political partisanship of some of the younger Peelites, but it was equally critical of the Protectionists.

Deprived of any normal party organisation, Peel's friends lacked cohesion as a parliamentary group and when the Houses divided often found themselves split between the two lobbies. No one was more conscious of these divisions than Gladstone who drew up an analysis of the votes of most of Peel's ex-colleagues on five controversial issues of the years 1848 and 1849, which showed a marked division on every one.[72] Gladstone's analysis was a selective one, however, and tells us nothing about the role of the larger body of Free Trade Conservatives. As Free Traders, would they follow Peel's example in giving regular support to the Liberal government to prevent the formation of a Protectionist one, or would they conclude, as some of Peel's ex-colleagues did, that Free Trade was no longer seriously challenged, and that their natural place was in a reunited Conservative party? To answer this question we should look first of all at the parliamentary scene in the years 1848–50.

During the first session of the new parliament, which opened in December 1847, there were a number of issues on which Peel and some of those Conservatives who still looked to him for a lead sided with the Government against the majority of the Protectionist Conservatives. One of the first matters to be discussed was the commercial distress of 1847, which had reached its climax in the autumn (see above, p 42). The Government proposed to appoint a committee of twenty-six members of the House of Commons, which included Peel, Goulburn, Graham, Cardwell, Bentinck and Herries, as well as four Liberal ministers and several Radicals.[73] Bentinck objected to the inclusion of so many ministers and ex-ministers, who might be expected to have a vested interest in defending the Bank Charter Act. Consequently the Protectionists divided the House on the inclusion of some of the proposed names, including that of Cardwell, as a Peelite ex-officeholder. This seemed to be a test as to which Conservatives were loyal to Peel, and of the 43 allegedly Free Trade Conservatives in the House 34, including Peel, supported the Government, which was sustained by a vote of 167 to 101.[74]

Bentinck himself, however, was dissatisfied with his Protectionist followers' lack of interest in such politico-economic questions. Opposition to the Jewish Emancipation Bill introduced by Lord John Russell early in the session was another matter. The Bill was strongly opposed by most of them, but surprisingly supported by Bentinck and, more understandably, by Disraeli.[75] The result was the forced resignation of Bentinck, leaving his party virtually leaderless and ineffective for the rest of the session.[76] The Jewish Emancipation Bill split Peel's followers; the more conservative joined the bulk of the Protectionists in opposing it, but Peel himself made one of the most effective speeches in support of the measure. Of the 72 Free Trade Conservatives who participated in the division on the second reading, 29 supported and 43 opposed the Bill, which passed by a vote of 277 to 204,[77] only to be defeated later in the House of Lords.

Another issue on which Peel's friends were understandably more unanimous in supporting the Government against the combined opposition of Protectionists and Radicals was the renewal of the income tax. Several of the ex-ministers joined in the debate resisting a hostile amendment introduced by Hume, Peel justifying his original introduction of the tax and its extension, Goulburn arguing against its opponents that it was no more unfair than any other tax, Cardwell pointing out that the Government needed the money and Gladstone vigorously combating Disraeli's slashing attack on the proposal.[78] The Ministers feared a Radical-Protectionist combination and were concerned that Peel's speech had stirred up the Protectionists by 'opening the old question of his financial policy'. However, in the view of Tufnell, the Liberal whip, the 'pulling off on the opposite benches' probably rallied some doubtful Free Traders in support of the Government.[79] Wood warned Russell in winding up the debate not to put any blame on the late government, for Peel's speech, he said, 'was very handsomely done'.[80] They were unnecessarily

D

apprehensive, however, for the motion was defeated by 363 to 138 with 75 of the 82 Free Trade Conservatives in the House entering the Government lobby.[81]

The Free Trade Conservatives also rallied behind Peel in support of the Government's Bill, introduced late in the session, for the repeal of the Navigation Acts. Towards the close of the debate on the second reading Peel made one of the most effective speeches in support of the Bill. He fully agreed that the time had come to tackle this anomalous code, already mutilated by reciprocal trade treaties, and cogently argued that Adam Smith's reservations were no longer relevant in the nineteenth century. He jeered at the shallowness of the Protectionists' arguments, asking what a great exporting nation such as Britain had to fear and pointing out that trade had increased since the introduction of a Free Trade policy.[82] His speech was so effective that Russell in winding up for the Government contented himself by observing that no more needed to be said.[83] The hostile amendment of the Protectionists' leader, Herries, was then defeated by a vote of 294–177,[84] but it was too late in the session to go on with such a large measure. Of the 73 Free Trade Conservatives participating in the division, 55 supported Peel and Russell.

The Government was pressed much harder on its West Indian policy and here Peel's friends were reluctant to follow him in supporting Russell. The Opposition made much of the plight of the West Indian colonies since the abolition of preference on colonial sugar and when Russell brought in a rather limited measure of relief, including a slight reduction in the duty on colonial sugar, Sir John Pakington moved an adverse amendment, appealing to Free Traders to join him, since, he claimed Free Trade was not the issue. Peel refused to accept his reasoning. He recognised the distress of the West Indians and expressed his sympathy with them, but argued that to support Pakington was to seek the defeat of the Government and reopen the whole policy of Protection, which he was not prepared to do.[85] Graham also came to the Government's support, stoutly defending the further reduction of the sugar duties as a boon to the poor. 'It is the only little luxury that many families can enjoy,' he argued with that moral fervour characteristic of the Free Traders of his day; 'it renders palatable their rice, their gruel, their crout, their indifferent tea and coffee'.[86] Gladstone, on the other hand, criticised the insufficiency of the Government relief measure and argued that the West Indies deserved pecuniary assistance in view of what they had suffered from the effects of imperial policy.[87] Although expressing his reluctance to support Pakington, in the end he entered the Opposition lobby, as did Cardwell, Goulburn, Herbert and Lincoln. The motion was only defeated by a vote of 260 to 245 and of the 92 Free Trade Conservatives participating in the division, 65 joined the Opposition.[88]

In 1849 the pattern of Free Trade Conservative voting was very similar to what it had been in the previous session. Indeed many of the main issues were the same. During the session, on the other hand, Disraeli became recognised as the leader of the Protectionists in the Commons, now beginning to assume more and more the name of Conservatives, although Stanley was not yet prepared to abandon the cause of Protection. These developments were not calculated to encourage ideas of reunion in the hearts of the Peelites, if we may use that name to describe those Free Trade Conservatives who still looked to Peel for leadership. The task of identifying them remains, since the continued lack of any overt direction on Peel's part still left them free to speak and vote as they saw fit, and consequently on some issues many of them found themselves in the same lobby as Disraeli; although, to their chagrin, Peel, who was most assiduous in his attendance in the House, chose almost always to vote with the ministers.

Following Stanley's lead in the House of Lords, Disraeli took a strong line against the Government from the start by moving an amendment to the address in response to the speech from the throne. He made a vigorous attack on the Government's foreign and domestic policy and decried the results of Free Trade. He was poorly supported, however, and when on a subsequent evening only 80 members voted for Lord Granby's motion to adjourn the debate, Disraeli abandoned his amendment.[89] Of 41 Free Trade Conservatives participating in the division, 34, including Peel and his former colleagues, supported the ministers.[90]

Irish affairs again accounted for a large part of the business of the session. One of the Government's limited measures to alleviate the hardship in Ireland was a Rates in Aid Bill to amend the Irish Poor Law. Peel gave his qualified support to the measure in the celebrated speech in which he made his own major proposals for social reform in Ireland.[91] Peel's scheme was applauded by Bright and criticised by Disraeli, but was not adopted by the Government. Their Bill, however, which passed its second reading by a vote of 193 to 138, was supported by 26 of the 54 Free Trade Conservatives who took part in the division. Peel was, as usual, accompanied by Graham, but Goulburn and Lincoln entered the Opposition lobby on this occasion.[92]

One of the first issues seized upon by Disraeli as *de facto* leader of the Protectionists in the Commons was that of local taxation. If the landowners had to bear the brunt of Free Trade by the repeal of the Corn Laws, why should they alone have to carry the burden of poor rates? In March Disraeli moved for a Committee to study the unequal distribution of local taxation, thinking that here was an issue on which he might rally support from the Free Trade Conservatives and thereby bring them back into the ranks of the larger party. To his disappointment, both Goulburn and Herbert spoke against his proposals and 37 of the 57 Free Trade Conservatives voting (including all of the ex-ministers) helped to defeat the motion in a division of 189 to 280.[93]

The most important accomplishment of the session of 1849 was the repeal of the Navigation Acts. This was a measure which the Protectionists again opposed at every stage, but the Free Trade Conservatives were more divided. Gladstone strongly favoured conditional legislation, that is to say, provision for negotiating reciprocal Free Trade with other countries. He, Goulburn, Cardwell and Clerk met Peel several times to discuss this proposal. Sir Robert, however, was unwilling to do anything to embarrass the Government, and only grudgingly agreed even to their sounding out the ministers as to their plan. Gladstone then saw Labouchere, but to no avail. Peel was anxious to see that the Government was not defeated. He told his doubtful colleagues that he foresaw a great battle for the re-imposition of protective duties and that he would resist this to the utmost and defend the Government 'when they were engaged in a measure for promoting liberty of commerce'. He observed 'that whatever might be said of the late Govt as adopting Whig measures, he certainly thought the present one was acting on Conservative principles, that they were generally acting in a manner to merit his approval, tho' Lord John seemed to have bid higher than he would have done for the support of the Church'.[94]

In the debate on the second reading of the Bill, Gladstone opposed Herries' hostile amendment, but spoke strongly in favour of the alternative approach of throwing open the British carrying trade to those countries who offered similar opportunities to British shipping.[95] In the Committee stage Gladstone did not press his proposals in the form of an amendment because he failed to find any support from the shipping interest. Consequently, although disappointed at the failure of the Government to adopt his proposals, he supported the Bill as preferable to leaving the existing Navigation Acts in operation.[96] The most effective speech in support of the measure came from Sir James Graham who warned that to repeal the Corn Laws and not the Navigation Acts would lead to the loss of Canada. (This was the year in which Montreal merchants, sore at losing their colonial preferences, talked openly of Canadian annexation to the United States.) Graham called the proposed measure the 'capital' that was to crown the pillar of Free Trade already erected. He saw it as the last round in the battle between Protection and Free Trade, between reaction and progress, and warned that without it the Free Trade edifice was imperfect.[97] Speaking after Graham, Russell avowed that he had great difficulty in finding anything more to say. Disraeli, rising at a late hour at the very end of the debate, was less inhibited. Jeering at Graham's apologia for the Bill, he suggested that Sir James's column was not worth the cost of a capital to adorn it, and as for the talk of progress, he asked whether it was to be 'progress to paradise or progress to the devil'.[98] On 23 April the Bill passed its third reading after the defeat of another hostile amendment of Herries by 275 to 214.[99] The Free Trade Conservatives were deeply divided on the issue. Of 78 members who voted on either the second or the third readings or both, 45 supported and 33 opposed it.[100] Goulburn, however, was the only ex-minister who broke with Peel in failing to support the Bill.

The Bill was eventually passed by a small majority in the House of Lords,[101] but, as we have seen (above, p 44), the Government feared the possibility of a defeat there and made strenuous efforts to prevent it. Palmerston urged Russell not to resign if they were defeated in the Lords. He argued that Stanley would be unable to form a government for lack of support in the Commons, with the result that the Queen would call Peel who could only govern with Whig support. Palmerston warned Russell that some Whigs might join a Peel government; 'but', he continued, 'you would be bound almost and obliged to hand your party over to Peel, and to abdicate your own Position as leader in his Favor—our Radicals would go to him whether you chose or not and a great many of our independent supporters might do the same so that at all events you would be left with a much reduced Band'.[102]

Russell, however, was prepared to resign if defeated in the Lords and expected that the Queen would call Peel rather than Stanley. '. . . I do not think that any of our colleagues could with decency leave our large party to join Peel,' he wrote to Palmerston, 'when all Peel's friends who have been asked have refused to leave his small party to join me.' Nevertheless, he would not oppose their doing so and he recognised that the Radicals would 'eagerly' support Peel; 'but if we kept together', he concluded, 'we should be able to support Peel in all good measures, and to counteract any mischievous policy—foreign or domestic'.[103]

The question of Jewish disabilities further divided the Free Trade Conservatives. In this session Lord John Russell endeavoured to solve the problem by introducing an Oaths Bill which sought to simplify or abolish the various oaths required of Members of Parliament in such a way as to make them acceptable to Jews and less offensive to Roman Catholics. Gladstone welcomed the measure, not only as an extension of civil rights to the Jews but also because, on theological grounds, he regarded the simplified form of oaths proposed to be more acceptable. Goulburn was again opposed, but Peel in supporting it indicated that he would be prepared to go further and enable Jews to hold some other civil offices from which they were still barred by the form of the oaths required.[104] The Bill finally passed its third reading in the Commons by a vote of 272 to 206, but was again rejected by the Lords. Of the 66 Free Trade Conservatives voting on the third reading only 26, including all the ex-Ministers except Goulburn, supported the Bill.[105]

Another issue that divided the Free Trade Conservatives in

their attitude towards the Government was the Rebellion Losses Bill passed by the Canadian legislature and signed by the Governor-General. The passage of this Bill has long been considered by Canadian historians as a notable landmark in the history of the attainment of responsible government, and Lord Elgin has been regarded as one of the wisest Governors-General because he accepted a Bill, which he himself did not like, since it had been supported by his ministers and the majority in the popular assembly. The passage of the Bill was, however, bitterly resented by the English-speaking minority in Lower Canada, for it was feared that former rebels would share in the compensation that the Bill proposed to pay to those whose property had been destroyed in the Rebellion of 1837. Conservative opinion in England reciprocated this feeling, and in June, when a Supply motion for the Canadian Militia gave the opportunity, Gladstone immediately introduced the matter. He argued that the Canadian Bill might provide for the indemnification of people guilty of high treason and that this was a matter of imperial concern and inconsistent with the honour of the Crown. He and Sidney Herbert both supported a motion of J. C. Herries petitioning that the Bill would not receive royal assent until Her Majesty had received assurances that no one involved in the rebellion should participate in the indemnification. Sir Robert Peel opposed the motion on the grounds that no objection had been made to a similar Act passed for Upper Canada and that to reject one for Lower Canada would be invidious. His advice was to leave the question of the honour of the Crown to the discretion of the Crown and not to involve the House in a contest with the majority in the Canadian Assembly. Lord John Russell reiterated this argument and stood by the principles of responsible government. The motion was easily defeated by 291 to 150; 41 Free Trade Conservatives opposed it and 25 voted in its favour.[106]

It is interesting to note that on several issues during these years Sir Robert Peel, who began his political life early in the century as the darling of the ultra Tories, took a distinctly more liberal line than did his young lieutenant whose name towards the end of the century was to be synonymous with advanced Liberalism.

Finally we may note a motion for a Select Committee on the

state of the nation introduced by Disraeli late in the session, which brought most of the Free Trade Conservatives in the House together against him. He painted a gloomy picture of the economic decline that he found had taken place in the country since the present Government had come into office and attributed this to the adoption of Free Trade. Inevitably Peel rose to challenge these conclusions, arguing that the policy of Free Trade had not caused the present distress, but rather had mitigated it. He made clear his reasons for generally supporting the present ministers since they had come into office and for opposing the present motion:

> I have thought that it was for the public interest that the energy and power of the Executive Government of this country during such a crisis of combined dangers [the Irish famine and the commercial distress], should not be impaired by a factious or captious opposition. At the same time, Sir, I wish it to be distinctly understood, that all I mean to imply by the vote I shall give tonight is this—that I cordially approve of the general principles of commercial policy by which Her Majesty's Government have been guided, and that I will not consent to a motion, the main object of which avowedly is, to censure them for their adherence to those principles, and to substitute in the place of that policy some other economic system.[107]

This statement admirably describes Peel's position in these last years of his public life.

The motion was defeated by a vote of 156 to 296, and of 60 Free Trade Conservatives participating in the division, 52 supported the Government against Disraeli. Indeed all but one of the nine who supported Disraeli may be regarded as having merged with the main body of the Conservatives if they would support Disraeli against Peel on such an issue.[108]

The unsatisfactory state of Peel's followers at the end of the session of 1849 was summed up fairly accurately and succinctly by the Whig statesman G. C. Lewis in a letter (of 4 September) to his friend Sir Edmund Head, Governor of New Brunswick:

> The Peelites were not only small in numbers, but disunited among themselves. Peel and Graham stood on several occasions nearly alone—Gladstone, Lincoln and the minor Peelites going off in other directions. Peel appears to me to have abandoned

definitively all idea of being a party leader or holding office. He is anxious, however, to maintain his own position in the House of Commons, and to be considered as the chief speaker in it when he thinks fit to exert himself. . . . The 'Chronicle' has been for some time a Peelite paper and is very ably written. Smyth and Hayward are two of the writers.[109]

There was no reason to suppose that the outlook would be any brighter for the Peelites in the following year.

The session of 1850 was not short of controversial measures, which continued to separate Peel and his close followers from the Protectionists, but which also often divided the ranks of the Free Trade Conservatives. The Protectionists continued to push the twin issues of agricultural distress and the plight of the West Indian planter. The former was made respectable by tying it to the question of local taxation, the latter by placing it under the anti-slavery mantle. A Protectionist amendment to the address in reply to the speech from the throne attributed the existing agricultural distress to the policy of Free Trade and found it aggravated by the existing system of local taxation. Of the 72 allegedly Free Trade Conservatives taking part in the division, 58 entered the Government lobby against the amendment.[110] A few weeks later Disraeli resumed the same complaint by moving for a Committee to consider the revision of local taxation as a means of alleviating the distress of the agricultural classes; in particular he proposed to transfer the cost of the Poor Law to the general revenue. Peel and Graham joined the ministers in opposing these proposals. Graham feared that such a major change in the fiscal system would lead to the return of Protection and that all classes would suffer from the consequent taxes on necessities. Moreover he did not think that the relief of the poor rates would be passed on by the landlord to the tenant. Gladstone openly disagreed with Graham, denying that the return of Protection was likely and that the tenant would receive no relief. Peel paid tribute to the ability and moderation of Disraeli's presentation, but observed that the current agricultural distress extended to other countries in Europe where agricultural protection continued. He also disagreed with Gladstone, pointing out that to charge the poor rates to the consolidated fund would either lead to a continuation of the income tax or to the imposition of revenue duties on imports. The result, he argued, would be the reversal of the successful commercial and financial policy of the preceding six years. Russell also attacked Gladstone's faulty logic and praised Peel's disinterested spirit. Fifty-six nominally Free Trade Conservatives supported Disraeli's motion, which was only defeated by a narrow majority of 21. Thirty-two Peelites, however, including Peel, Graham and Goulburn, voted with the Government to ensure the defeat of the motion.[111]

On this occasion Sir John Young, representing the Irish agricultural constituency of Cavan, felt himself compelled to vote with the Protectionists. He wrote to Peel to explain his action and to point out the significance of the division in which 35 friends of Peel had voted in the minority while 28, including Peel himself, had helped to give the Government a bare majority of seven. He enclosed two lists with the names of these 63 Peelites whom he described as 'mostly men of considerable local influence, good fortune and high character'. 'They will stand by Free Trade . . .', he wrote. 'But they have no sympathies with and no confidence in the present Government. . . . These two lists, about half as many more absent, and nearly an equal number favourably inclined but generally voting with the Protectionists—say about 160—would rally around you personally, or any organization distinctly formed under your auspices and guided by your advice. . . .'[112] This was Young's last effort to persuade Peel to resume his role as a party leader, but to no avail.

A more thoroughly Protectionist attack on the Government was made later in the session in a motion by Grantley Berkley who demanded a Committee on the importation of corn. Here was a challenge to the genuine Free Trade Conservatives to rally behind Peel and Russell, and 50 of them helped to defeat the motion by a vote of 298 to 184. The nine who supported the motion appeared (with one exception) by this time to have thrown in their lot with the Derbyites.[113]

On 31 May Sir Edward Buxton, a Liberal and son of the great opponent of the slave trade, revived the sugar controversy with a motion that aroused the combined emotional enthusiasm of humanitarians and Protectionists. He condemned the policy of exposing free-grown sugar to competition with slave-grown sugar and, although alluding to the consequent economic distress in the

West Indian colonies, said that he was primarily speaking in the interests of humanity. Gladstone supported the motion, but concentrated his attention on the conditions in the West Indies. He maintained that the problem was not emancipation but the artificial labour scarcity, yet at the same time he claimed that the social conditions of the Negroes were worse than before emancipation. Lord Palmerston, not unnaturally, charged him with inconsistency. Fifty-one Free Trade Conservatives supported the motion, including Cardwell, Gladstone, Goulburn and Herbert, but 24, including Peel and Graham, helped to ensure its defeat by a vote of 275 to 234.[114]

On the sugar issue the Government were charged with giving support to slavery, but from another direction they were criticised for their quixotic attempt to suppress the slave trade. In 1849 a Commons Committee, chaired by William Hutt, an advanced Liberal, had brought in a report, carried by the chairman's casting vote, recommending that Britain give up its attempt to suppress the slave trade, but a similar committee in the Lords had made the opposite recommendation. Hutt now introduced a motion directing the Government to enter negotiations to relieve Britain of her responsibilities in this regard.

The motion cut across party lines and the Liberal chief whip was seriously afraid that the Government might be defeated by a combination of Radicals and Conservatives. As a result Russell summoned a party meeting, telling his followers that a vote for the motion was a vote for the restoration of slavery and that the defeat of the Government would be a matter of confidence.[115] The debate on the motion was short and confusing.[116] All speakers protested their detestation of slavery, but the supporters of the motion argued that the Africa Squadron had failed, that it only made the conditions of the middle passage worse for the slaves and that it wasted a lot of tax-payers' money. The Protectionists in particular accused the Government of hypocrisy by encouraging the importation of slave-grown sugar, while going through the motions of suppressing the trade in slaves. The opponents dwelt on the horrors of the slave trade, the progress that was being made in stamping it out and the gross betrayal that it would be to the cause to abandon it now. Cardwell, the Peelite member for Liverpool, spoke against the motion on humanitarian grounds, but his ex-colleague Gladstone, member for Oxford University, supported it. 'When I see the fact', he said, 'that with the assistance of our squadron we are making no advance, but on the contrary losing ground, I am compelled to consider the question in its whole breadth, and to set aside those feelings which certainly would have inclined me, if I could have done so, to accede to the policy which has been hitherto pursued. . . .'[117] The original sin of natural conservatism in Gladstone died hard, but, ironically, on this issue his High Tory colleague at Oxford, Sir Robert Inglis, voted with the angels. The motion was defeated by 232 to 154. It was supported by 24 Free Trade Conservatives and some 70 Protectionists and 50 Liberals (of the *laissez-faire*-radical variety); 36 Free Trade Conservatives, including Peel, Sidney Herbert and Cardwell, were in the majority.[118]

The Government's fiscal policy came in for many attacks from both Protectionists and Radicals, that again saw the ranks of the Free Trade Conservatives divided, although Peel and Graham always sided with the ministers. On 15 April, 27 of 35 Free Trade Conservatives participating supported a Conservative amendment aimed at increasing the proposed reduction of the stamp duties, and the Government was defeated by 164 to 135,[119] but on 30 April 46 Free Trade Conservatives supported and 18 opposed the Government in a division on Henley's unsuccessful motion for a reduction in official salaries.[120] The Derbyites were also very anxious to stop a Government Bill to extend the Parliamentary franchise in Ireland, which had been left untouched by the Reform Act of 1832. Peel and Graham supported the measure and 18 Free Trade Conservatives voted against a hostile amendment on the third reading, but it was supported by 30 others (see below, pp 72-4).[121]

The one occasion on which Peel was reluctantly persuaded to turn against the Russell government was, of course, the famous Don Pacifico debate of June 1850. The incident from which it sprang was long-drawn-out, and in its early stages Aberdeen urged Peel to criticise Palmerston's policy, without success. '. . . I really cannot see any reason why,' he wrote to Peel, 'if the occasion offered, after an hour spent in approving of the measures of the Government, five minutes might not be employed in

letting it be known that this laudation did not extend indiscrimi-
nately to all Departments.'[122]

Peel rejected Aberdeen's 'virtuous theory', which he said did
'not suit the rough practice of what is called Parliamentary
Government'.

> It becomes necessary [he told Aberdeen] to consider not only
> the particular vote, but its Consequences.
> If you mean to arraign the foreign Policy of a Government, it
> should be done in Earnest. To do it in Earnest there must be a
> concerted and combined attack. The speech of an Individual
> member—hinting a fault and hesitating dislike—would be a very
> innocuous proceeding. . . .
> This may be a very good reason for men acting in concert, that
> is forming party connections, or for those who have had enough
> of party connection and are resolved to maintain themselves free
> from these Engagements to retire altogether.[123]

Peel informed Graham of this exchange and, in their last
letters to each other, they rejoiced that they were so entirely in
agreement, as they usually were in these days. To criticise the
Government, argued Graham, implied a readiness to support a
motion that may consequently be brought against the Government, and responsibility for the consequences should the Government fall; 'and it is the wise remark of Mr. Burke', he added,
'that no coalition, which, under any specious name, carries in its
bosom the unreconciled principles of the original discord of
Parties, ever was or ever will be an healing Coalition'.[124]

Yet despite these lofty resolutions Palmerston's obstinate pug-
nacity eventually led Peel and Graham to change their minds—
presumably when they learnt of the withdrawal of the French
ambassador from London, and realised the full extent of the
crisis in Anglo-French relations. Lord Derby led the attack with
a motion of censure in the House of Lords, strongly supported by
Lords Aberdeen and Canning, Peel's former foreign minister and
his deputy minister, which was carried on 18 June by a majority
of 37. A few days later Roebuck moved his famous motion of
confidence in Palmerston's foreign policy and in the great four-
night debate that followed Peel and three of his former colleagues
spoke against the motion. Graham led the attack with a general
indictment of Palmerston's policy since 1846,[125] and Sidney

Herbert continued the same theme, concentrating his criticisms on Palmerston's policy in Italy.[126] Gladstone repudiated Palmerston's arrogant concept of *civis Romanus sum* and took the high moral ground that was to characterise his approach to foreign policy over the next forty-five years.[127] The most significant speech was Peel's, for it was his last public utterance and his only major speech against the Whig Government. He denied that he was taking part in any conspiracy against them. Indeed he had given his cordial support to their domestic policy but he could not in honesty subscribe to the declaration of Roebuck's motion nor approve of the course that Palmerston had taken against Greece.[128]

The Roebuck motion was passed on 28 June in a very full House by a vote of 310 to 264.[129] Of the 89 Free Trade Conservatives participating in the division, 67, including all the ex-ministers, joined Disraeli in the Opposition lobby, Peel, according to Gladstone, 'with visible signs of repugnance'.[130] We may be sure that he was not unhappy to see 22 of his former followers help to save the Government by voting in the majority.[131] The sequel is well known. The very next day he suffered the fatal fall from his horse that removed him forever from the House that he had dominated for so long.

It is clear that of the leading Peelites Gladstone was the most restive and dissatisfied during these years. In his unpublished paper on the party politics of the period, written five years after Peel's death, he sets forth his views frankly and fully. An examination of it throws some further light on the Peelite story of the years 1846 to 1850.

Surveying the parliamentary history of these years, Gladstone found that with one notable exception Peel always supported the Government. Upon questions involving the principle of Free Trade Gladstone admitted that the Government had the support of 'the whole body' of Peel's friends. 'But upon other questions such as that of the admission of slave grown sugar, the Canada Rebellion Losses Bill, and the Commutation of burdens on Real Property', he wrote, 'Sir Robert Peel always accompanied by a small minority of the Peelites and exercising a general influence on the House was able to win a majority for the Government.

And yet none of these votes were votes in accordance with his own personal leanings or disposition.' Whenever his former colleagues resorted to him for advice his answer could always be summed up in one sentence: 'get what you can in the right sense from the Government: but do not convulse the country by letting in the Protectionists'.[132]

The explanation for Peel's strange conduct Gladstone saw to be in this fear, but he argued that it was an unfounded one in marked contrast to the 'jovial confidence' of those two staunch Free Traders, Cobden and Bright, who 'had none of these qualms' and no fear of 'the phantom of a Derby Government'. He proceeds:

> ... The question may fairly be raised whether he would not have set as a greater luminary if he had been taken from us in 1846. ...
> The course taken by him both postponed the extinction of Protection as a Party creed and symbol; and moreover has even to this day been probably the means of preventing Parliament from resuming its natural and usual organization in the form of two political parties, a Government and an opposition.[133]

Still more serious, according to Gladstone, was the effect that Peel's course had 'upon the organization of Party and the state and working of Parliament'. As in the case of a broken china plate, he suggests, 'so should the fragments of a political party, shattered by a crisis, be reunited before a new surface has been formed by the constant attrition ... of public life'. The friends of Peel, however, did not feel disposed 'to enter into a political combination without either his participation or his countenance', and these were not forthcoming. 'But it was impossible for them alike as a matter of feeling and as a matter of honour to enter upon communications which if pursued might end in a formal separation between them and Sir Robert Peel.'

Gladstone then went on to speculate as to Peel's motives:

> ... Did he mean them to be eternally divorced from their old friends and eternally prohibited from making new? Did he contemplate the dying out of party connection altogether and the substitution of philosophical for Parliamentary Government? Could the practical mind of Sir Robert Peel overlook the necessity of working the Parliamentary Government of England by means of one or other of the great and stable subsisting combinations ...?

Had he in a remote corner of his capacious mind so much yet remaining of an idea that he himself might yet be wanted, as to be not unwilling that his trusted Staff should be kept in order and at hand? Or did he expect that Protectionism would die out while in Opposition and that thus his friends would in the natural progression of events again find the Conservative party surrounding them?[134]

What conclusions may we draw about the last four years of Peel's life? Are we to consider them with Gladstone as an unfortunate anti-climax to a great career, or may we agree with Professor Gash that their significant feature lay in the movement of Peel in the direction of the coalition that Aberdeen actually formed thirty months after Peel's death? The Don Pacifico vote was an exceptional one and did not indicate the end of the understanding between Peel and the Whigs. Yet his attitude to them was a negative one. His opinion of them was not very high, but he infinitely preferred them to the Protectionists. His strong aversion to any idea of his returning to office was not a pose, but the possibility could not be ruled out as long as he remained an active Member of Parliament, which he did almost to the day of his death. Aberdeen formed a coalition in 1852 on surprisingly good terms for the Peelites and one cannot deny that Peel might have been persuaded to do the same. It would not have been incompatible with his disinclination to countenance piecemeal adhesions of individual Peelites to the Liberals. There is of course no question of his superiority to Aberdeen as a prime minister, but I doubt whether he would have been as successful in getting along with the Whigs. Indeed, he might not have succeeded in inducing them to serve under him, as the respected and amiable Scottish aristocrat was able to do. (Even the Peelites showed greater affection for Aberdeen than for Peel.)

Gladstone's strictures on Peel bear some reassessment more than a century later. During this period Gladstone himself was still a Conservative party man at heart, although there was much on which he differed from the existing leaders of the party. He still looked back with nostalgia to the Peelite Conservative party and forward to its eventual revival. This is why he was so exasperated with Peel who had no interest in such a possibility and was genuinely content to support Russell's domestic policy.

Gladstone viewed that policy with a more jaundiced eye because it was the policy of the party which he had always opposed. The more support it received from Peel and his friends the less hope there was for the revival of a Peelite Conservative party. Gladstone and subsequent historians have tended to look upon the Peelite course in these years in terms of the official men, those who had held office under Peel. Insufficient attention has been paid to the 120 Members of Parliament whom we have tentatively classified as Liberal or Free Trade Conservatives (above, pp 30–1). An analysis of the divisions that we have examined reveals that some 48 (14 of them former officeholders) voted fairly consistently with Peel during these years and that another 24 did so more often than not. Of these, 6 had died or left the Commons before the end of the session of 1850 so that it would appear that Peel had left some 66 members still inclined towards him, of whom some 45 may be regarded as safe Peelites.[135]

We may define a Peelite, then, as a Free Trade Conservative who instinctively looked to Peel for a lead and normally voted with him in the years 1847–50 in support of the Liberal government and against the Protectionist opposition on those questions which the latter made an issue. Cardwell put the matter clearly when he observed to Lincoln in 1849 that to protect Free Trade the Peelites must 'walk into the lobby with the Government on those questions on which alone they will be seriously assailed by the Protectionists'.[136]

The Peelite was a Conservative in that he disliked change for change's sake and was concerned to preserve existing institutions in church and state and the existing class structure, but his approach to political questions was rational rather than emotional. His inclination was to treat an issue on its merits. He believed that existing institutions, including the church, would be healthier and more enduring if they worked efficiently and without creating injustices, and that democratic radicals would most easily be frustrated if legitimate popular grievances were removed. In a kingdom where the great majority of the population and almost all the ruling class were Protestant it was absurd, the Peelites thought, to see any great threat from the mostly poor Roman Catholic minority. On the other hand, no matter how misguided that minority might be, it was both unjust and im-

E

politic to give them unnecessary grievances.[137] Consequently the Peelite normally supported the Maynooth grant and was less likely to be upset by the alleged threat of papal aggression. He instinctively recoiled from the blatant bigotry of Conservatives such as Spooner or Newdegate and the corrupt practices of a politician like William Beresford. Above all the typical Peelite was a Free Trader, who generally accepted the current orthodoxy of the political economists, and here his views were in many respects similar to those of the Manchester School. His predilection was for *laissez-faire*, although he was not a complete doctrinaire and recognised that there were some areas where the state must interfere, but for social or political rather than economic reasons. Peel and his friends were prepared to take more positive steps to meet the extraordinary problems of the Irish famine than was Sir Charles Trevelyan, the mentor of the Whigs. Likewise the Peelite instinct was to encourage colonial autonomy for economic as much as political reasons, and here at least some of them shared common opinions with various Radicals.

Not all the Peelites, of course, held all these views *in toto* or lived up to all these ideals, but their general tendency was in this direction, Gladstone as much as any of them, and this is why they ultimately had a more likely future with the Liberals than with the Derbyite Conservatives. They disagreed in principle with the Derbyites on commercial policy and religious toleration; they criticised the Whigs for lack of judgement and expertise and for their subordination of ability to connection. This dual outlook was well expressed by Lincoln in the autumn of 1850 in a letter to Gladstone advancing the view that it remained the duty of the Peelites to complete Peel's commercial policy, a task in which Derby could have no interest and with which the Liberals alone were not to be trusted. It was up to them, he argued, to develop a counter-project 'to the wild schemes of Cobden on the one hand and the impotent frettings of Wood on the other'.[138]

Dr E. J. Hobsbawm has said that the Peelites in Parliament represented very much the 'group of business families assimilated into a landed oligarchy, though at odds with it when the economic interests of land and business clashed'.[139] The names of Peel, Gladstone, Baring, Cardwell and Walter seem to bear this point out, but in actual fact Professor Aydelotte has shown that there was no appreciable difference in the social composition of the two sections of the Conservative party that split in 1846 on the repeal of the Corn Laws.[140] The same is true of the smaller group of 48 whom we have identified as continuing Peelites in the Parliament of 1847–52. Only seven or eight appear to have come from a business background and only five to have been directly involved in business, of whom only two could be called self-made business men.[141] Five had been or were engaged in an active legal career, but the great majority were men of leisure drawn from the landed classes. Indeed 22 had close connections by marriage or birth with the peerage. A third of the total had once held government or household appointments and in this respect only did they differ sociologically from the main body of the Conservatives.[142]

It might in any event have been supposed that through their parliamentary constituencies the Peelites had a close connection with the world of industry, commerce and finance, but if we examine the geographical distribution of their seats we shall find that even this was not the case. They composed only 6–7 per cent of the membership of the House of Commons in the parliament of 1847, but they were spread surprisingly widely throughout the United Kingdom, except in Ireland, holding some 7 per cent of the English, 9 per cent of the Scottish, 17 per cent of the Welsh, but only 3 per cent of the Irish seats. Only 6 Peelites represented English counties, but the 27 holding borough seats were evenly spread, 6 in the north, 7 in the midlands, 7 in the southwest and 7 in the southeast. Only 8 Peelites represented boroughs with over 1,000 electors, and of these only one, Edward Cardwell, sat for a major city, Liverpool, which he lost in 1852. Oldham and Stockport were the only industrial towns returning Peelites, John Duncuft and James Heald respectively, two backbenchers of business background, of whom the former died and the latter was defeated in 1852. For the most part the English Peelites sat for boroughs with old historic names such as Lancaster, Warwick, Nottingham, Devizes, Plymouth, Salisbury, Bury St Edmunds and Canterbury, as well as more obscure places such as Ripon, Tamworth, Honiton, Thetford and Grantham. Three of them represented boroughs from that small category with less than 300 voters, while nine were comfortably installed in proprietary boroughs. Although progressive in their views on the commercial policy of the newly industrialised Britain, to a curious extent the Peelites represented in their constituencies the old England of the past; and of course in Gladstone and Goulburn they held two of the four English university seats. Nevertheless, despite such ties the political differences between the Peelites and the main body of the Conservative party survived, as we shall see, the death of their great leader.[143]

*Notes to this chapter are on pages 184–91*

# Chapter 3 THE PEELITES WITHOUT PEEL 1850–1

Now is the stately column broke,
The beacon's light is quenched in smoke;
The trumpet's silver voice is still;
The warder silent on the hill.

THESE LINES, written by Sir Walter Scott to commemorate the death of the younger Pitt, were appropriately quoted by Gladstone in the Commons the day after Peel's death. Although he died out of office in a time of peace, the national sense of loss was not unlike that experienced in 1806.[1] As with Pitt, there was a widespread feeling in the country that Peel was a statesman who towered above his contemporaries and who might be relied upon to take the helm with a firm hand in time of crisis. As long as he remained in the House of Commons no ministry could afford to depart too far from the principles of sound government for which he stood. As we have seen, Russell leaned heavily on his support and Stanley could scarcely hope to secure any firm tenure of office without it. 'He was pre-eminently the "representative man" of the nineteenth century in its political aspect', in the words of the *Morning Chronicle* (3 July 1850) '. . . the statesman of an age when a powerful and enlightened public opinion was gradually obtaining a more and more complete sway over the mechanism of government.' Now all this was over; the magic spell that Peel had exerted in his last years was broken. Many instinctively regarded his death as disastrous, but some saw that it was in the natural order of things. 'He had done his work,' commented Bulwer Lytton, '. . . There was nothing left for him to do.'[2] More significant, perhaps, was Cornewall Lewis's observation that upon Gladstone the death of Peel would 'have the effect of removing a weight from a spring'.[3]

Joseph Hume, the veteran Radical, anticipated Russell before he reached the House by moving its adjournment. Gladstone, the only former colleague of Peel's present, seconded the motion in a speech comparing Peel to Pitt and quoting the lines cited above.[4] Gladstone voiced the general sense as to the prematurity of Peel's death, but in a private memorandum written the following year he noted that the closing years of Peel's life were 'beneath those that had preceded them'.[5] In another memorandum written years later he reiterated his view that Peel was mistaken in making such efforts to keep the Protectionists out of office, since in fact that only postponed a final settlement of the Free Trade issue which they were really powerless to reverse. In this respect, Gladstone then maintained, the death of Peel was not a great calamity, although 'in all other respects it was indeed great'.

> The moral atmosphere of the House of Commons [he continued] has never since his death been quite the same and is now [1876] widely different. He had a kind of authority that was possessed by no one else. Lord Russell might in some respects compete with, in some even excel him: but to him as leader of the Liberals, the loss of such an opponent was immense.[6]

Lincoln, who had none of Gladstone's reservations, regarded Peel's death as a 'national calamity'. He rejoiced that the dead leader's last speech and vote had been an assertion of independence. 'To our dying hours', he wrote to Gladstone, 'those of us who have been associated with him in political life must retain our sorrow for his loss.'[7] In this sentence we may see one of the main ingredients of Peelism in the years that followed.

Peel's death left his followers leaderless for the time being. Although Lord Aberdeen was eventually recognised as the heir, he was not the sort of man consciously to seek the dead leader's mantle, as he indicated in a letter to Guizot, in which he discounted the probability of a reunion with the Conservative party:

> Many look to me as the means of effecting this union from my good-will towards all and the absence of any extreme opinions on those subjects by which they are divided; but the difficulties

would be enormous and probably insurmountable. I must confess
. . . I feel no great disposition for a work requiring so much
exertion, and the result of which is so doubtful.[8]

In terms of age and experience Graham was the most obvious
leader in the House of Commons, but he had no inclination to
head an independent party and some of the younger Peelites did
not at this time have complete confidence in him as a political
ally. Goulburn was a less impressive figure than Graham; on
grounds of seniority and closeness to Peel he might also have been
considered as a candidate for Peelite leadership, but in fact his
political career was almost over, and his general outlook was too
conservative to satisfy some of the younger Peelites. Discussing
the possibility of Conservative reunion on the eve of Peel's death,
Disraeli commented years later that he had always thought 'that
old Goulburn was the man whom Sir Robert Peel and Lord
Derby [then Stanley] would have brought forward, and furnished
up like an old piece of dusty furniture', under whom they 'might
have all served without any great outrage of personal feelings'.[9]
Goulburn was not the man to galvanise the remnant of the
Peelites to united action; indeed, rusticating on Putney Heath, he
complained to Cardwell about this time that he saw nobody and
heard nothing.[10]

Gladstone, Herbert and Lincoln were the trio who were to do
most to keep the Peelites together in the two years that followed,
but in the latter half of 1850 they were all preoccupied with other
matters. Herbert was still busily involved in the operation of his
female emigration scheme, and as soon as the session was over
Gladstone departed for Italy for reasons of family health and
there he became deeply interested in the cause of Italian national-
ism. Lincoln, already estranged from his father, now faced the
final rupture of his unhappy marriage. The previous year his wife
had run off to the Continent with Lord Walpole, with whom she
was living in Italy. Gladstone had pursued her on his friend's
behalf and vainly attempted to persuade her to return to the path
of virtue. Some friends thought it just as well that he failed.[11]
Following the birth of a child Lincoln instituted divorce proceedings against his wife that resulted in a private Bill being
passed in the summer of 1850.[12] Lincoln remained out of the

country for the greater part of the session of 1850 and he expressed his sense of shock at the news of Peel's death in a letter to Gladstone in which he wrote:

> . . . the sorrows of my domestic life have been so associated with his ready and friendly Counsels and I have ever found in him so delicate a sympathy and so sagacious advice that the termination of my married life and the simultaneous death of my Friend and Councillor seems to leave me in a void which yet appears bewildering.[13]

Shortly after his return to England the Duke of Newcastle's health began to fail and Lincoln was faced with the prospect of an early translation to the House of Lords. He wondered whether he should not 'abandon public life altogether', but politics were in his blood and in the same letter he discussed the outlook eagerly with Gladstone, hoping that they might continue the close co-operation which for many years he had found 'invariably agreeable'. 'I think it is due to the memory of our great leader', he wrote, '. . . to show to the country what can be done to render complete our great commercial policy. . . .' This meant the extension of Free Trade which in his opinion ruled out the possibility of co-operation with Stanley.[14]

Lincoln spent the autumn months by his father's bedside, but late in November the old man experienced a temporary recovery and all the old animosity returned as he ordered his grandchildren out of the house. 'You know not the misery I have to undergo,' Lincoln lamented to Bonham, whom he asked to find him some inexpensive quarters in London for his family.[15] Finally on 12 January 1851 the old Duke died[16] and Lincoln's promising career in the House of Commons was over. A few months later he took his seat in the House of Lords as the fifth Duke of Newcastle.

At the time of Peel's death the Don Pacifico debate had seemed to indicate some *rapprochement* between Peelites and Conservatives, but another issue shaping up at the same time, which Stanley had hoped would strengthen the connection, in the end contributed to a continuation of the estrangement. In the spring of 1850, as we have seen, the Liberals had introduced an Irish Franchise Bill, seeking to remedy the injustice done to the Irish by the Reform Act of 1832, which had left Ireland with a much smaller ratio of voters to population than the rest of the United Kingdom (one adult male in twenty compared to one in five in England and Wales; see above, p 60). The Conservative peers took fright at the proposal to enfranchise £8 ratepayers, which would have increased the electorate by about a quarter of a million, and Stanley made great efforts to persuade Aberdeen that the Peelites should join them in thwarting it. He passed on the views of one critic who said of the Bill: 'It altogether destroys the influence of the aristocracy, and will place *at once* the *whole* constituency of Ireland in the hands of the Priests, demagogues and infidels with the solitary exception of the Representation of the University of Dublin.'[17] He considered a £15 franchise the minimum acceptable and rejected one Peelite compromise proposal of £12, while deploring the impossibility of finding anybody capable of speaking for the Peelites as a body. He professed an interest in the reunion of the Conservative party, but not at the cost of this measure. 'If this Bill passes,' he warned, 'it creates a Constituency for Ireland, which apart from its bearing on England, will render the existence of a Conservative Government hereafter hopeless.' He went on, therefore, to argue that they should avoid being drawn into a dangerous compromise. 'On the other hand,' he added, 'an election with the present Constituency, it is notorious would add to the strength, I will not say of the Protectionist, but of the Conservative party; and surely this is a card which is not lightly to be thrown away.'[18]

While this correspondence did not have any positive results it shows clearly how ready the Protectionist leader was to welcome the Peelites back into the fold and that no personal barrier divided him from the Peelite leader in the Lords. He said that he would be disposed to act on Lord Aberdeen's advice in matters of foreign policy. 'I wish to God', he added, 'that in this I could induce you not only to act, but to influence others to act in accordance with mine'[19]

The views of the Peelite peers on the matter varied. The Duke of Argyll, as a large Highland landlord, feared the enfranchisement of such voters whom he regarded as 'totally devoid of independence in character'.[20] The Duke of Buccleuch, on the other hand, who had originally sided with Stanley in the Peel cabinet in opposing the repeal of the Corn Laws, took a more liberal attitude on this issue. He supported the principle of extending the franchise, recalling that the Peel cabinet had agreed to it in 1844. 'I cannot look upon this solely as a party question,' he wrote to Aberdeen; 'it is too serious to be so treated, and tho' out of personal feeling and friendship towards Stanley I would make a great sacrifice; the more I consider this point the more convinced do I become in my own conscience that he is wrong as to present policy and future results.'[21]

In the end Stanley reluctantly accepted the second reading of the Bill in the Lords, but obtained an amendment raising the franchise to £15. On 30 July, however, 19 Peelites in the Commons, including Graham, Goulburn and Cardwell, joined the Government in reducing the £15 requirement to £12. The alliance made in the Lords and continued in the Commons on the Don Pacifico issue was already broken. Young, one of the more conservative Peelites, reflected the continuing coolness of that group when he wrote to Gladstone that he had no fear of Stanley, but that 'the party to which he is allied are rash and violent and all their sayings and doings augur a thoroughly reactionary policy'. He believed that if the Protectionists were only less unreasonable reunion could be achieved. 'But it is union alone that could make it such a force,' he added, 'and disunion and irreconcilable hostility are all that the Protectionists ever breathe.'[22] Stanley, himself, was of course unhappy at the way in which things had gone. He told Aberdeen that he had given proof of his desire to act with the Peelites in the House of Lords and asked even before the vote in the Commons if Aberdeen 'did not think it a strange evidence of friendship that men in the House of Commons, not connected with the Government, should vote against their own opinions and convictions, in order to place themselves in opposition to him'. 'He seemed a good deal hurt', Aberdeen told Gladstone, 'at the course which had been pursued, and said that if it had not been for my assurances he should have been disposed to regard it as proof of the most inveterate hostility.'[23]

The session of 1850 ended therefore with the Peelites apparently leaderless, but with a reunion of the Conservative party no closer. There were ample grounds for asking whether the

Peelites had any legitimate role left to play, but suddenly before the next session opened an issue arose which brought together most of the Peelite ex-ministers and some of their followers as leading defenders of the liberal principle of religious toleration in a Parliament that seemed to have forgotten its meaning.

On 29 September 1850 a papal brief was published in Rome restoring the Roman Catholic episcopacy in England after a break of almost four centuries. In the choice of territorial titles care was taken to avoid the names of existing dioceses of the Church of England, but the wording of the brief and still more of the inaugural pastoral letter of the new Cardinal Archbishop of Westminster (Wiseman), issued 'from out of the Flaminian Gate' at Rome, was indiscreet.[24] The step had been under discussion for some years and friendly conversations with Lord Minto in 1848 and more recent utterances by Lord John Russell had led the papal authorities to expect no difficulties. The climate of opinion had changed, however, as a result of the Revolution of 1848, and Pio Nono was no longer the popular figure that he had been before that event. Consequently reaction in Protestant England was hostile from the very beginning. Listing the territorial names of the new sees *The Times* indignantly commented that 'all this laid down with the authority and minuteness of an Act of Parliament, by a Papal Bull, certainly constitutes one of the strangest pieces of mummery we ever remember to have witnessed'.[25]

A month later, on 4 November, the Prime Minister addressed his unfortunate letter to the Bishop of Durham, in which he roundly condemned the papal action and forecast countermeasures by his government.[26] Up and down the country Protestant spokesmen, including many Anglican bishops, denounced the papacy and its latest abominations in language that harked back to Tudor times. Protest meetings were organised in almost every county and images of the Pope and his new cardinal replaced Guy Fawkes in that November's bonfires. Poor Wiseman on his return from Rome was shocked to discover the intensity of the storm that he had unwittingly helped to stir up and hastened to issue a reasonable explanation of all that had happened, but only time could calm the tempest.[27]

Lord John Russell's name will always be associated with most of the great reforms of the second quarter of the nineteenth century, especially those connected with the cause of religious liberty. Yet it is an irony of history that one of the few measures that his own ministry of 1846–52 produced which is still remembered today was the illiberal and reactionary Ecclesiastical Titles Act. It may be asked whether he really believed all that he said in his letter to the Bishop of Durham in view of the fact that Roman Catholic territorial bishoprics had long existed in Ireland and in Canada and that he himself in 1845 had advocated the repeal of the clauses of the Act of 1829 forbidding the assumption of the titles of Protestant sees in Ireland. Nor can it be suggested that he acted on impulse since his Durham letter was written four weeks after the publication of Wiseman's pastoral, and a few days before he had written to the Queen to say that there was nothing to be alarmed at in the Pope's action since it could only affect Roman Catholics. 'The matter to create rational alarm is, as Your Majesty says,' he added, 'the growth of Roman Catholic doctrines and practices within the bosom of the Church.'[28] Herein lies the explanation of the intensity of the anti-Catholic Protestant outburst against 'papal aggression' at this time when Tractarianism seemed so widespread. But it is difficult to avoid the conclusion that there was an element of calculation in Lord John's public indignation and that he saw the situation as an opportunity to take a popular stand and to bolster up the unsteady position of his tottering government. Graham had no doubts on this score when he wrote to Herbert: 'Lord John's letter was hasty, intemperate and ill-advised. He sought to catch some fleeting popularity at the expense of the principles of his political life; and in his eagerness to strike a blow at "Gladstonianism" he forgot that the "superstitious mummeries" which he enumerates are part of the creed of one-half of the British Army, and of eight millions of his fellow subjects.'[29] It may be presumed that some of Russell's own colleagues regretted the course that he took, but as a cabinet they accepted the *fait accompli* of the Durham letter and were resigned to its legislative implications.[30] On this issue it may be noted that the Queen took a more level-headed view of the situation than did her Prime Minister in his unfortunate letter.[31]

In a memorandum written for his colleagues, however, Russell was somewhat more judicial. 'It seems to me that we ought neither to leave the matter alone nor to proceed in a hurry,' he wrote. He proposed to ask the Pope for an explanation, and if it transpired that he was merely seeking to regulate his own spiritual relations with the Roman Catholics then they could only say to him that he had been 'very unfortunate in his expressions'.[32] Palmerston, however, advised against opening up any direct conversations with Rome, since, he argued, the Pope would have no real inducement to retract, knowing that the British Government could not go back to the Penal Laws and persecution.[33] Despite the assurances of Cardinal Wiseman and others, some sort of legislation was deemed politically necessary.

The point of view of the more enlightened Peelites was well expressed by Roundell Palmer in a letter to Bishop Blomfield, who had asked for advice on some form of legislation. 'The longer I have lived, the more attached I have become to the principle of religious liberty, and more distinctly I have learnt to see the interest which every man, who is in earnest about his Religion, has in the maintenance of that principle,' he wrote. While abhorring the teachings of the Roman Catholic Church he was strongly opposed to the idea of punitive legislation, which, he said with foresight, would be impossible to enforce without a return to persecution. 'Under these circumstances', he argued, 'I think it unnecessary, unprofitable and at variance with an intelligent adherence to the principles of civil and religious liberty, to enter upon a legislative crusade against the mere phraseology, by which a voluntary church naturally, according to its own religious ideas, designates its own Episcopacy.'[34]

When Parliament met on 4 February 1851 the speech from the throne promised legislation to deal with 'papal aggression', and in the ensuing debate the long argument began that was to dominate the whole session. Three days later Russell moved for leave to introduce his Ecclesiastical Titles Bill in a speech which Bright said would have been very good if delivered three hundred years earlier.[35]

The debates on the Bill were interminable, although it was passed by large majorities at every reading.[36] It was strenuously opposed, of course, by most of the Irish Liberals who received stout support from some of the leading Radicals.[37] In the debate on the second reading, however, the most striking opposition came from Peel's former colleagues, with the exception only of Goulburn. They all demonstrated their Protestant allegiance by denouncing the papal action, but none of them believed that it warranted legislation. Sidney Herbert, ridiculing the ministry for its inconsistencies, made a powerful plea for the principle of religious liberty and pronounced the Bill a nullity. He refused to believe that Roman Catholicism offered any serious threat to England since he thought that 'the doctrines of the Church of Rome were foreign to the genius of the English people'.[38] Gladstone, recently returned from Italy where he had been championing the cause of Italian liberals and anti-clericals, made a speech which Morley describes as one of 'his three or four most conspicuous masterpieces', but all his eloquence could not win the House. 'Through it all', Morley writes, 'the House watched and listened in enchantment, as to a magnificent tragedian playing a noble part in a foreign tongue.'[39] Sir James Graham said that he considered the proposal to be a reversal of the Emancipation Act and he expressed his amazement to find on the back of such a Bill the names of Russell, Grey and Romilly, all so closely connected in former times with the cause of religious liberty. He denied that English Protestantism needed statutory protection against Roman Catholicism and appealed to the spirit of the champions of Emancipation, living and dead. In a splendid peroration he concluded:

> There may have been some movement towards Rome on the surface of what are called the higher ranks, but the deep undercurrent of the feeling of this country is essentially Protestant. It is written in their very heart's core—and, what is more, it is written in those Bibles to which they have free access; and while they enjoy those privileges and possess those feelings we have no occasion for a Bill like this. I say there is no danger in England which justifies it—every feeling in Ireland condemns it. It is a brand of discord cast down to inflame the passions of the people. . . .[40]

The second reading was passed on 25 March by an overwhelming vote of 438 to 95. Only 18 Liberal Conservatives were in the minority but this number included all the prominent Peelites except Goulburn.[41]

The debate on the third reading was finally passed on 4 July by 263 to 46, with the Irish Catholic members abstaining in protest against the acceptance of fresh amendments at that late stage.[42] The House of Lords disposed of the Bill after three nights of brisk debate in which Peelite peers (Aberdeen, Newcastle, Canning and St Germans) led the opposition; but the second reading was passed by 265 to 38, including proxies. On the final night Lord Lansdowne made the interesting admission that had the Pope informed the Government of his intentions and made certain adjustments in the wording of the proposed episcopal titles, there would have been no objection to his action. Thus after six months' debate it appeared that 'papal aggression' amounted to no more than the way in which an inherently harmless act was done. The minority of opponents in the Lords felt so strongly about this anomaly that they entered two lengthy protests in the Journal of the House.[43]

We are not here concerned with the sequel, but it may be noted that the Act was never enforced and that eventually, when its most formidable opponent found himself in Lord John's shoes, it was quietly repealed, but by this time Gladstone was disestablishing the Irish Church and an Ecclesiastical Titles Act was as archaic as an Elizabethan penal law. The immediate political significance of the legislation was that it further postponed the day when a Liberal-Peelite juncture might be arranged. It may also have widened the gap between the Peelite leaders and many of the more Protestant of the Conservative backbench Free Traders. On the other hand it inevitably raised the reputation—and the influence—of the former with the Irish Liberals, now mostly cut off from Lord John. Moreover the large majorities for the Government did not represent any real political strength, for on the very night before the second reading was passed the Government only succeeded in repelling an attack from Disraeli on the subject of agricultural distress by 14 votes and a week later it was defeated in a small House on Locke King's famous reform motion.

The Protectionists made Disraeli's motion on agricultural distress the basis of a fresh overture to Graham. Disraeli promised that in return for support on this matter they would be ready to 'listen with the utmost deference and willingness to any suggestions on his part which [might] otherwise accomplish the

common purpose',[44] and Londonderry, as an old friend, appealed
to him saying that he had 'no object whatsoever but to see the
Great Conservative party consolidated once more under the best
statesmen whom we have yet left to depend on'.[45] Graham dis-
claimed any pretension to occupy the role of Peel. He recognised
the necessity of a two-party system, but maintained that the
policy of Protection, in which Stanley persisted, placed an 'in-
separable barrier' between them.[46] When Disraeli's motion on
agricultural distress was debated a few weeks later, Graham and
Cardwell spoke against it and were joined by some 37 other
Liberal Conservatives (including Goulburn and Herbert).[47] The
incident is important in that it coincided with the 'papal aggression' debate and showed that, while this was opening up a
serious rift between Liberals and Peelites for the time being, they
still had basic principles in common that might yet bring them
together. Indeed, Russell made Graham's friendly speech against
the Disraeli motion the occasion to attempt yet another approach.
In a long and amicable interview with Graham he offered him a
seat in the cabinet replacing either George Grey at the Home
Office or Hobhouse at the Board of Control. Graham declined,
alluding to their differences over the Ecclesiastical Titles Bill, and
told Russell that he thought he could be of more use giving
independent assistance outside the Government. In Russell's
view, as expressed to the Queen, he 'did not wish to embark in
a boat which was going to sink'.[48]

In the midst of the debate on the Ecclesiastical Titles Bill one
of those sudden political crises blew up on an entirely different
matter, that were so typical of the 1850s. The Government was
defeated on 20 February 1851, by a majority of its own followers
(100 to 52), on Locke King's motion for the extension of the
franchise.[49] The result was a political crisis that in some ways
foreshadowed December 1852. Russell, differing with his cabinet
on the matter of Parliamentary Reform, pressed hard by the
Opposition on their agricultural resolution, and perhaps, in view
of old difficulties with Palmerston and new difficulties with the
Irish, not too sorry to get out of the mess altogether, resigned
from office, although there was clearly no constitutional requirement for him to do so.

When Stanley was called upon to form a government he frankly doubted his ability to carry out the royal command without assistance from some of Peel's former ministers, and so he suggested to the Queen that she should first seek to obtain a coalition ministry of Whigs and Peelites.[50] The Queen and Prince Albert, who bristled at Stanley's proposal of reimposing a duty on corn, welcomed this advice and proceeded to summon Russell, Aberdeen and Graham to the Palace. A strange series of interviews followed between the royal couple and the three statesmen and various combinations of them; in the middle of it all the old Duke of Wellington came to dinner and roundly condemned the Protectionists for their foolish goings on. Aberdeen was most co-operative; he 'declared his inability to join a Protectionist Ministry; he did not pretend to understand the question of Free Trade, but it was a point of honour with him not to abandon it, and now since Sir R. Peel's death a matter of piety'. He was even prepared to accept an extension of the franchise. But all sorts of difficulties were put up by Sir James Graham who persuaded Aberdeen to turn down formal proposals put to them by Russell in writing. In their reply on 24 February Aberdeen and Graham said that they could not even accept a watered-down Ecclesiastical Titles Bill and expressed doubts about the way in which Russell proposed to tackle Reform. Graham also asserted the need for a more rigorous economy than he thought Russell was prepared to accept. Russell naturally took this answer as a refusal and gave up his commission.[51]

That evening the Queen called on Aberdeen and Graham to form a government. The former appears to have been ready to act on the Queen's wish, but Graham threw cold water on it. Once again the 'papal aggression' issue was made the scapegoat, for Aberdeen and Graham recognised that they were probably 'two of the most unpopular men in England at the moment'. There was now a growing feeling among some of the Peelites that Stanley should be given a chance to form a ministry. This would make a realignment of parties easier, and indeed there would be a much better chance of a future Whig-Peelite coalition, entered into 'on a footing of perfect equality' after they had experienced a period of joint opposition.[52]

Stanley now accepted the Queen's commission, but with no

F

illusions. He indicated to her that his chances of success largely turned on the willingness of Gladstone to join him and he was even ready to give the latter the lead in the House of Commons. Gladstone arrived home from Naples on 26 February to find a pressing letter from Stanley awaiting him, but before he could leave his house in Carlton Gardens the Duke of Newcastle arrived to urge him not to join the Protectionists. Newcastle was also against a coalition. 'I am sure our rule of conduct at this juncture', he wrote in a note of welcome preceding his visit, 'must be a prudent waiting on events and perfect readiness for any self sacrifice which those events may prove to be a duty. I think a Coalition at the moment would be fatal to character and most mischievous to the Queen and the country.'[53]

Stanley proposed to offer Canning the Foreign Office and Gladstone any other office he might choose, but he made the latter's refusal easy and inevitable by proposing to reintroduce a small duty on corn. On hearing of Gladstone's refusal Canning did likewise. Lord Ellenborough, when asked, first accepted office, 'but having been sent on a mission to Mr. Goulburn in order to see whether he could convert him, he came home himself converted, and withdrew his acceptance again'.[54] As a result of these refusals Stanley gave up the commission with obvious relief and advised the Queen to recall Lord John.

The Queen then discussed with Russell the possibility of a temporary Whig administration to pass the Ecclesiastical Titles Bill, after which a coalition with the Peelites might follow. This project, however, was given up on the ground that it would be unacceptable to the Whigs (let alone the Peelites), especially those Whig ministers who might be displaced and who told Russell they 'would not be *warming pans*'.[55] Consequently there was nothing for it but for the old ministry to resume office. Russell told the Queen that the most natural solution to the existing political quandary was 'a Coalition sooner or later with the Peel party', but this could not be done until the Ecclesiastical Titles Bill had been disposed of. That done, 'it would be seen whether the Ministry had sufficient strength to go on'. In that event they might, as the occasion arose, seek assistance from the Peelites. Otherwise the Queen could then form a new (coalition) government, 'free from the obstacles which have lately been fatal'.[56]

In the subsequent explanations in Parliament Stanley placed the burden of his failure on the refusal of the Peelites and spoke with an appalling frankness (scarcely to be equalled until the days of Stanley Baldwin) of lack of ministerial material among his own followers.[57] In the Lower House both Russell and Graham attributed the failure of their negotiations to the Ecclesiastical Titles Bill, but they alluded to each other in such friendly terms that the door was left open for future discussions.[58]

Greville took a low view of what had happened. Although each of the participants appeared to have acted with unselfishness and public spirit, he detected 'no little jealousy, dislike and ill-will' beneath the surface. Indeed, in his view, 'in all that passed, nobody was in *earnest*'.[59]

Gladstone deplored the tacit support given by Graham in his speech to Russell's Reform proposals, but he now hoped that Graham would take the lead of an independent Peelite party. He pressed Sir James hard on this point, but the latter declined to act.[60] Graham told Londonderry, who was still advocating Conservative reunion, that a third party would be 'fatal to the country', that no one else could take Peel's place, and that 'ere long' he 'would embrace one of the two great organizations'. Londonderry, of course, agreed that a separate Peelite party would be 'perfectly preposterous and absurd' and in July once more appealed to Aberdeen to act, telling him that he had it in his power 'to weld the scattered fragments into some consolidated shape'.[61] Aberdeen, however, had no ambition to assume such a role.

When Gladstone arrived in London in the midst of the constitutional crisis of 1851 he had come hot from Naples, anxious to do what was in his power to help the Italian liberals languishing in Neapolitan prisons. Since the British Foreign Secretary, Palmerston, was *persona non grata* with the government of Naples and its ally, Austria, there could be no hope of action on his intercession. What alternative was there, Gladstone asked, but publicly to expose the horrors he had discovered and bring the Neapolitan government to book before the tribunal of European public opinion. But first he must consult his friend and leader Lord Aberdeen, whose sagacity in the realm of foreign affairs was always esteemed by the friends of Peel. All this is a familiar chapter in Gladstone's biography, but it is also an important episode in the Peelite story. Foreign policy was a field in which the Peelites had remained aloof from the Liberals, since in Lord Aberdeen was to be found the opposite pole to Palmerston, and Derby would have been delighted to have had Aberdeen as a Foreign Secretary whenever he formed a government.

Gladstone, hitherto one of the more conservative of the younger Peelites, now seemed headed to the other camp unless Aberdeen could restrain him or he could convert Aberdeen. Such was the great respect each had for the other that their political and personal friendship survived the shock of the ensuing clash of wills.

Aberdeen showed sympathy with Gladstone's views; how could he help but be disturbed by such shocking information obtained at first hand from a trustworthy witness? But as a natural conservative and a pacifically minded diplomat, who had never forgotten the horrors of the Napoleonic wars, which he had witnessed with his own eyes, his normal disposition was to favour the *status quo*. At all costs a head-on collision of the Palmerstonian sort should be avoided. He persuaded Gladstone to let him see what he could do by private overtures through Prince Schwarzenberg, the Austrian minister, and suggested that Gladstone should submit a 'statement of the case' for his consideration. Early in April Gladstone presented his celebrated Letter to Lord Aberdeen 'about the proceedings of the Neapolitan government', urging that any action should be taken 'with all practicable despatch', and suggesting that he should know the results by the beginning of June.[62] Aberdeen proceeded to address Prince Schwarzenberg on the basis of this information and then they settled back to await the reply.

Weeks turned into months and Gladstone became restive as he thought of his friend Poerio, suffering in his dungeon. On 12 June he urged Aberdeen to renew his enquiries.[63] By 7 July he had given up all hope and proposed publication of the letter.[64] On Aberdeen's plea he promised to restrain the printer another week. Then his patience finally ran out, and he announced that he was going ahead, since Aberdeen's interference had failed. The latter gently asked him 'by some insertion, to let it appear that I do not share your conviction that all remedy is hopeless'.[65]

No sooner had Gladstone rushed into print than Prince Schwarzenberg's long-awaited letter arrived, promising, as a grudging concession to Aberdeen, to bring Gladstone's representations before the Neapolitan government, but at the same time exonerating the latter from doing any more than the English did in Ireland or with the Chartist leaders.[66] A fruitless controversy then developed between spokesmen for the Neapolitan government and Gladstone, with poor Aberdeen caught in the middle. The survival of the warm friendship of the two under the circumstances is to the credit of both, for Gladstone was disappointed at Aberdeen's caution and Aberdeen annoyed by Gladstone's precipitancy. 'The only thing of which I think I have any reason to complain', Aberdeen wrote after the event, 'is that you did not allow me a fair chance of effecting the object which you had in view.' He admitted that the Neapolitan reaction had been discouraging, 'but I am by no means prepared', he went on, 'to say that a more urgent remonstrance on my part would have been unsuccessful. . . . I always trusted much more to the weight of Austrian influence. . . . A publication therefore without waiting for his [Schwarzenberg's] answer to my application, not only placed me in a very awkward position with respect to him, but deprived him also of the means of most efficiently making his own representation. . . .' He had, however, written once again to Schwarzenberg urging him still to intervene since 'the interests of humanity and of monarchical government in Italy were equally at stake'. For all his sorrow at Gladstone's rashness, Aberdeen showed his continued affection, affirming his 'firm conviction' that Gladstone had acted in the whole matter under the conscientious belief that he was 'discharging a solemn duty' imposed upon him.[67]

To his old friend Princess Lieven Aberdeen expressed his feelings towards Gladstone with great candour. 'I have certainly much reason to complain of Gladstone,' he wrote on 30 August (he was unhappy that Gladstone's published letter should have been addressed to him); 'but he is so honest and so perfectly sincere; and we are both personally and politically connected so closely, that although I have not concealed my feelings from him,

it is impossible for me to entertain any resentment.'[68] Gladstone's
persistence in the same line may account for a slightly sharper
note in another letter a few months later, where Aberdeen wrote
of him: 'He is one of the best men in existence, but he has done
more mischief by his ill-advised proceeding than it is possible to
estimate, and unless I am much mistaken, he will, in the course
of his life, do much more.'[69] From Aberdeen's point of view
these were prophetic words that might have been uttered by
many of Gladstone's friends over the following forty years. That
old trouble-maker, Lord Brougham, rubbed salt into the wound
by writing to Aberdeen from Paris: 'I need not tell you that
Gladstone has gained golden opinions from the republicans . . .
and that those whom you, and I, and Gladstone himself, would
call the right thinking are vexed, not by Gladstone's name being
to the statement so much as by yours being there,—for they
all say, "Gladstone is nothing and no name,—yours of course
is".'[70]

In October Aberdeen heard again from Schwarzenberg, who
protested that the publicity brought about by Gladstone's action
had 'entirely deprived him of the means of exercising any influence'. In communicating this news to Gladstone Aberdeen
assured him that he would 'be always ready and happy to do
anything in [his] power calculated to diminish human suffering',
and expressed a belief that Gladstone would be distressed at 'the
practical encouragement given to the promotion of revolution
throughout Europe'.[71] When he heard that Gladstone was considering another pamphlet he hoped that advantage would be
taken 'of the opportunity to shake off the radical alliance'; for he
could not bear the thought of seeing Gladstone practically 'united
with Kossuth and Mazzini!'[72] He added a wish that the next
pamphlet should not be addressed to him! In an answering letter
Gladstone assured him: 'You need not be afraid I think of
Mazzinism from me, still less of Kossuth-ism, which means the
other plus imposture, Lord Palmerston and his nationalities.'[73] In
the end Gladstone gave up his idea of another pamphlet and
Aberdeen wound up the correspondence congratulating him on
this decision and reminding him that his only difference with
Gladstone related to the mode of his proceeding. 'I would as
willingly as yourself use every endeavour to mitigate the horrors

of Poerio's treatment and that of his associates', he wrote, 'but it is my conviction that the course you have adopted is less likely to be successful than mine.'[74]

This correspondence is significant as illustrating one of the strains in the Peelite connection that was turning it slowly in the direction of Liberalism. The incident is of greatest importance, of course, for its effect on Gladstone personally, since up to this time he was generally considered to be to the right of most of his friends, but even in the guarded reactions of Aberdeen we see some readiness to accept principles that one day would be called Gladstonian liberalism and that were generally repellant to the typical nineteenth-century conservative.

The main hurdle that faced the Russell government in the session of 1851 lay in the Budget proposals. Sir Charles Wood was in the fortunate position of having an anticipated surplus, but this raised difficult questions as to what to do with it. His first proposals, made before the ministerial crisis, were received without enthusiasm and in April he came back to the House with a modified programme. Since he could not sacrifice as much revenue as £5,500,000 he proposed to renew the income tax for another three years, but as a boon to the working classes he recommended as a substitution for the hated window tax a limited house tax on houses worth more than £20 annual rental. He would also make a small bow to Free Traders by reducing duties on timber and coffee.[75] The Peelites were always condescending towards Whig finance, regarding it, as Gladstone once said, as the lesser of two evils. Yet when some of them gathered at Lord Aberdeen's house to discuss these proposals, Gladstone was highly critical of them. He attacked the financial feebleness of the Government and questioned the wisdom of keeping them in office (and thereby incurring the danger of a new Reform Bill) when nothing was really to be feared from a Stanley ministry. It was only after long discussion and much argument that he agreed not to join the Opposition in resisting the Budget.[76] The result was that some 53 Liberal Conservatives, including Graham, Goulburn, Gladstone, Herbert and Cardwell, supported the Government on 7 April against an adverse Protectionist motion that was defeated by 278 to 230.[77] Four days after

this Disraeli moved another amendment, demanding some relief
to agricultural distress. Gladstone, who had supported such a
motion in the previous year, now spoke strongly against it on the
grounds that he could no longer support Protectionist proposals,
now that Derby avowedly sought to reimpose a duty on corn. On
this occasion he again entered the Government lobby in the
company of Graham, Goulburn, Herbert, Cardwell and about
thirty-seven other Liberal Conservatives, while twenty-five
Liberal Conservatives, five Whig protectionists and 28 Irish
Liberals voted with the opposition.[78]

Nevertheless, in Graham's view, Gladstone remained dis-
gruntled with the Government and looked forward to the time
when they would be turned out.[79] When Greville approached
Graham, acting as an unofficial intermediary, Sir James once
more made clear his own disinclination to any close connection,
but he 'promised that he would communicate more frankly and
freely with J. R. in respect to any matters of difference and when
he was disposed to take any adverse part'.[80] Two days later he
widened the gap by his speech against the Ecclesiastical Titles
Bill, although, as he told Greville, 'he had studiously avoided
saying anything disagreeable to John Russell'.[81] On 24 March
Graham had an amicable conversation with Russell and promised
'to do all he could to help them with the Budget'. On 2 May,
despite a speech in its defence from Sidney Herbert and the
votes of some thirty Liberal Conservatives, the Government was
defeated by a combination of Protectionists, Radicals and 21
Liberal Conservatives on a motion of Hume's limiting the income
tax to one year.[82]

As the session dragged on, overcast by the ridiculous Ecclesiastical Titles Bill imbroglio, Peelite confidence in the Government grew ever cooler. Graham looked forward to its downfall,
saying to Aberdeen that there was 'no public advantage in delay-
ing it', but he declared himself 'unwilling to take any step which
might precipitate the event'. He added in his characteristically
gloomy vein:

> The country is weary of the 'Family Compact', and is quite
> willing to run some risks rather than remain under the thraldom
> of a clique. The misfortune is, that the risk on this occasion is too
> great. My forebodings are always gloomy. . . . I shudder on the

brink of the Torrent and hesitate to plunge into it. I often think of our dear Friend, whose remains we followed to the Grave; and I am disposed to think that in mercy he has been taken from the Evil to come. Solitude, you see, has not enlivened me; and I return again to the accustomed task with a heavy heart.[83]

In the meantime Lord Londonderry continued to press Aberdeen and Graham towards a reunion of all Conservatives[84] and in June Stanley urged Aberdeen to persuade his friends in the Commons to support some financial resolutions that Disraeli proposed to introduce.[85] The Peelite leaders discussed the matter inconclusively and in the end Gladstone decided to register his dissatisfaction with the Government's fiscal policy by speaking in favour of Disraeli's motion. Only three Peelites, Herbert, Smythe, and Young, joined him in the Opposition lobby, but 31 Liberal Conservatives, including Graham and Cardwell, helped the Government to defeat the motion by 242 to 129.[86] Towards the end of the session Gladstone also joined the Radicals on several occasions in attacking the Government's colonial policy.[87]

August finally brought release from Westminster and members of both Houses dispersed, for the most part, to their country seats and more congenial pursuits. 'I have been among the hills,' Graham wrote to Aberdeen from Scotland, 'enjoying as much sport as the weather would permit, and glad to forget "Papal Aggression" and public affairs.' He went on to speculate gloomily on the Government's plans for Reform and the likelihood of Russell's enlisting the support of the Queen and her husband for his proposed measure. 'When Princes yield it is vain for subjects to resist . . .' he commented pessimistically. 'To know when to yield and what to yield is the Triumph of Statesmanship. This glory still survives poor Peel; and will not be won by Ecclesiastical Titles Bills, or by constant and repeated changes in the System of Representative Government. We must look to Aberdeenshire for our future safety.'[88] Aberdeen took a more optimistic view of affairs. The editor of The Times had told him that Russell had shown him his plan for Reform in confidence and had asked him 'to moderate the expectation of the Public'. Aberdeen believed that the Queen would support Russell's proposals, which would make them irresistible. 'We seem to be drifting towards democracy in politics, and to separation of Church and State in religion,' he concluded. 'But the country is rich, prosperous and contented. Vogue la galère !'[89]

Politics pursued Sir James Graham to Netherby in the shape of his Whig friend, George Cornewall Lewis, bearing yet another invitation from Russell, acting with the full approval of the cabinet. Graham was again offered the Board of Control, with the possibility held out of Cardwell being brought in later as Secretary at War and Frederick Peel as Under-Secretary for the Colonies. Russell intimated that the Ecclesiastical Titles Act would not be enforced without cabinet sanction, which 'would be guided by their known opinions and convictions in favour of religious liberty on the one hand, and their determination to uphold the independence of the Crown and the nation on the other'. Since no sensible person could imagine that the latter were in peril, the 'papal aggression' issue seemed as good as closed, unless Sir James, for tactical reasons, chose to think otherwise— which he did. 'Sir James Graham views with sorrow and apprehension', he wrote in a formal memorandum of reply, 'every step which moves in the directions of the reenactment of the Penal Code.' He was not prepared, he said, 'to partake of the responsibility of the Cabinet in encountering evils which have their origin in the recorded votes of members of the Administration'. He also expressed doubts about the authors of the Reform Bill proposing its extension, especially when so many ministers had expressed their support of the ballot. At the same time he reiterated his continued friendly feelings personally towards Lord John Russell.[90] After this refusal Cardwell apparently was not approached, but Peel's son, Frederick, after some consultation with Graham, accepted the under-secretaryship for the colonies,[91] feeling that it was the Tories who had been unfair to his father and that he was in general agreement with the principles on which the Government claimed to act. 'This is no unimportant transaction,' Graham observed to Aberdeen. 'Ld John will derive great strength and advantage from it. I might have prevented it but I think I should have acted unworthily in so doing.'[92]

Graham corresponded frequently with both Aberdeen and Greville about Russell's Reform plans. He was always pessimistic[93] and his attitude was somewhat oracular. He emphasised the dangers arising from the reopening of the Reform question, since the Tories would oppose any Bill and the Radicals would not accept a moderate one. He continued in his most melodramatic manner:

Then will arise a most fearful struggle of Parties and a collision of Classes and of Interests for which they alone will be responsible, who have opened the closed door, & most assuredly the Crown must lose what Democracy will not fail to gain; numbers will be in the ascendent; and deputations from Finsbury and Marylebone, under the auspices of Wakley and the guidance of Mazzini and Kossuth will then revisit Downing Street perhaps to be warmly caressed by Palmerston as when they lately spoke of 'Despots' and 'Assassins'.[94]

Nevertheless, Graham was likewise emphatic that any attempt at a sham Bill would be equally dangerous. Since the subject had been reopened, they must find a real solution. He himself felt that it would be better to apply what he called 'the Rule of 1832', namely to 'disfranchise where you cannot trust, & transfer to large Constituencies the Right, which for malfeasance has been forfeited'.[95]

Meanwhile, some of the younger Peelites had been taking stock of their position. On 22 October Gladstone wrote to Newcastle deploring their disorganised state. Co-operation between Herbert, Young and the two of them, as Newcastle had suggested, was all very well but scarcely enough. He argued that they could not continue in their present leaderless state and that either Aberdeen or Newcastle ought definitely to take the lead. He urged that they should take a more resolute line on policy in the future, especially with respect to colonial problems, and expressed some regret at the harshness with which they had treated the Protectionists.[96]

Newcastle passed this letter on to Herbert. He sensibly ruled out the possibility of his own leadership and observed: 'Unless, therefore, Lord A. will seize the reins, I think, notwithstanding G.'s strong opinion, we must still go on without a leader. Still, I think a meeting of the few who will talk freely to one another may be very useful.'[97] Herbert fully concurred in Newcastle's views.

In December, of course, everybody's interest shifted to the renewed indiscretions of Palmerston, first in the matter of his projected entertainment of Kossuth, then in his reception of the

radical delegations from Finsbury and Islington, who denounced
General Haynau to him, and finally in his light-hearted approval
of Louis Napoleon's *coup d'état*. Aberdeen and his friends were
especially scandalised by all this levity. On hearing the inside
story of the Kossuth incident from Greville, Graham wrote in
indignation of Palmerston who valued 'the applause of the lowest
Radicals and the scum of Europe' above the 'confidence and good
will of honourable Colleagues'.

'The Queen and Lord John have been deceived and outraged
by him before', he continued, 'and have failed to resent it: and
it now remains for them to reap the fruits of past imprudent
subserviency. They will find him a hard task master and we have
not yet seen the end of the difficulties and dangers in which he
will involve them.'

Graham ironically paid tribute to the services Palmerston had
'rendered to the cause of Revolution and Republicanism throughout Europe. He has been indeed the "Bottle Holder" of Rebels;
ever in the ring encouraging others to fight, but ready to leave
them in the lurch when they are beaten; and never intending to
fight himself unless indeed some opportunity presents itself of
Bullying a weak power such as Naples or Greece; or of making
war on Barbarians in Africa or in Asia'.[98]

Then came the great news. Graham had it in a letter from
Greville written on 22 December 'in strictest confidence and to
you only'. 'I will impart to you an event that will make an
indescribable sensation all over Europe and even the world,'
Greville wrote in great excitement, '—Palmerston is out—irre-
trievably out . . . and the offer of the F.O. is now on the way to
Clarendon. . . . I am so overwhelmed by the importance of the
event that I can say nothing on the subject. . . .'[99]

Next day Greville sent news of Clarendon's refusal and Granville's acceptance of the Foreign Office. 'This has been a most
extraordinary affair . . .,' he wrote. 'Johnny has acted with great
[? dexterity] resolution and decision—he may say "alone I did
it"—not one of his colleagues had a notion of what was in
preparation. . . . Figure to yourself the joy of the Queen!—the
Radicals, his bottleholders, will be sorely puzzled. . . .'[100]

Graham, in thanking Greville for the news, commented that if
the change took place it was 'likely in its results to be more

important than even the death of Peel'.[101] He rejoiced at the appointment of Granville and dwelt on 'the grand opportunity for the legitimate exercise of British influence on the Continent' that lay before him. 'Whether the Serpent will beguile in the shape of Protection, or Anarchy triumph by the allurements of Finsbury and Marylebone it is too soon to predict', he added, 'but the Times is quite mistaken in supposing that we have seen or heard the last of Palmerston.'[102] Graham foresaw that Palmerston would be bent on revenge,[103] while Aberdeen anticipated another offer of office to Graham, which this time he thought should be given serious consideration.[104] Graham acknowledged that Palmerston's 'crooked policy' had been the chief reason for his last refusal, but he thought that the obstacles to a better understanding had been effected too late.[105]

From Bear Ellice, a former Whig whip, Aberdeen learned the gossip from the Whig camp, where there was some sympathy for Palmerston and a tendency to blame other members of the cabinet and Prince Albert for intriguing behind his back.

> With all his faults [Ellice wrote] the ex-Secretary was a good party man. While he offended foreigners, he flattered and was faithful to his followers—his house and table were open to them —his manners affable and courteous—and he had a larger following, from a successful application of the arts of personal popularity, than all the other members of the Government put together. You know Lord John's manner,—cold and indifferent, thinking he should command, rather than stoop to the policy of encouraging adherents by showing sympathy for their opinions or feelings. The Greys are certainly not popular; the Colonial and Financial Administrations more open to *general* criticism, and, I fear, condemnation, than our Foreign Affairs. . . .
>
> On the other hand, he finds no enemies or even opponents in the Protectionist camp. . . . Dizzy will be perfectly ready to become bottleholder, in any fight, against all comers.[106]

Clearly it was impossible to predict what the New Year might bring in the way of fresh political surprises.

*Notes to this chapter are on pages 191–7*

# Chapter 4 DERBY AND THE PEELITES
## 1852

THE YEAR 1852 opened with a renewed flurry of Liberal overtures to the Peelites. Indeed all Russell's colleagues put their offices at his disposal and some of them showed more conviction as to the necessity of a Peelite alliance than did the Prime Minister himself. They feared that, lacking heart in the proposals, Lord John would not offer acceptable terms, but others were all too ready to welcome their failure.[1] The first approach was made to the Duke of Newcastle, who had a long conversation with Russell on 30 December and some subsequent correspondence that reflected the prickly natures of the two men. Russell invited Newcastle to succeed Clarendon as Lord Lieutenant of Ireland and asked him to sound out other Peelites about taking office. The Duke made difficulties from the beginning, criticising the Government's ecclesiastical appointments and its colonial policy, but in particular he refused to administer in Ireland the Ecclesiastical Titles Act, which Russell would not abandon. He gave it as his opinion to Russell 'that, generally speaking, junctions of this kind did not strengthen the existing Government, and injured those who joined it'.[2] In the subsequent correspondence Russell defended himself against Newcastle's criticism with some acerbity[3] and so the offer fell through. Herbert likewise made it clear that he too was disinclined and Cardwell refused a direct offer on the grounds that he would not act separately from his friends.[4] According to Greville this offer was contingent on the expected demise of Fox Maule's father, Lord Panmure, which, in Graham's view, was less likely than that of the Government.[5] Russell also made a last half-hearted effort to get Graham to discuss the state of the Government with Lansdowne and himself, but Graham replied that despite Palmerston's departure his other objections, made earlier, still held good, and consequently he doubted the value of an interview that could have no result, a conclusion with which Russell agreed.[6]

Graham told Aberdeen that he doubted Russell's good faith in these negotiations. 'I believe that he intends to rule alone', Sir James commented, 'and if he fall, to lay the blame on Peel's friends, who have refused to cooperate with him.'[7] The Court obviously feared this, because in a letter to Russell at the time of his approach to Graham the Queen shrewdly asked whether the object was 'really to effect a junction with the Peelites' or whether it was simply to strengthen the Government's '*case* in Parliament' by giving the appearance of having made the attempt, in which case she was sure that anyone as canny as Graham would see through it. She distinguished between two kinds of junctions:

> ... one, a *fusion* of Parties; the other, the *absorption* of one Party by the other. For a fusion, the Queen thinks the Peelites to be quite ready; then, however, they must be treated as a political Party, and no *exclusion* should be pronounced against particular members of it, nor should it be insisted upon that the new Government and Party is still emphatically the *Whig* Party.
>
> An *absorption* of the most liberal talents amongst the Peelites into the Whig Government, the Queen considers unlikely to succeed, and she can fully understand that reasons of honour and public and private engagement must make it difficult to members of a political Party to go over to another in order to receive office.[8]

This was an acute appraisal of the Peelite position and fully borne out by events.

Greville, whom Graham had fully informed of the abortive negotiations between the Government and the Peelites, summed up the relationship between the two in these caustic terms:

> It is pretty evident that, however plausible may be the scheme of a comprehensive administration, the personal predilections and antipathies will create enormous difficulties. The Whigs generally hate the Peelites, and Graham especially. The Peelites hate the Whigs. Mutual dislike exists between G[raham] on one side, and Newcastle, Gladstone, and S. Herbert on the other. The three latter are High Churchmen of a deep colour, which makes it difficult to mix them up with any other party, so that the Peelite leaders are extremely divided, and the party is so scattered that it can

hardly be called a party. The Whigs, who really are a party, and, though in a state of great insubordination, do generally consider themselves one army under one chief, don't at all like the idea of treating with the Peelites on anything like equal terms. And if ever the time comes I fully expect they will all resist any such basis of arrangement, and that John Russell will not be disposed to agree to a Government being formed by himself *and* anybody else.[9]

There was some truth in what Greville wrote, but his natural cynicism tended to make him exaggerate these tendencies, as the correspondence between Russell and his colleagues and the sequel at the end of the year went to prove.

It is clear that church differences were a big factor in the failure of the two parties to come together at this time. The triumvirate of Newcastle, Gladstone and Herbert were looked upon with suspicion both in Whig circles and at Court for their high-church views, and both Aberdeen and Graham when visiting the Queen were at pains to reassure her that there was no danger in this direction.[10] The attitude of many Whigs may be seen in a letter from Lord Wriothesley Russell to Lord John in which he wrote: 'We are talking much of an infusion of Peelites, but it seems to me that the best of them as Newcastle Sidney Herbert and Gladstone must be quite impracticable on Church matters. The very name of the last would scamp any Cabinet. They are, I take it, too much in earnest to throw overboard their High Churchmanship; and as they are, of course you could not work with them.'[11] On secular matters, such as Russell's projected Reform Bill, there were fewer difficulties. Graham, thinking the time unpropitious, refused to comment, but Newcastle and Cardwell when they were approached made no objections.[12]

Shortly before the opening of Parliament Newcastle was host of what Graham called an 'anti-government meeting' at Clumber. It was attended by Aberdeen, Goulburn, Gladstone, Herbert, Canning, Young, and Lord Lyttelton (Gladstone's brother-in-law). Graham declined to attend, fearing that it would lead to an irreconcilable break with Russell and be interpreted by Lord John and the Queen as a 'high church intrigue'. Cardwell also stayed away, to Graham's delight, but Aberdeen parried Sir James's warning by promising to be discreet and to put the meeting to good use. Newcastle realised too late that the timing of the meeting was unpropitious, but, having issued his invitations, was reluctant to cancel what he called his 'very innocent Cabal'. As usual, Graham was overfearful, and there is no evidence that any harm was done.[13]

Parliament opened on 3 February and Russell asked permission to bring in his Reform Bill on the 9th. The Peelites did not participate in the brief debate on the first reading, which passed without a division, and the Government had fallen before the second reading was moved. The end came suddenly on the evening of 20 February when Palmerston moved an amendment to Russell's Militia Bill, which was carried to give him his 'tit for tat' with Lord John. Only two Peelites participated in the short debate, Herbert, who supported Palmerston, and Charteris who spoke against him. Ten Peelites, including Herbert, Gladstone and Young, voted for the amendment, and seven against it, while the rest, including Graham and Cardwell, stayed away. Russell, with little evidence, suspected that there had been 'a pre-arranged determination' between Palmerston, the Protectionists and the Peelites.[14] Refusing to risk the humiliation of further defeats, he resigned immediately. The *Morning Chronicle*, which had criticised the Bill on its first appearance, argued that the resignation was quite unnecessary, that the amendment merely strengthened the Bill and that the real reason for Russell's precipitancy was probably apprehension over the coming debate on the Kaffir War.[15]

This time Stanley, now Lord Derby, succeeded in forming a government, which, owing to the obscurity of its membership and the deafness of the Duke of Wellington, has gone down in history as the 'Who? Who?' ministry. It was formed without recourse to the Peelites, except for Lord Hardinge, a military figure who accepted the office of Master-General of the Ordnance on the understanding that 'he was not to be expected to give a vote which would reverse the policy of Sir R. Peel'.[16] On 27 February Derby announced the formation of the new administration in the House of Lords and outlined the policy he proposed to follow. In foreign affairs he would aim at peace and tranquillity; he refused to abandon Protection, but indicated that nothing

G

could be done in this connection until the 'intelligent portion of the community' had expressed their views upon it.[17] In responding to this speech Aberdeen promised to oppose any attempt to put a duty back on corn, but he welcomed Derby's statement on foreign policy and concluded his remarks in a friendly tone by assuring the new Prime Minister that 'he may rely on receiving from me, whenever it lies in my power, the most cordial and the most sincere support'.[18]

Derby wrote to Aberdeen to thank him for the friendly tenour of his concluding remarks, saying that he had not renewed the overtures of the previous year, in view of their failure then and the unlikelihood of any other termination on this occasion. He expressed regret at the violent tone of some of his own political followers and was willing to believe that the more violent views expressed by the Peelites in the Commons did not represent Aberdeen's attitude.[19]

The formation of a Protectionist government posed difficult problems for the Peelites, to which they reacted in different ways. The young Duke of Argyll was among those whose reaction was adverse. Although he had previously thought otherwise, he now suggested to Lord Aberdeen that a third party might 'be required in the times which [were] at hand to preserve a balance'. On the same occasion he expressed the interesting opinion that 'activity' was 'the best conservative policy' in their time; 'it is the only way of guiding that progress which is inevitable, in a safe direction', he asserted, '. . . it was the secret, as it seemed to me, of the success of the government to which you belonged. . . .'[20]

One of the shrewdest assessments of the situation from a Peelite viewpoint was made by Roundell Palmer, the future Lord Selborne. Although his church views were much closer to those of Gladstone, Herbert and Newcastle, he was a closer personal friend of Cardwell, to whom he wrote at length on the political prospects. He assumed that the new ministry could not survive an election while sticking to Protection and looked to the formation of a 'Conservative Liberal' party of Peelites and moderate Whigs to succeed them. 'But to make this possible', he continued, 'it seems to me essential, that the Peelites should preserve their Conservative character and keep on as good terms as they can with the whole moderate section of the present Conservative party in the House and the country.' He rejected 'a mere junction of the Peelites with the Whigs' for the purpose of turning out the Protectionists as unacceptable, since it would not effect any separation from the Radicals and the subsequent government would be faced with the same problems that had bedevilled Russell's. He saw 'the tendency of the Radicals' to be towards democracy and asserted: 'We shall deprive ourselves of all power to resist it effectively if we break forever with the Conservatism of the country; and we shall be abandoning forever the whole moral power of that Conservatism to those whom we now oppose, and paving the way for their return to office . . . unless we choose (like the Whigs, when they are hard pressed) to sacrifice our sense of public duty for the sake of keeping the Radicals in good humour.' He believed that there was a large body of Conservatives in Parliament and in the country who would vote for Derby's government while it lasted, but who would support the kind of 'modification of parties' that he proposed. 'The leading influence over all this moderate and rational Conservatism will revert to the Peelites . . . if they do nothing in the meantime to reject or forfeit it,' he wrote; 'and by cultivating this influence we may secure a really Conservative basis, upon terms as liberal as we like, for a future constitutional party and government.' He recognised that the Peelites could not 'flinch in the least degree from maintaining the policy of their great Chief', but urged a policy of forbearance and the avoidance of personal antipathies towards the Protectionists, arguing that they had the advantage in being 'a small body of men, with heads upon their shoulders, instead of a numerous and unmanageable party'. He was anxious to avoid alienating moderate Conservatives in and even more outside of the House who did not care about Protection. 'If we do not offend and alienate these men now, by our mode of dealing with the transitory Ministry which they support,' he concluded, 'they will be ours for ever, as soon as the Ministry falls to pieces; and they will bring with them all the real strength of the Conservatism of the country, without the illiberal tendencies which have been a drawback upon it hitherto.'[21]

This long letter is worth attention, not only for the light that it throws on the viewpoint of thoughtful Peelites and on the course taken by many moderate Conservatives in the following

year, but also for the evidence that it provides of the extent to
which Conservatism had replaced Toryism by the mid-nine-
teenth century. We also might accept Palmer's pithy definition of
the Peelites as a 'small body of men with heads upon their
shoulders' for want of a better one.

No Peelite took greater interest in these developments than
Gladstone, who made it his business to sound out the opinion of
the others individually.[22] Gladstone found Lord Aberdeen 'as
usual very accessible and kind'. Although he spoke in a friendly
way about Derby personally (wishing that '*he* could be extricated
from the company with which he associated'), Gladstone formed
the impression that Aberdeen leaned more in the liberal direction,
expressing his readiness for instance to drop his former opposition
to Jewish emancipation. He said that he, himself, favoured steer-
ing clear of both Derby and Russell for the time being, and he
urged Aberdeen to aim at bringing the Peelites 'together for
common counsels'.[23] Gladstone found Graham, as he thought,
unduly apprehensive of the Protectionist government, and looking forward to a future junction of Peelites and Liberals. Indeed
Graham told Gladstone that he had recently called on Russell and
told him that he had held aloof while Lord John was in office, but
that '*now* he recurred to the relations in which they stood more
than twenty years ago when in opposition together'. Gladstone
concluded that 'Graham contemplated his own virtual reincor-
poration with the Liberal party' and feared that to act with him
would 'have the analogous effect' for the rest of them. Gladstone
next saw Lord Hardinge and accepted the explanation that the
latter had taken the office as a military one. Indeed he informed
Hardinge that he thought his position would be useful as a
channel of communication between Derby and the Peelites. 'I
told him', Gladstone recorded, 'that what I longed for was to
maintain our separate and independent position that we might be
in a condition to take our own line after Lord Derby's failure.'

Gladstone found Newcastle 'extremely incensed with Har-
dinge' whom, to Gladstone's indignation, 'he declared to be a
shabby fellow'. Newcastle spoke 'with great asperity against Lord
Derby and his party' and was particularly irritated by their whip,
Beresford, who was reported to have told his men to let the
Peelites 'go to hell', and to have instructed Tory newspapers to

run them down. He 'thought that this government must be opposed and overthrown; that those who led the charge against them would reap the reward'.

The conversation was resumed at the Carlton, where, by Gladstone's account, seated together on a sofa they became 'rather warm'. Newcastle denounced the baseness of the Tories who hoped to remain in office without tackling Protection or dissolving, and he also suspected that they would make capital out of Maynooth. Gladstone professed more confidence in Derby and urged a policy of 'wait and see'.

> I said to him [Gladstone recorded], 'It appears to me that you do not believe this party to be composed even of men of honour or of gentlemen'. He on the other hand insisted that I was advising a negative policy or a virtual support of Government, and said that he was afraid that I should separate from the rest of the Peelites if I acted on my opinions: to which I demurred . . . but he evidently clung to the idea that we were hereafter to form a party of our own, containing all the good elements of both parties to which I replied the country cannot be governed by a third or middle party unless it be for a time only . . . and on the whole I thought that a Liberal policy would be worked out with the greatest security to the country through the medium of the Conservative party, and I thought a position like Peel's on the Liberal side of that party preferable . . . to the Conservative side of the Liberal party.[24]

The argument continued the next evening at a dinner meeting of most of the Peelite leaders.[25] Herbert and Gladstone favoured their moving to the seats below the gangway on the Government side of the House of Commons, while Cardwell and Newcastle favoured their remaining in the seats below the gangway on the Opposition side which they had occupied for the past six years. Newcastle accused Gladstone of drifting towards the Government and again the differences between the two of them became 'rather hot'. Graham, admitting that his case was different (as an ex-Whig), said that he would sit with the Liberals and Cardwell took the same position, although he later admitted that had the rest been firm he would have joined them, since he believed in keeping together, which Graham did not. Aberdeen, Herbert and Canning took little part in the discussion, which continued to a late hour, but remained unresolved, and the next day several of the participants avoided the House for that reason. Eventually the differences between Gladstone and Newcastle blew over and Gladstone apparently accepted the decision to sit below the gangway on the Opposition side.[26] It was also agreed at another meeting on 28 February that a Free Trade resolution against the Government as suggested by Villiers should be avoided, but that the Government should be put on short supply if necessary and that the Liberals should be informed of this decision.

When he heard of the differences coming out of the first meeting Sir John Young wrote in great distress to Gladstone deploring what seemed to him to be the dissolution of the Peelite party.[27] On receiving further news of the final seating arrangements he wrote again in some perplexity:

> I did not quite understand about the places. I thought you meant to take below the gangway on the Ministerial side. Will not Cobden, Bright, Hume and their friends take most of the places on the opposite side—and along with them will not Reynolds, Moore and the Brass Band be ranged? I doubt whether they will be pleasant neighbours or make room for us complaisantly. Perhaps Hayter [the Whig whip] would arrange for his friends not to invade the upper end of those benches which we have so long occupied—for six years nearly.[28]

In the end Graham and Cardwell, who had made up their minds before the rest decided to remain on the Opposition side, sat with the Liberals. Of the others Gladstone later wrote:

> But . . . I think with these exceptions only the body [of the Peelites] determined on giving the new Government what is called a fair trial. Mr. Sidney Herbert and I took pains to bring them together in the recognized modes. They sat on the Opposition side, but below the gangway, full, or about forty strong; and Sir James Graham, I recollect, once complimented me on the excellent appearance they had presented to him as he passed them in walking up the House.[29]

This account is an intriguing one and a rare description of the Peelites as a Parliamentary group and not just the half-dozen ex-ministers who continued to confer together over the years.[30] They appear to have started with a general meeting on the urging of Newcastle from the Lords who warned that if early action were not taken the English Peelites would be lost to Derby along with the Irish Brigade, with whom Disraeli was flirting at that time.[31] Graham, Gladstone was glad to find, made no objection to the idea of a meeting.[32] There is also some evidence that Gladstone and Herbert made special efforts to keep the Peelites together socially.[33]

When the Commons resumed its meetings in the middle of March, Villiers immediately challenged the Government on the Free Trade issue and received a question-begging answer from Disraeli, who refused to make any promises for the future on that issue, but contented himself with outlining the Government's immediate legislative programme, which consisted in the main of carrying on measures already promised or initiated by their predecessors.[34] Graham made a speech, described by Disraeli as 'elaborate, malignant and mischievous', in which he promised no factious opposition, but challenged the Government sharply on the question of Protection. He expounded the magic charms of the doctrine of Free Trade, concluding with reference to his very last conversation with Sir Robert Peel, who, facing the danger of Russell's Free Trade government being defeated on the Don Pacifico debate, had said to him: 'I know that in this country, without party connections, no man can govern. I know that my party ties are dissolved and I am not prepared to renew them, and do not desire to renew them. But, come what may, there is no effort that I will not make to maintain that free trade policy, which I believe to be indispensable for the maintenance of peace and happiness in this country.' Graham proclaimed that his policy remained that of Peel's.[35]

Gladstone was more conciliatory than Graham and anxious to indicate the terms on which the Free Traders might be expected to hold their fire. He welcomed the formation of the Derby government in order to bring to a head the issue of Free Trade which had been under attack from Derby's followers for the past six years. Recognising the anomaly of a minority government, he demanded from them 'a distinct assurance that, after the despatch of necessary business—and I do not mean to give an unduly narrow construction to the term necessary—', he added, 'the Crown should be advised to appeal to the country'.[36] This in effect was Peelite policy for the rest of the session.

In the House of Lords Derby skirted the contentious issue of the Corn Laws and appealed to all Free Traders and Protectionists to support a government which took over the helm in an hour of peril and to help it 'maintain and uphold the Protestant institutions of the country' and to resist 'the encroaching democratic influence' that faced them.[37]

At another meeting of the Peelite leaders (including Graham) at Lord Aberdeen's on the following day, 16 March, Gladstone proposed certain terms regarding the amount of public business the Peelites would sanction prior to a dissolution. These were approved and passed on to Lord Derby in the form of a memorandum, transmitted via Lord Hardinge.[38] Two days later they discussed a second memorandum setting forth the objectives of the negotiation—an early dissolution, the settlement of the Protection issue at an autumn session of the new Parliament, the renewal of the income tax for a year, the avoidance of 'all symptoms tending towards collusion'.[39] The next day, 19 March, Hardinge brought Gladstone a message from Derby that was recognised as an acquiescence and that became 'in substance the basis of the declarations in the Lords and Commons the same evening'.[40]

On the same day the Duke of Newcastle spoke in the House of Lords, but to Gladstone's relief his language was moderate. While calling for an early dissolution and settlement of the Protection issue, his tone towards Lord Derby personally was not unfriendly and he promised to avoid any factious opposition.[41] Derby made a cautious reply, but assured the House that as soon as the business of the session was finished he was anxious to have the matter settled at an early election and an autumn meeting of Parliament.[42] Both Aberdeen and Grey professed to be satisfied with this answer.[43]

Meanwhile, not anticipating Derby's assurances in the Lords on 19 March, Graham had been conspiring with Cobden and Russell about ways and means of using the Free Trade majority in the Commons to extract a commitment from Disraeli on the subject of an early dissolution. After some sparring on the floor of the House, Graham and Russell decided, in view of Derby's assurances, not to press the matter to a vote and so informed Cobden, who expressed his regret at the decision.[44]

Thus the Derby government could breathe for the time being, thanks to the moderating influence of the Peelites, but the future of the latter group remained obscure. Gladstone summed up their situation as follows:

The truth is these last weeks have been spent in an endeavour to keep the House of Commons together and prevent it coming into a state of crisis by means of a body which does not cohere spontaneously but only holds any kind of unity by constant effort. There are at least four distinct shades among the Peelites. Newcastle stands nearly alone if not quite in the rather high flown idea that we are to create and lead a great virtuous powerful intelligent party, neither the actual Conservative nor the actual Liberal party but a new one. Apart from these witcheries, Graham was ready to take his place in the Liberal ranks; Cardwell Fitzroy and Oswald would I think have gone with him, as F. Peel and Sir C. Douglas went before him. But this section has been arrested, not thoroughly amalgamated, owing to Graham. Thirdly there are the great bulk of the Peelites from Goulburn downwards, more or less undisguisedly anticipating junction with Lord Derby and avowing that free trade is their only point of difference. Lastly, I myself, & I think I am with Lord Aberdeen and S. Herbert, have nearly the same desire, but feel the matter is too crude, & too difficult & important for anticipating any conclusion, & that our clear line of duty is independence, until the question of Protection shall be settled.[45]

The problem of Graham's relations with the Liberals came to a head when he accepted an invitation to become a Free Trade candidate for his old constituency of Carlisle in the company of an advanced Radical. His speech on this occasion when he said of himself that 'the wanderer has returned' and indicated his readiness to accept some further extension of Parliamentary Reform, was looked upon askance by the main body of the Peelites. Gladstone insisted that it must be repudiated and, over some objections from Newcastle, persuaded a meeting of Peelite leaders that the rank and file of the party should be told that their political connection with Graham was dissolved by the Carlisle speech. Gladstone also wrote personally to say with regret that as long as he represented Oxford it would be impossible for him any longer to continue a political connection with Graham.[46] In reply Graham said that he recognised that his age and 'the habits and connections' of his early political life made it natural, though regrettable, that he should take a different course now that Peel was dead from that of his former colleagues in Peel's cabinet.[47] Herbert agreed with Gladstone, saying of Graham: 'With all his ability and experience and his love of straining his sight into the future, he had none of what the French call "esprit de conduit". He had a great game before him and has thrown the cards away, tho' I doubt whether he is conscious of it.'[48]

Now that he was out of office and perhaps aware that he had lost the allegiance of some of his followers as a result of his conduct over the dismissal of Palmerston, the Locke King Reform motion and the Militia Bill, Russell became more friendly towards the Peelites. Indeed he actually called on Lord Aberdeen to discuss the position of Gladstone, who received an account of the meeting from his chief. 'The tenour of his conversation', Gladstone recorded, 'was that my opinions were quite as liberal as his; that in regard to Colonies I went beyond him; that my Naples pamphlets would have been called revolutionary if he had written them; nay that in regard to church matters he saw no reason why there should not be joint action, for he was cordially disposed to maintain the Church of England, & so, he believed, was I.'[49] Gladstone was suspicious of Russell's motives, but there was much truth in what Russell said about his views, as the future was to prove. The strange paradox of Gladstone's position at this time was that potentially he was the most advanced Peelite in his liberal thinking, but that actually he was the most critical of the Liberals and most suspicious of any close co-operation with them.[50]

The first challenge to the Government came on their Militia Bill which was attacked by the Radicals and, rashly in view of his own failure, by Russell. Some Liberals, including Palmerston, and all but five of the Peelites supported the Government, which received a large majority of 315 to 165 on the second reading.[51]

Disraeli's budget was of necessity provisional and made no changes in the system of taxation. It was presented with great lucidity and the new Chancellor of the Exchequer, to the chagrin of his friends and the delight of the Opposition, fully admitted the benefits of the Free Trade commercial policy of the preceding decade. 'It is difficult to say what may be the effect of this speech', commented Greville, 'but it seems impossible that any sort of Protection in any shape can be attempted after it; and it certainly opens a door to the admission of any Peelites who may be disposed to join a Conservative Government, for even their personal feelings against Dizzy will be mitigated by this speech.'[52] This was borne out by Gladstone, who urged the House to support the budget and who was very complimentary to Disraeli.[53]

In the House of Lords, where Derby's pronouncements had been more equivocal on the subject of Protection, Newcastle, while supporting the interim budget proposals, warned the Government in a strong Free Trade speech that the country and Parliament would not stand for any reversal after the election. 'I repeat, my Lords,' he concluded in a sentence which summarised the essence of Peelism, 'the policy of a Conservative Government is that of steady progress; to stand still, again I say, is dangerous; and in my conscience I believe that at the present day a Government of reaction, however slow, is a Government of revolution.'[54]

There was only one occasion in this session when the Peelites, led by Gladstone, turned against the Government, and that was on a modest proposal to redistribute the four seats taken from the corrupt boroughs of Sudbury and St Albans. Several Reform proposals had been made in the course of the session by the Radicals, but all had been successfully resisted by the Government with Whig and Peelite support. Indeed the keynote of Derby's first administration was anti-democratic,[55] but Disraeli did seek to gain some virtue with Reformers by the 'baby' Reform Bill which he brought in on 10 May. Gladstone considered that this broke the understanding that the Government would not introduce any new and unnecessary measures. The Peelite leaders[56] met at Gladstone's house to decide what their course should be and determined to resist the Government's Bill. Russell, who had been looking all the session for an opportunity for joint action against the Government, told Gladstone he would support the amendment that the latter proposed to make, and Graham expressed his delight at this co-operation between Free Traders.[57]

When Derby heard of Gladstone's intention he endeavoured to dissuade the latter by writing to him 'as to a private friend, not as to a personal supporter, or opponent, of the Government'.[58]

But Gladstone was not to be deterred and he answered Derby the following day, courteously but firmly, to the effect that as a matter of principle he must oppose the proposed Bill since it did not come within the class of measures which it was agreed would be introduced prior to the dissolution.[59]

When Disraeli introduced his unfortunate proposal Gladstone easily demolished his arguments and killed the motion with an amendment that was passed by 234 to 148, with 37 Liberal Conservatives or Peelites in the Opposition majority. 'This was the only occasion of conflict that arose,' Gladstone noted years later; 'and it was provoked, as we thought, by the Government itself.'[60]

A few weeks before the end of the session Russell, without consulting his colleagues, opened up a general attack on the Government, accusing them of lack of consistency and principles.[61]

Disraeli, in reply, gave as good as he got, quipping in characteristic fashion: 'And when the noble Lord the Member for the city of London talks of our being a party without principles, why, he seems plainly to admit that he is an Opposition without a cry.'[62] It is doubtful whether Russell gained anything from the exchange and he probably only further irritated some of his former colleagues. 'I hear, that the Whigs are not well pleased with Lord John's intended move of this Evening,' Graham wrote to Aberdeen. 'They were not consulted: Ld Lansdowne never heard of it, till the Notice was printed in the Votes of the House of Commons; and if it is not successful, Lord John will fall into greater disrepute than ever with his old Followers.'[63]

The session, which was finally concluded on 1 July, was on the whole a more successful one for the Derby government than had been generally anticipated four months earlier. Besides the Militia Act and the budget, already alluded to, useful measures of a non-controversial nature were passed with respect to law and sanitary reform, as well as an Act for the government of New Zealand, in which Gladstone took great interest.[64] It is true that much time was lost over fruitless debates on various religious issues, but this was characteristic of all parliamentary sessions of the period.[65] Most of the legislation of the session had been forecast by the previous government, but the framing of many of the Bills and their passage through Parliament was to the credit of this untried administration. It is doubtful whether anything could have been accomplished, however, had it not been for the understanding worked out by Gladstone, which saved the Government from facing endless partisan opposition, and perhaps premature defeat. Lord Derby, himself, in the course of a curious 'conversation' that took place in the House of Lords at the end of the session, while preening himself on the Government's legislative achievement, admitted as much when he said: 'we have met with no factious opposition; we have encountered nothing but a fair, legitimate, and constitutional opposition in the other House of Parliament'. He was sure that if they had dissolved immediately upon coming into office they could not have achieved so many useful measures in so short a time in the new Parliament.[66] Gladstone, many years later, attributed the Government's survival entirely to 'the deliberate and united action of a body of about forty gentlemen called Peelites', and gave it as his opinion that the case was 'unique in our Parliamentary history'.[67]

The circumstances under which the Peelites helped to keep the Protectionists in office for the last few months of this Parliament's life were, however, exceptional and non-recurring. For the greater part of the Parliament of 1847–52 the Peelites were to be distinguished from the majority of the Conservative opposition by their efforts to prevent the formation of a Protectionist government, and consequently by their reluctant support of the Russell administration. Indeed to determine the names and numbers of genuine Peelites in this Parliament as distinct from the 120 nominally Free Trade Conservatives elected in 1847 or at subsequent by-elections (see above, pp 30–1) we may make a further analysis of its division lists. A selection of 27 of the larger and more significant divisions for the five years, 19 of them divisions in which Peel himself led a varying number of these former followers and new recruits into the Government lobby against the Protectionist opposition, will suit our purpose. An examination of these lists reveals that of our original list of 120 names 32 (a number reduced to 30 by 1852) were actually Derbyites, to judge by their voting pattern (ie a ratio of 2:1 or higher with the Derbyites), and can thus be excluded from our consideration, although 18 of them had supported the repeal of the Corn Laws in the previous Parliament. Of the remaining 88 we can reasonably identify 48 as Peelites, to judge from their voting pattern, although three deaths and two successions to the peerage reduced their numbers to 43 by the end of the Parliament. The voting pattern of the remaining 40 (reduced to 30 by the end of the Parliament) is too mixed or deficient to allow us to categorise them safely, but clearly they remained potential Peelite recruits; indeed 15 of them voted more often than not as Peelites. It will be observed, however, that 8 members who voted frequently with Peel when he was alive voted regularly with the Derbyites after his death.[68]

Unfortunately we do not have the names of the 40 Peelites whom Gladstone describes as sitting together below the gangway during the session of 1852, but we may suppose that most of them were in the list of 48 whom we have identified on the basis of their voting pattern. Some of the latter, however, appear by now to have been sitting with the Liberals[69] and some of Gladstone's 40 probably come from the 30 whom we have regarded as uncertain. Voting patterns are the only objective means of identification that we have been able to use and consequently we have had to limit our list of identifiable Peelites to those Free Trade Conservatives who generally voted independently of the Protectionists over the five-year life of the parliament. A more mixed voting pattern does not bar a member from being considered a Peelite, but we lack other evidence to make a judgement in these cases. Gladstone and Herbert, on the other hand, knew their men and no doubt regarded some whom we have been forced to consider uncertain as genuine Peelites because they shared common traditions, views and prejudices. In short, it is impossible to draw up a precise and definitive list of Peelites in this Parliament, and the most that we can claim for our list of 48 is that their voting pattern clearly differentiates them from the Derbyites. The election of 1852 helped to polarise the Peelite and Derbyite camps, but, as we shall see, those in the best position to judge were not always agreed when it came to counting heads.

*Notes to this chapter are on pages 197-200*

# Chapter 5 THE ELECTION OF 1852
## AND ITS SEQUEL

PARLIAMENT WAS prorogued on 1 July and dissolved on the following day. The general election began five days later and polling continued until 28 July.[1] It was not a particularly significant or exciting election, but it was quite typical of the period. It was characterised by the corruption that had survived the Reform Act of 1832, despite the recent disfranchisement of Sudbury and St Albans and the passing of legislation designed to stop such practices. *The Times* (6 July) professed to see some improvement since the bad old days prior to 1832,[2] but the more radical *Economist* (3 July) gloomily foresaw 'a sort of saturnalia—a licensed holiday for all the mean and bad passions of humanity', and bewailed the anomaly of a prosperous and enlightened country stooping to such methods to elect its legislators. When events bore out its worst prognostications it bitterly protested (24 July) that if the Derby government survived 'it would exclusively be the consequences of coercion, bribery and corruption' and asserted that these charges were 'a stigma on Lord Derby's Parliament and on Lord Derby's power' that would never be thrown off. A particularly flagrant case of bribery was revealed at Derby where an agent of Major Beresford, the Tory Secretary of War, was caught in the act and arrested by the police with a letter of instruction on his person initialled by the minister.[3]

Since there were no great issues at stake there was a general lack of excitement over the election, many seats were not contested and many voters failed to register their votes. The country was prosperous and the public could comprehend no precise issues between the parties. An attempt was made, in the words of *The Economist* (24 July), 'to excite the slumbering bigotry of the nation, and fan into a flame the ancient animosity between Protestants and Catholics', but in England, according to this source, there was little response, outside of Liverpool, which was probably one of the few constituencies in which it had any decided influence on the results. No one really supposed that Free Trade was in serious danger, but some Derbyite candidates still made Protectionist speeches, especially in the counties, and Free Traders felt that the issue should be treated as a serious one and settled decisively by the election.[4] *The Times* (8 July) was particularly indignant at the way in which the Derbyites spoke with two voices on this issue, according to whether the constituency was urban or rural.

The Derby government had done little to inspire enthusiasm or to arouse popular outrage, but it was not clear what might be the alternative, since Russell's stock was low in his own party and the position of the Peelites was still uncertain. Party lines, long unclear, became even more blurred; with no pressing national issues to distract public attention there was a natural tendency to fight the election on the familiar constituency basis, where local issues and prejudices and local personalities loomed large. 'The division into Whig, Tory and Peelite is felt to be no longer an exhaustive one, and the present election has considerably swelled the number of those who come under none of these denominations,' *The Times* commented (24 July). 'The election found all parties weak, and has left them weaker.' Nevertheless individual Peelite candidates (eg Roundell Palmer in Plymouth) undoubtedly found it difficult to contest seats without traditional party affiliations. The *Spectator* (10 July) attributed the losses of the Peelites to this cause, observing that 'in quitting the old camp they have in great measure been obliged to leave their *impedimenta* —the bulk of the influences derived from property and local position—behind them'. Clearly the fate of the Peelite and other independent candidates was one of the several imponderables of this election.

The position and prospects of the Peelites were obviously very different in 1852 from what they had been in 1847. Thus the rump that Gladstone and Sidney Herbert had pulled together in the last session of the old parliament was little more than a third of the Conservatives elected five years earlier professing loyalty to Peel's Free Trade principles. Lord Aberdeen was the titular leader of the Peelite remnant, but, cut off in the Lords, he made little effort to rally it. This was not for lack of prodding. For instance, a few months earlier J. E. Denison, a conservative Whig of Canningite origins, wrote to him to urge that the country should be given another alternative to Derby. He looked to the Peelites to rally 'all the best elements now in opposition', under the leadership of 'the man who would inspire the most general confidence, who would enlist under his banner the largest amount of support, especially of support of a conservative character'.[5]

This appeal is interesting in that it helps to explain Aberdeen's success in forming a coalition government later in the year, but at this stage, while not unsympathetic to the ideas expressed, he did little to promote their development, and potential supporters were left without a lead at the election. For instance when one correspondent wrote to urge that the Peelite leaders should issue a joint election address to advise Liberal Conservative voters such as himself, who, he declared, were proportionately more numerous in the constituencies than in Parliament, Aberdeen merely replied that they should vote for those candidates most likely to ensure 'the maintenance of Peel's commercial and financial reforms'.[6]

The Derbyites made no approaches to the Peelites for an electoral pact; indeed in some constituencies the former bitterly attacked the latter and their policies. 'I am thoroughly disgusted at the conduct of the whole Ministerial body!' Newcastle wrote to Gladstone while the contest was still proceeding. 'Truth is a word unknown to them and honour no more regarded than if it were only a garment intended for special use. I have seldom read speeches less creditable than Pakington's, Walpole's and Henley's.'[7]

On the other hand, Newcastle himself was criticised by one of Gladstone's Conservative friends and supporters at Oxford. 'I cannot imagine', wrote Sir William Heathcote, 'what made the Duke of Newcastle take the very bitter tone of hostility which marked his speeches. I know how very intimate he is with you and with Sidney Herbert, whose line has been very different, and I know too . . . how estimable he is—& yet he seemed to be doing all he could to prevent reconciliation, on which depends our

H

only chance of avoiding such a radical Govt. as we have never seen.'[8]

Religious bigotry was too much for several of the Peelites, such as Cardwell in Liverpool[9] and Roundell Palmer in Plymouth. Herbert and Gladstone faced stiff opposition for the same reason, but survived. Gladstone held the second seat for Oxford with 1,108 votes to 758 for the Warden of Merton, who was put up against him by the reactionaries of the University.[10] Lord Aberdeen congratulated him warmly, observing that it was 'indeed no small matter that Oxford should have proved superior to the bigotry and injustice which in other quarters have been triumphant'.[11] Some of Gladstone's Oxford supporters, however, would have liked to see him less remote from Lord Derby. 'It has sometimes seemed to me', wrote Heathcote, 'that you stand too much at the exact antipodes to poor old Inglis.'[12] Gladstone's victory was also significantly applauded by such Liberal organs as *The Economist* (17 July) which commented: 'though Mr. Gladstone is not exactly one of our foremost friends, we regard his success at the present circumstances as one of the great triumphs of the elections'. 'He has become both politically and religiously much more liberal,' it observed; 'his mind expands with time and the necessities of office.' It was for this reason that his return had been opposed.

*The Times* frequently alluded in sorrow to the losses of the Peelites. Commenting on the capriciousness and illiberality of the electors of Liverpool it observed (8 July): 'We may admit, perhaps, that the so-called Peelites are in a very embarrassed and crippled condition, too good for Earth, and not good enough for Heaven; but their splendid contribution to the most important debates of the day show that they cannot well be missed, even if they happen to be thrown out of the play of political parties.' A few days later it returned to the subject, noting the defeat of Lord Mahon at Hertford and Sir George Clerk at Dover, and on the 24th it sadly compared the Peelite losses in two elections to those of 'a crack regiment which had served with distinction through two bloody and desperate campaigns'.

Observing that the friends of Sir Robert Peel must seek consolation in the triumph of his policies, *The Times* (10 July) proceeded to explain the cause of their electoral discomfiture:

. . . Sir ROBERT PEEL broke from party: he scattered his party to the four winds of heaven, and substituted a policy in its place. His followers ceased to be partisans and at this moment it is only a convenient fiction to describe any number of men as 'Peelites', for, besides their original diversity of character, the men so described seem to have received an additional impulse of separation and independence from the example of their late chief. Their present difficulty is that they are not a party; they have not its ties; they have not its facilities; they have not its obligations. They have not acted together, and no one can argue from the course taken by one what the other will do, or what opinions may be presumed from a mere historical connexion with Sir ROBERT PEEL.

The post-election correspondence of Gladstone, Bonham and Young, as we shall see, bears out the truth of these observations; certainly the term Peelite cannot appropriately be used to describe all of the 111 candidates whom *The Times* described as 'liberal conservative'. As in the previous parliament, many of these were simply independent-minded Conservatives with Free Trade leanings and no love for Derby or more particularly Disraeli, but their support could by no means be counted upon by the Peelite leaders.

No firm figures can be given as to the final results of the general election of 1852 because of the uncertain affiliation of many of the members elected, especially the so-called Liberal Conservatives of whom *The Times* (28 July) listed 58 and *The Economist* (24 July) 63. One ministerial paper put the Government's majority as high as 43 (giving it a total of 346 seats), while an Opposition paper claimed an anti-ministerial majority of 86 (leaving the ministry only 284 seats). 'All computations vary,' the *Spectator* commented in citing these figures (31 July). Some of the many calculations will be found on the accompanying table, with minor discrepancies arising from the fact that three candidates tied for the two seats at Knaresborough and that two seats were vacated before the elections were completed.

Russell was ready to grant the Government 310–20 supporters,[13] but Derby was less sanguine, telling the Prince Consort in December that he had never counted on more than the 286 who supported him in the last division preceding his resignation.[14] The *Spectator* (31 July), although unfriendly to the

Government, listed 60 Government gains as against only 40 losses, but a calculation in the Russell Papers shows 48 Opposition gains as against 58 Government gains.[15] Joseph Parkes, the Liberal election agent, wrote to Russell on 19 July: 'I can't see how we can fail of 20 or 25 majority—certain—and I calculate on full 40 more M.P.s reckoned Derbyites *now* who when the Cabinet is overthrown will support a liberal administration.'[16] On

| | Maximum minis- terial | Safe Derby- ite | Anti- or non-minis- terial | Liberal | Irish Bri- gade | Peel- ite or L.C. | Un- accounted for |
|---|---|---|---|---|---|---|---|
| The Times (28 July) | | 284 | | 309 | | 58 | 3 |
| Economist (24 & 31 July) | 317 | | 337 | | | | |
| Spectator (31 July) | 310 | | 344 | | | | |
| Morning Chronicle (31 July) | | 283 | 370 | | | | 1 |
| Bonham[17] | | 288 | | 313 | | 50 | 3 |
| Young[18] | 315 | 272 | | 304 | | 34 | 1 |
| Goulburn[19] | 307 | 301 | | 266 | 42 | 36 | 3 |
| Hayter[20] | 309 | | 331 | | | | 14 |
| Derby[21] | (310) | 286 | | 270 | 50 | 30 | 18 |

24 July he allowed the Government 315–16 of whom he reckoned 30 or 40 on the fall of the Government would support a Liberal cabinet. 'The Pure Whigs have lost & the Peelites most,' he added, perhaps with some satisfaction: 'the latter all but annihilated'. He concluded his letter by expressing trust 'in the good sense of the country and in the thing called the "British Constitution" '.[22] Sir Charles Wood was sceptical of such calculations, noting that Hayter's 331 anti-ministerialists included the names of a number of Conservatives who made the potential majority very doubtful.[23] Greville thought there might be fifty or sixty members who would 'not consider themselves as belonging to the Government nor to the Opposition', but of whom the majority would 'probably support the Government, except on particular questions'.[24] Clarendon observed to Russell that 'the 45 Irish Brigands' might 'be more correctly said to hold the balance than the 30 Peelites'.[25] Edward Ellice wrote to Aberdeen: 'the balance

of power will be in a small brass band whose violence and folly will be worth double their numbers to this, or to any other Government'. He viewed the election results as a clear majority against both Protection and Reform.[26]

Graham told Russell that he heard 'that the Government calculated on having 315 supporters, 303 opponents and 32 Neutrals or Doubtfuls', but he considered this 'a sanguine view on their part'.[27] He and Russell exchanged information about the respective calculations of Parkes and Bonham. Sending Graham one of Parkes's letters Russell wrote, 'I believe he calculates rightly that 50 of the 316 wd support a new Ministry. But those 50 may be the same who figure in Bonham's list as Liberal Conservatives or perhaps 30 of them.'[28]

The newspapers recognised the impossibility of making exact or precise lists of the results. The *Spectator*, for instance, commented that it did not remember a general election in which the calculations as to probable votes were so utterly baffling.[29] *The Economist* noted that although the Government had failed to win the 336 seats that it had expected,[30] its forces were 'a compact host', while the Opposition consisted 'of four very imperfectly amalgamated sections', the Whigs, the Peelites, the Radicals and the Irish Brigade. In the view of *The Economist* (31 July) it was all-important that these four groups should be kept together to produce a better government than the existing one. In particular it maintained 'that no Reform party or Liberal Ministry could be strong or permanent that did not command the support and include the leaders of the section of which Sir James Graham, Mr. Gladstone, and Mr. Sidney Herbert are the representatives and chiefs'. It estimated that 'the followers, or rather the companions of those gentlemen, as Peelites, will number between 40 and 50 in the new House of Commons—sufficient to give to the Liberals they join a decisive, steady, working majority'.

*The Times* (24 July), while contemptuous of the ministerialists as a party without a soul (now that they had abandoned Protection) whose members for the most part represented 'safe' constituencies, was more detached in assessing the prospects of the Opposition. Although sympathetic to the Peelites, it continually harped upon their losses. It also dwelt upon the losses of the Whigs, noting the failure of such candidates as Sir George

Grey, Sir John Romilly, Sir David Dundas, G. Cornewall Lewis and others to retain their seats. Indeed, *The Times* was obviously pleased that the elections had disposed of the fear of 'a reconstruction of the Whig party on its old exclusive and dynastic principles'. It found the old Whigs 'in a state of disorganization and dissolution' and the name of Russell discredited. 'If the Liberal party is to be held together, and become a really efficient instrument of Parliamentary party warfare', it maintained, 'its leaders must be content to submit their opinions and projects in private to those whom they expect to follow them in public.' In short, the Liberals needed to develop the American art of 'caucus'.

The Peelite *Morning Chronicle* (31 July) placed the Peelites clearly in the anti-ministerial camp and dismissed 'the so-called Derbyite free-traders' as supporters of the Government. 'On the other and stronger side', it observed, 'will be found all those members who are pledged to oppose any of the indirect substitutes for Protection which Mr. Disraeli and his colleagues are irrevocably pledged to bring forward.' It lost no opportunity to criticise and belittle the Government. 'If we may judge from their addresses', it noted at the outset (2 July), 'Ministerial candidates think that the less they say about Protection the better, "Protestantism" is now their chief stalking-horse, Bigotry their main source of hope, and No Popery their cry.' When the elections were concluded the *Chronicle* (31 July) counted 283 ministerialists against 370 anti-ministerialists of whom some 55 were Conservatives, but it made no effort to identify Peelites as such.

Of the 43 members whom we have identified as Peelites in the House of Commons when the previous parliament was dissolved 27 were re-elected, of whom one, William Keogh, was now an Irish Independent, and another, John Duncuft, died very shortly after the election. Three did not stand and 13 were defeated or forced to withdraw on the eve of the election, although 4 of these were shortly returned at by-elections or as a result of petitions.[31] In addition there were some new Liberal Conservatives elected, not in the previous Parliament, 8 or 9 of whom proved themselves to be Peelites in the new one.[32] Finally, of the 30 uncertain Liberal Conservatives in the old Parliament when it was dissolved, 19 were re-elected, half of whom took a Peelite line in the new one, bringing the Peelite total to between 40 and 50.[33]

The uncertainties of the election results are nowhere more strikingly revealed than in the discussions that the Peelites themselves conducted as to their numbers. Gladstone, their most active leader in the Commons, asked the faithful Bonham to give him, when the returns were 'sufficiently ripe', the best account he could make of the relative strength of the parties.[34] This was a question for professionals, and who was better qualified than Peel's old party agent to answer it?[35]

Bonham undertook the task with alacrity and a week later sent Gladstone his analysis.[36] In doubtful cases he leaned toward the ministerial calculation and was sure of the 313 as 'declared opponents' of the Government. He was less certain of some of the 50 Peelites whose action would depend on circumstances, but he was sure the Government could rely on none of them. He noted that there were 39 Irish Derbyites and of the 63 Irish opposed to the Government only 3 were Whigs and 3 Peelites.

Gladstone broke down Bonham's 50 Peelites into 26 pure, 6 inclined towards Russell, 5 inclined to Derby, 8 of whom he would call 'real though moderate Derbyites' and 5 of whom he had no personal knowledge.[37] Bonham disputed some of Gladstone's analysis as being too pessimistic. He believed that Gladstone was wrong about 6[38] of the 8 whom he had listed as moderate Derbyites and gave evidence to prove them to be dependable Peelites. Of Gladstone's 26 pure Peelites he only questioned 2, Pennant and Smollett, whom he thought might lean to Derby. He assured Gladstone that Wortley and Jocelyn had no tendency in that direction, as Gladstone apparently suspected. Of the 5 whom Gladstone did not know, Bonham professed to have information that 3 were ready to follow Gladstone.[39]

Gladstone also sought the views of Sir John Young, Peel's old whip, who reported as follows:[40]

| Supporters of the Government who are nowise tainted by Free Trade or any other noxious liberality | 272 |
|---|---|
| Whigs and Radicals | 304 |
| Remain[der] | 78 |
| | 654 |

With these 78 or the majority of them the balance rests. Many of them are unknown to me—new names etc.—but I class them thus:

| | |
|---|---:|
| Free Trade Derbyites on whom the Govt. may confidently rely | 25 |
| Doubtful | 18 |
| Oldham vacant | 1 |
| Firm Free Traders who do not admit the fallacy that Conservatism does not or could not exist outside Lord Derby's ranks | 34 |
| | 78 |

| | |
|---|---:|
| Supposing a division to take place on which the 25 Free Trade Derbyites and all the doubtful went with Govt. the numbers would be 272—[plus] 25 and 18 | 315 |
| Whigs etc | 304 |

| | |
|---|---:|
| Giving a Govt. majority of | 11 |

but when the 34 are absent—if all present and voting together they would convert the Govt. majority into a minority of 23 or augment it into a majority of 45. This is as near the mark as I can bring the estimate.

Gladstone then sent to Young the list of 50 that he and Bonham had been discussing. Young crossed off ten[41] as sure to support the Government on all occasions, and listed another nine upon whom he doubted whether they could depend.[42] This reduced the list to 31, but he added three other names (Mostyn, Hanmer, Milnes) and also put more reliance on two whom Bonham considered leaning to Derby (Whitmore and D. Pennant). Young was sceptical of the Peelites' power for independent action:

> Twenty of this 31 or 35 [he wrote] might go with you (by you I mean Newcastle, S. Herbert and yourself) in the event of your splitting with Lord Derby and joining the Whigs but several of these would not like it.
> What has kept the members together so long has been mainly the adherence to Sir R. Peel's commercial policy and the hope of seeing you, i.e., those who served in Sir R.P.'s cabinet, called to power and enabled to dictate alliances and their policy to the rival parties.

The commercial policy is now out of peril and the hope above alluded to has I fear been much chilled by Graham's defection to the Radicals and the defeats our friends met with at the recent election.
Still undoubtedly we hold the balance.[43]

Young concluded by saying that 'we must not lay too much stress on names without considering the question on which we may be called to vote'; this was a sensible point at which to leave the matter until Parliament met.

Early in September Bonham wrote again saying that 'as to numbers I see no reason to change the *proportions*, but some difference as to individuals'.[44] 'Something, however, depends', he added, 'on each man's definition of "L.C.".' He did not think there would be much desire for a direct vote of want of confidence. 'After all any trifling difference as to numbers', he concluded, 'is of less importance as the general tendency of things in the absence of events is to keep together an existing Government, and I am sure they are *now* to be destroyed by their own blunders alone.' Gladstone told him that he and Young reckoned the 'L.C.'s' lower than he (Bonham) did, but observed that 'the number who will consent thus to be kept together even if not absolutely large may be large enough to exercise an important influence on the course of events'.[45]

In the meantime Bonham and Young had been exchanging lists and in the end Bonham told Young he did not think they differed widely as things stood, but that '*actively exerted influence & power*' would cause many changes before the session opened.[46] Bonham also sent his calculations to Newcastle, who in reply observed that 'no two persons will exactly agree as to the precise strength of the Ministers in the new Parliament'. He said the Government had not the strength to follow a policy of its own since it depended upon the division of its opponents.[47]

Finally in October Bonham sent Gladstone a list of friends to be counted on, observing: 'the names are more than I anticipated (23) but we have thirty more favourably disposed if they are allowed *to declare themselves*'. He anticipated the return of Frederick Peel, 'who has altogether left Ld John', but considered Goulburn 'to have withdrawn from political strife'.[48]

On 30 July Gladstone wrote to Aberdeen saying that Derby

was left dependent on Peelite votes. He spoke of the heavy losses of 'our small section', but thought they might claim fifty 'without much danger', of whom forty would be opposed to overthrowing Derby at the outset.[49]

Lord Aberdeen's followers approached the coming session with varying hopes and fears. Young, perhaps, typified the solid core. Although initially apprehensive about the future,[50] as time went on he became more belligerent towards the Government.

> It seems to me [he wrote] of paramount importance & necessity to let the country know as speedily as may be consistent with fair play the secret of the ministerial weakness, and disabuse the public mind of the audacious falsehoods and false reckonings of the Ministerial journals. If Newdigate be proposed for the Chairmanship [of the Ways and Means Committee] as is rumoured, how can we assist the Ministerial triumph in so placing so rabid a partisan and defamer of Sir R. Peel. If Beresford, the Secretary of War and now Commander-in-Chief [Wellington had just died] has dirtied his hands in circulating secret service money, & providing agents to bribe, I cannot see how we can with any degree of regard for our own character, or for public opinion interpose our votes to save him from searching enquiry, or the Govt. from defeat, if they refuse enquiry—then again as to alleged mal-practices of the Admiralty—I do not know what the particulars may be, but I do know Stafford's character, and I know it to be that of a most arbitrary unscrupulous partisan, & I am persuaded that . . . there is nothing he would stick at to procure or ensure success. . . .
>
> So long as three of us can stand together the Peel party shall have my best adherence but we must be cautious how we vote— public opinion is not with the present government—but it is the Government & Englishmen hate the risk and trouble of changes.[51]

Young seemed to have a lower opinion of the Derbyites than Gladstone, but the tone of this letter reveals the chasm that had opened and helps to explain the step the Peelites finally took.

Gladstone was detached, agreeing with those such as Bonham,[52] who advised against an immediate motion of confidence, but sceptical of the advantages of friendly intervention; 'each successive speech at Aylesbury', he wrote to Aberdeen, 'has been

more quackish in its flavour than its predecessor'.[53] He opposed
junction with the Derbyites because he 'for one' was not prepared
to accept Disraeli as a financial expert. On the other hand he was
opposed to immediate juncture with the Whigs. 'To follow
Graham's example', he said, 'would not so much make the
Liberals rich as make us poor indeed. . . . A change of party
requires thorough and harmonious concurrence between those
whom you join as a party.'

Aberdeen's reply reflected his natural distaste for politics. He
told Gladstone that he tore himself with difficulty from the sight
of 'the blue and beautiful sea' and 'the various forms and colours
of my granite cliffs' to contemplate the vagaries of politics. He
supposed that 'long habit, the desire of association with friends,
and perhaps, in some small degree, a sense of duty must account
for it', and proceeded to express his views of the situation:

> I confess, after the events of the last six years, I would look with
> no common satisfaction to the formation of a Government, mainly
> under the auspices of Peel's friends. I still think that Lord John,
> from his station and life, is the fittest person to be at the head of
> any liberal government; but he appears by common consent to be
> out of the question. Can Peel's friends supply his place? If high
> character and ability only were required, you would be the
> person; but I am sure that at present at least this would not be
> practicable. Whether it would be possible for Newcastle, or me,
> to undertake the concern is more than I can say; but I am sure
> that it must be essentially with liberal support, and with little
> chance of much accession from the Protectionist camp.
>     . . . I am not afraid of the effects of Reform; and I have no
> doubt the abuses are sufficiently great to justify those who seek
> for change. But I much doubt the probability of any great
> improvement. Influence, intimidation and corruption are in-
> separable from our Representative system; and the English are
> as venal as any people in Europe.[54]

In replying to a letter from Goulburn, who professed distrust
of both Whigs and Protectionists,[55] he maintained that the
Government must be made to show its hand, 'that Disraeli, in
Graham's phrase, should be made to jump into his bottle'. He
made clear his own contempt for the Government, saying that
their position was 'so immoral as to deprive them of all sym-

pathy'. He considered Free Trade to be safe, but asked what was to follow:

> I think it clear that all Government in these times must be a Government of progress; conservative progress, if you please; but we can no more be stationary, than reactionary. I do not know that there is any great reason to fear Democracy at this moment. Perhaps there is even less than at any former period. Whig and Tory have become titles without meaning; and I am almost inclined to think that Conservative and Radical are growing to be cant terms, better suited to the language of the Clubs, than accurately descriptive of any great divisions of the political world.[56]

Many Liberals were now looking to the Peelites to join them in replacing this despised Protectionist government. *The Economist* (31 July) strongly championed this idea. A Peelite alliance, it was argued, would be a guarantee, on the one hand, against the danger of organic changes, on the other hand ensuring 'that the essential administrative business of the country would be conducted on principles of liberal and effective reformation; that abuses would be everywhere honestly searched out and courageously rectified; and that many great public and imperial affairs, that urgently press for a settlement, would be approached in an earnest, statesmanlike, and philosophic temper'. Such an alliance in *The Economist's* view, would produce 'essentially the party of CONSERVATIVE PROGRESS AND PRACTICAL REFORM'.

James Wilson, proprietor of that paper, and a Liberal MP, had already been in correspondence with Russell urging the merits of the Peelite leaders, especially Graham. 'And I am not without hope', he added, 'that the treatment which Mr. Gladstone has received at Oxford and Mr. Sidney Herbert here [in Wiltshire] from the supporters of Ld Derby will show them that they can never join his government.' He told Russell that he had had a long conversation with Herbert who 'seemed more than ever alienated from the present Government'.[57]

The cordial relations developing between Graham and Russell, who had been exchanging friendly letters for some time, and the continued friendship between Graham and Aberdeen, pointed the way to an understanding.[58] On 17 July Graham wrote to

Russell about the election results, the prospect of a new administration and the policy on which it might be based. He thought agreement might be reached on Finance, Parliamentary Reform and National Education, but foresaw difficulties over Religion and the Ballot.[59] As to his former colleagues, he told Russell, 'I know not what effect the unsparing attacks of the Gov't on the Peelites . . . may have produced on the minds of Gladstone and the D. of Newcastle; but I should imagine that the Vision is dispelled, which flickered with a hope of reunion with Ld Derby'. Russell rejoined: 'The very first thing of all is to ascertain whether Gladstone and Herbert would act with the Whigs, & whether the two could act with the Radicals.'[60]

Graham replied that since his alliance with a Radical at Carlisle his communications with Gladstone were 'reserved and indirect'.[61] Herbert, he said, was more friendly, but in full agreement with Gladstone. He repeated that the recent attacks of the Derbyites on them were bound to have widened the breach, but he doubted whether they would ever serve under Russell as a prime minister, although they might accept him as a House leader with a peer as prime minister. He told Russell that Roebuck had urged him 'to take a prominent part in concerting a combined Opposition', but that he had declined to take any leading role, although expressing sympathy with the objective.[62]

Clarendon also wrote to say that he had had several hours' conversation with Graham who had spoken very warmly of Lord John:

> Upon the whole I gathered that he was aware of the mischievous part he had played and that he wishes to be a good boy for the future—that he thinks the present Govt. the worst we have ever had but has no idea how another can be formed, owing to the quirks, the conceit, the personal feelings and the obstinacy of the different sections into wh. the Liberal party is divided.[63]

It appears to have been agreed among Russell's friends that fresh approaches should be made to the Peelites, for Wood had cautioned him, on 19 July, to write to Aberdeen 'in very general terms & leaving the future course quite open', and advised against any attempt to turn the Government out prematurely. 'I am quite convinced', he wrote, 'that the *centre* at present has a strong free trade, but also a strong conservative tendency & wants to be quiet. We must get the Government thoroughly in the wrong before we can do any good with them.'[64]

On 21 July, Russell made a significant approach to Aberdeen in a long letter setting out his views on the situation. He allowed the Ministry 310–20 votes, which he himself would have looked upon as defeat, but not so Disraeli. The Government's two rallying cries had been abuse of Peel's Corn Law and 'the hounding on the Protestants to run down the Catholics', neither of which were likely to attract Peelite support to them. Consequently, the Peelites might continue to remain aloof, which Russell thought would only perpetuate the present unsatisfactory state of affairs; they might co-operate with the Whigs from a position of independence; or they might 'join with the Whigs and form a fusion, either with or without Cobden'. As to the course when Parliament met, he opposed a vote of want of confidence but favoured a Free Trade amendment to the address. He also favoured a 'vigorous attack on the glaring corruption' of the present elections, but would postpone reform until February and then make quite limited proposals. He continued:

> The main point, however, is to ascertain whether Mr. Gladstone and Mr. Sidney Herbert would be disposed with you and the D. of Newcastle to concert with the Whigs the course to be adopted when Parlt. meets. And I beg of you the favour to ascertain this point for me.

He made it clear that he would be ready to support a Liberal ministry out of office if 'the Radical and Irish members would be gratified by my exclusion'.[65]

Aberdeen responded with alacrity and promised to sound out his friends as requested.[66] Both Russell and Aberdeen kept Graham informed of their correspondence, the former indicating that, if he stood aside as prime minister, he would not lead the House for a peer prime minister.[67] Graham agreed with Russell's proposal for a Free Trade amendment to the Address, and condemned the Government, saying:

> Men like Beresford and the D. of Northumberland are not suddenly raised to Offices of great Authority and Power without

danger to the State; and I have always foreseen that this Government of Ld Derby's will give a greater impulse to Democracy than the quiet Rule of progressive Reform could have effected in the natural course of two or three Generations. At the same time it is right to remember, that in Opposition the Principles of good Government must be respected, and no changes ought to be pressed, which in Power it would be inexpedient to carry.

He proceeded to sketch a tactical plan of operations for the Opposition to follow when Parliament met, 'but the Grand Attack, without being indefinitely postponed, should not be hurried', he warned. 'As at Salamanca, the two Armies in presence must move in parallel lines. . . .'[68]

Graham also wrote to Aberdeen to let him know exactly how matters stood between Lord John and himself. He indicated that he had taken the 'opportunity of raising the point whether he himself [Russell] insisted on being Prime Minister'. He felt the answer was 'distinct & final'. 'It is not possible to press on a gentleman', Graham commented, 'what beforehand he declares to be "Personal Degradation".'[69] Aberdeen thought that nothing could be done without Russell, but did not despair of persuading the latter to change his views.[70]

On 25 July Aberdeen wrote at length to the Duke of Newcastle enclosing Russell's letter and asking him to forward both letters to Gladstone and Herbert. He trusted the four of them would continue to agree as in the past and regretted they could not come together to discuss Russell's proposals. 'The late elections', he said, 'have thinned our ranks and deprived us of several friends whom we could ill spare; but the country must still be disposed to regard us as the representatives of Peel's policy, and as the party of Conservative progress.' Despite the Government's hostility in the elections he foresaw the possibility of approaches to 'some of Peel's friends'. He confessed his own attitude towards them had changed:

The only test proposed at the elections involved a principle of religious bigotry pregnant with mischief for the future, and more objectionable to me than Protection itself. Altogether the conduct of the Government is quite unprecedented, and their whole proceeding is the most dishonest I have ever witnessed. From the course which has been pursued, both before and during the elections, it is clear to me that any principle will be sacrificed with the view of obtaining Parliamentary support.

He told Newcastle that personally he would like to see a Russell government 'supported and in some measure directed by a portion of Peel's friends', although not in office himself. However, if some Whigs and some Peelites were not prepared to accept Russell they 'must look for some other combination' of which Russell must be 'an essential part'. He gave it as his opinion that the Derby government would stand as long as its opponents were divided and that the time had come for concert with the Whigs. He argued that there were no real differences between them, that difficulties with regard to education and the Church were theoretical rather than practical. Parliamentary Reform was the only difficult question but Russell's proposals appeared 'reasonable enough'. He himself was ready for some change in view of the amount of corruption in the present system.[71] The last survivor of Wellingtonian Toryism was showing himself remarkably liberal in his old age.

Aberdeen sent a copy of this letter to Graham who was delighted to find it reflecting sentiments so similar to his own.

> In acting with you [he wrote to Aberdeen], I often have the same proof of unity of feeling and opinion, which constantly attended my intercourse with our departed friend, Sir R. Peel. Without concert we come to the same conclusions; and without comparing notes, there is no diversity of thought or of expression between us. This pleasant circumstance is remarkably illustrated by your letter to the D. of Newcastle. I return the copy of it and am ready to subscribe to every word.

He went on to tell Aberdeen that Tufnell (a former Whig whip) had reported to him 'that a large portion of the old Whig party would not serve in a Government, or even support it, if Lord John were the head'. Graham continued:

> He evidently was recruiting for adherents to Ld. Lansdowne, and led me to believe that Ld. Lansdowne would not be found unwilling, if duty pressed. I urged the necessity of satisfying Ld. John; I dwelt on his superior claims and merits as a Reformer when contrasted with the pretensions of Lord Lansdowne, whose

formal retirement from active public life had been recorded by a subscription to his Bust, which was regarded as the honourable Termination of his Party Warfare. Tufnell was somewhat shaken by this in his advocacy of Ld. Lansdowne's claims, but remained unshaken in his assertion, that Ld. John could not at present return to power as Prime Minister. I found from Tufnell, that the D. of Newcastle had during the Elections been in constant and confidential communication with the Whig political Agents.[72]

On 2 August, in a long letter setting forth the essentials of the Peelite programme, the Duke of Newcastle expressed his general agreement with Aberdeen's views, except perhaps on the subject of direct taxation, which he believed to be an important part of the revenue. 'On the great subjects of Free Trade, Civil and Religious Liberty, Colonial and Law Reform', he wrote, 'a careful and Popular (but not Democratic) Revision of our Representative System, a Foreign policy at once respecting the rights of other Countries and firmly Maintaining our own, and generally—a policy of Conservative Progress,—upon all these I believe there is no difference of opinion between us.' After their recent un-scrupulous and unprecedented sacrifice of principle in order to obtain Parliamentary support he considered co-operation with the Derby government out of the question. Therefore, he argued, Derby must go and be replaced by a government of a 'Liberal' character which might obtain the support 'of many of the more moderate & sagacious members who will adhere to the present Government as long as it lasts'.

He ruled Russell out as a possible prime minister, saying that even his own friends admitted he could not head a new govern-ment. The English Radicals deprecated Russell's Whiggishness, while many Peelites would desert to Derby if any of their friends accepted office under him. As for the Irish, 'now a powerful and on the whole less corrupt and more fanatical party than in the last Parliament', he maintained they would 'pursue to the death' any government of which Lord John was the head. He under-stood Russell's objections to following in the steps of Lord Sidmouth or Lord Goderich, but urged that his support was essential and his participation would be a great advantage to the country.

Newcastle also ruled out Lord Lansdowne since he had for-

I

mally retired from public life and was 72. He believed that Aberdeen was the man despite his lack of experience with domestic affairs. Thus with respect to Russell's three courses for the Peelites, Newcastle concluded:

1. Union with Ld. Derby is impossible.
2. Isolation is pleasant but not patriotic.
3. Co-operation with other Liberals *requisite*.[73]

On the following day Newcastle wrote again strongly urging 'with a view to real fusion of all Liberals', the abandonment of the names '*Whig*' and '*Peelite*', since names meant so much to the public and some MPs, even though, as he himself realised, they were only nicknames. He believed the change from Tory to Conservative in 1832 'had a very great effect in drawing to Sir Robert Peel's standard many who would never have joined a Tory opposition'. Many would work with Russell, Clarendon, Grey, *et al*, who would refuse to join a Whig administration. 'Moreover', he wrote, 'those who *call themselves Whigs* are as few as the *Peelites* in the present Parliament.' A new Liberal party, he suggested significantly, must be constructed, on a new basis, 'not by one party *joining* another'.[74]

On 5 August Gladstone wrote to express his reaction to the Russell letter, saying that he was not free to join Lord John without resigning his seat; 'any alliance or fusion', he asserted, 'to be lawful for me must grow out of circumstances which have not yet risen'. He was convinced 'from personal communications' that the great majority of the Peelites in the House of Commons would 'not consent to merge themselves in the Liberal party'. 'From these men,' he wrote, 'except under strong necessity, I do not wish to part.' 'The shifting and the shuffling that I complain of', he added, 'have been due partly to a miserably false position and the giddy prominence of inferior men; partly to the (surely not unexpected) unscrupulousness and second motives of Mr. D'Israeli, at once the necessity of Lord Derby and his curse.' Gladstone was not as critical of the Derby government, however, as were Aberdeen and Newcastle; moreover, he made a distinction between the government and the party. 'I look to the sober-minded portion of that party', he declared, 'as the most valuable raw material of political party in the country.'

He condemned the religious bigotry of the Derbyites, but said it was not as bad as the 1850–1 anti-papal outburst of Russell, 'the person to whom I am now invited to transfer my confidence'. He also condemned the immorality of Derby, forming his opposition on a principle (Protection) and then abandoning it, again comparing it to a similar action of the Whigs with respect to the Appropriation Clause in 1835 and Coercion in 1846. To join with the Whigs, he argued, would be to cut themselves off from the intelligent and sober-minded portion of the Conservative party who were no more retrograde than in Peel's day. He was not willing that D'Israeli should leave office with three hundred men behind him 'including almost every person', he said, 'with whom I have been accustomed to vote'. He preferred to wait and deal with Derby's measures and professed greater sympathy with their colonial and ecclesiastical policy and no great liking for Reform. He looked forward, however, to the end of the Peelites' 'intermediate position'.[75]

Herbert told Gladstone that he was in agreement with his view. "The "little man" [Russell] seems to me never to have understood the nature or amount of the change effected by his own reform bill,' he wrote from Homburg. '. . . Lord John is not aware how sick the country is of the Whigs & of himself, nor how much they fear the Radicals.' Herbert was, however, even more caustic in his criticism of the government for its two-faced attitude. He thought the ministers if left to themselves would be their own undoing, but recognised that if Disraeli had his own way he might produce measures acceptable to the House. 'He has a great sagacity & no scruple', Herbert wrote, '& his preference, in so far as he has any for any set of opinions, has no doubt always been in favour of Free Trade.'[76]

Aberdeen forwarded Newcastle's and Gladstone's letters to Lord John. He had not yet heard from Herbert, who was abroad, but supposed his views would 'not materially differ from those expressed by Gladstone', although he believed Herbert 'to be altogether more liberally disposed'. He considered Gladstone to be 'hampered by his Oxford constituency', but was sure that he considered the overthrow of the government to be 'quite indispensable' before any acceptable government could be formed:

The plan of proceeding proposed by you, on the meeting of Parliament, will encounter no objection; indeed Gladstone himself had previously suggested it to me and you may therefore fully expect his concurrence. I do not know, however, that any further concert is possible at the moment. It is evident that I am at present considerably in advance of my friends; although I do not despair of seeing them ultimately brought to an entire agreement with me.

. . . You must now allow me to avert to your own position, which I can venture to do the more readily in consequence of my personal situation, and the nature of the views which I entertain.

I do not mean to say, after the great sacrifice made by Peel and his friends, if I thought that either I, or any of his Party, had been in condition to form such a Government as was required by the exigency of the times, that I should not have looked at such a result with satisfaction. It would have seemed to me to be the natural triumph of his policy, and a fitting termination to the contest of the last six years. But feeling that any attempt of this kind is out of the question, I think that a cordial concert with you is the course which it now most becomes his friends to adopt.

With respect to the difficulties in the way of your being placed at the head of a new Administration, I am very imperfectly informed. You will see that the Duke of Newcastle entertains very strong opinions on the subject; and I have received various intimations of the same kind; but whatever may be the cause and however real these difficulties may be at the moment, I can only regard them as merely temporary. It is probable that you may not yourself be aware of the nature and extent of such objections, or of the quarters in which they exist. At any rate in the actual state of affairs, I would venture strongly to recommend that you should come to no decision calculated to interfere with your perfect liberty of action in the course of any future events which may occur, and the character of which it is impossible accurately to foresee.

Perhaps I ought to apologise for writing with so much freedom; but I am sure you will forgive me.[77]

Aberdeen had received word about the rumblings against Russell's leadership among the Whigs from Ellice, and in more detail from Graham, who had it both from Ellice and later directly from the Duke of Bedford.[78] The plan promoted by Palmerston was to form an anti-Reform government under Lansdowne, 'which would include many of the Whigs, all the Peelites wishing to join, and possibly some of the Derbyites'. Graham scouted the possibility of the project succeeding and said it would have no attraction to the Peelites. 'I do not think that the D. of Newcastle or Gladstone will be parties to a Sham Reform Bill,' he said.[79]

Russell thanked Aberdeen for his 'very friendly and very open conduct' and proposed to show the correspondence to Sir George Grey, Lord Minto and Lord Panmure. He commented on the letters: 'The Duke of Newcastle is very fair and candid. Mr. Gladstone seems disposed to the Derby party without Disraeli.'[80] Two days later he wrote at greater length. He promised to follow Aberdeen's 'wise advice' and come to no hasty decision binding his future course of action. He explained that he would not lead the House of Commons under a peer prime minister since the Irish Brigade would be as much opposed to him in that capacity as they would be to him as Prime Minister, but he promised his 'cordial support' to Aberdeen if he 'would take the lead in a Ministry'. Although there was much in Newcastle's letter with which he could not agree, he saw grounds for understanding in the three main propositions that Newcastle made. Gladstone's line he judged was 'very different' since he still looked to reconciliation with Derby. He was, of course, indignant at the jibes Gladstone made on past Whig actions in 1835 and 1846. 'I do not see any chance of agreement with a man who entertains such sentiments of us,' he commented. He pointed out that Gladstone himself had changed his views with respect to the Corn Laws, but gave him credit for being sincere in doing so. 'I ask him to give the same credit to me,' said Russell, and proceeded to vindicate his actions in 1835 and 1846. 'Sir Robert Peel while he lived did all he could to maintain the late ministry in power. After his death his followers in the House of Commons have thought it best to contribute to its fall. Their work is complete; I cannot say that it is very satisfactory; the wisdom and honesty of their great leader is only more fully proved.'[81]

Aberdeen sought to soothe Russell's ruffled feelings, expressing regret that Gladstone's remarks had upset him. He thought that perhaps he should not have forwarded Gladstone's letter, which he had done in the belief that Russell should be 'fully in possession of everything that had passed'. 'But if these [remarks] were never intended to be seen by you,' Aberdeen pleaded, 'in that case, you must forgive him for repeating sentiments which we have all of us been in the habit of expressing for years. . . .' He continued:

> . . . I doubt not that you have yourself sometimes attributed motives to Tory opponents, which further experience has taught you to abandon.
> Gladstone possesses so much that is excellent and amiable in character, that you may be fully persuaded, if it should ever be your fate to act together, you will find in him nothing but frankness and cordiality.

He concluded that for the present nothing further could be done, and that they 'must wait for events to decide the future', laying aside 'all prejudice and feelings of personality'. 'You have made a suggestion respecting myself', he added, 'which there is no necessity now to discuss; but which under the most favourable circumstances would be entertained by me with the utmost reluctance, and of which I cannot even contemplate the possibility.'[82]

Russell replied on 21 August, saying:

> No doubt party men engaged in the heat of conflict throw sundry imputations at each other without being very particular and often without the means of ascertaining their correctness—Like the rest I have often believed the worst of my opponents.
> But it struck me that in reviving those imputations in a letter to you & on such an occasion, could only be done to mark a desire for separation, if not hostility.
> I agree with you as to the practical decision—I think it would be very foolish in the leaders of those who adhere to Sir R. Peel's policy to make any move which would draw away from them to the Govt. any portion of those adherents. I therefore entirely subscribe to the present suspense.

He went on to make some carping allusions to the election calculations of Newcastle and Herbert, in which he indicated that he himself now regarded Graham and Cardwell as Whigs.

> As to the name of Whig [he continued] a name of which Mr. Pitt (as Ld Harrowby assured me) was as tenacious as Mr. Fox,

it does not belong to me to give it up. If people do not continue to use that name well and good—I shan't insist on being called a Whig rather than a Liberal. We have no Whig Club—no other use of the word than quem volet usus—I do not see any advantage therefore in making any formal agreement on the subject.

. . . I fear Cobden is bent upon an amendment the first day. He told C. Villiers so. . . .[83]

Russell wound up the correspondence two days later, returning Gladstone's and Newcastle's letters, and again thanking Aberdeen for his 'kindly conduct'. He summed up the situation by saying that they were all agreed in defending the Free Trade policy, but they would have to wait on events to decide how this could best be done.[84]

In mid-September Russell sent Aberdeen a letter he had received from Lansdowne, which suggested that Russell was the most likely leader to rally both the Whigs and the Peelites.[85] In returning the letter Aberdeen expressed the opinion that Russell had painted too gloomy a picture of the results of the recent conversations to Lansdowne and professed the belief that 'a real fusion . . . is best produced by events and the force of circumstances, rather than by previous stipulations and discussions'. He granted that Newcastle had gone rather far in suggesting that Lord John should surrender the title of Whig, which he was no more likely to do than were the Peelites to forsake a 'Conservative policy'. He himself suggested that the best policy should be one of 'Conservative progress' and he had no objection if the progress was more rapid than Peel ever intended.

With respect to Whig and Tory [he continued], so far as I understand the terms, I must confess to having been frequently both one and the other in the course of my life; and such I think must be the case with any honest man who acts under the influence of natural impressions. When Power assumes an arbitrary character, especially if accompanied by anything like injustice or oppression, we at once side with the People. On the other hand when popular licence knows no bounds . . . we are naturally disposed to support Authority and to strengthen the means of resistance.

At all events the present fear of Democracy seems to me to be more unreasonable than at any former period.

He hoped that they might see Lord and Lady John at Haddo or in London.[86]

Russell expressed his regrets at being unable to visit Haddo, but he suggested that Newcastle might visit them at Gort if he returned from Haddo by land. He continued in humorous vein: 'I forgive him his proposal to get rid of the name of Whig as I hold that it is out of my power, if I wished it, to do so—& if I attempted it, Fitzwilliam & others would seize upon it as their exclusive possession. It has the convenience of expressing in one syllable what Conservative Liberal expresses in seven, & Whiggism in two syllables means what Conservative Progress means in [an]other seven.'[87]

Although the discussion had come to an end for the time being without any very concrete result, new ground had been broken that made the formation of a coalition of Liberals and Peelites more possible than at any time in the past six years. There was as yet no certainty of this and the outcome was to depend on circumstances, but there was a distinct advance in the relationship between the two leaders, Russell and Aberdeen. Their relationship was more relaxed and more intimate, their discussions franker and more positive than when they had last discussed a juncture eighteen months earlier. There were still formidable difficulties, but after this useful exchange of views the door was left open pending further developments. Much would depend upon the course which the Derbyites would take when Parliament met and it remained to be seen whether the younger Peelites would then take the plunge that Aberdeen and Graham were now virtually ready to make.

Political speculation continued throughout the autumn, interrupted only by the engrossing news of the Duke of Wellington's death, which for some weeks filled the public mind. Graham, linking the Duke's passing with that of Peel, uttered a typically Victorian lament:

> ... the deep conviction is driven home to the Heart [he wrote to Aberdeen], that our worldly cares are empty and all our aspirations vain. Still we must return to life and its sad realities for a season; but with minds subdued and tempers mollified by the Thoughts, which these solemn warnings carry from beyond the Grave.[88]

Before long, however, the absorbing topic of the course to be taken in the coming session once more began to preoccupy the minds of the politicians. A sampling of the interminable letters that passed between the country seats of the leading actors in the play throws some light on the eventual formation of a Liberal-Peelite coalition. We may first look briefly at some of the interchanges among the Liberals.

Several of Russell's ex-colleagues were ready to ply him with advice on the course he should take in the coming session. Clarendon warned him against any hasty attack that might drive Derby out of office because of the difficulty that he himself would have in forming an administration. 'To think of anybody but yourself as head of a liberal Govt as some folks may idly or pettishly do is sheer nonsense but it is on that acct that I am so anxious for a policy of caution,' he wrote.[89] Wood took a similar line, urging the necessity of courting Peelite support which he claimed would bring the Irish members too, since in his view they looked to Newcastle and Graham for a lead.[90] He reported that Disraeli was heading the Free Trade wing within the Government in order to guard against the danger of his being supplanted by Gladstone.

> Dislike (personal I mean) of Disraeli [Wood wrote] in the first place, & of Derby in the second is a ruling passion with the Peelites; and it has always struck me that the personal difficulty as to Disraeli would stand in the way of any junction between even the Gladstonian section & the present Government.[91]

Russell's brother, the Duke of Bedford, warmly approved his co-operation with Aberdeen, but his father-in-law, Lord Minto, took a more jaundiced view of the Peelites. He too warned Russell not to make an early attempt to form a Liberal government.[92] 'In opposition you will recover your *individuality*', he advised, 'instead of being seen as the impersonation of other men's errors.'[93] Minto was especially indignant at news of an alleged intrigue among the Whigs against Russell's leadership. He made little of all the obvious reasons for Liberal discontent with it, such as the Durham letter, the dismissal of Palmerston, the resignation, the failure to bring in some Peelites, and suggested that it had its source in the ambitions of Palmerston and

Newcastle.[94] Bedford, who was more in touch with other elements in the party, reassured Russell that there was no intrigue,[95] as did Clarendon,[96] but Lord Broughton's diary reveals Whig unrest with Russell's leadership.[97]

Early in October Palmerston happened to meet the Duke of Bedford at Brocket and took the opportunity of telling him at great length why, despite his warm personal regard for Lord John, he could not again serve under him. He was, however, prepared to serve with him on equal terms and suggested Lord Lansdowne as the most likely leader under whom all sections of the Liberal party and some moderate Conservatives might unite.[98] He made this proposal to Lansdowne, who expressed his gratification, but said bluntly that he considered Russell to be in the best position to form a government.[99] A few weeks later, after hearing of the conversation with Palmerston from his brother, Russell called on Lansdowne, told him that he would be willing to serve under him and asked him so to inform Palmerston.[100] The latter expressed his delight at this news. 'John Russell's decision does him great credit . . .,' he wrote. 'I now for the first time begin to see daylight.'[101] In the end gout ruled Lord Lansdowne out, but it is doubtful whether he could have formed a coalition with the Peelites. The incident, however, narrowed the gap separating Russell and Palmerston.

The gap separating Whigs and Peelites was in fact a narrow one, formed for the most part by lingering political traditions that no longer had any great significance. Indeed, the Duke of Newcastle observed that the differences lay more between generations. In a revealing passage in a letter to Lord Granville shortly after they became colleagues he commented that there was no more difference between them 'than there must always be between any two men who think for themselves'.

> The fact is [he continued] that among men of Liberal opinions the difference is not Whig and Peelite, but the men of forty years of age (more or less) and those of the former generation. *Peelism*— if I must still use the word—is really the more advanced form of Liberal opinion, cleared of that demagogic Liberalism which characterised the Liberalism of twenty years ago, and on the other hand of that oligarchic tendency of the old Whigs, who, wishing to extend freedom, sought to do it by making use of the

people, instead of identifying themselves and their own interests with the people.[102]

In actual fact a wider gulf separated the Whigs and the more extreme Radicals who for the most part spoke a different language and moved in different social circles than the aristocrats on whose side of the house they sat in uneasy alliance. In a letter to Cobden John Bright has left an amusing description of a chance meeting with Russell in the Scottish Highlands where they were both holidaying after the elections. 'We met the little man jogging along on his pony, & looking as well satisfied with himself as when he is insulting the Catholics, or arguing for a Militia in the House of Commons,' Bright wrote. He told Russell that he thought the atmosphere of the north was doing him good and that he 'hoped it would brace up his politics as well as his health'. He seized the opportunity to impress upon Russell the necessity of obtaining a 'better representation' and observed 'that Sir Jas Graham was stepping out a little on the Reform question & on the Ballot'. But he had little confidence in Lord John. 'It is a pity a man in his position should be so incapable of doing a right thing with courage', he commented to Cobden, '& yet unhappily it is difficult at present to see what can be done without him.'[103]

Cobden replied:

I was amused at your description of Lord John. Depend on it however there is more of obstruction than of progress in that quarter. It is true that his family antecedents make him of necessity a *theoretical* liberal in constitutional questions, & he will be found as a parliamentary reformer a little & but very little ahead of the Tory or Peel party. But he has no love for the work which history has bequeathed to the Russells & he is more intent upon preserving the aristocracy than encroaching upon their privileges. It is my settled conviction, after long consideration of the question, that we have more to gain in the way of practical & administrative reforms (apart from Parliamentary Reform) from either the Tories or Peelites than the Whigs. The latter are wrong on almost every administrative measure. . . . Whilst professing free trade principles, to serve the ends of party, they seem to be quite unable or unwilling to accept its logical consequences;—for they are extending our territorial dominion in all directions.[104]

Meanwhile endless correspondence was also going on in the Peelite camp. Lord Aberdeen continued to profess his confidence in Lord John but Newcastle complained of Russell's peevish temper and fossilised Whiggery. 'The Whigs are buried with Mr. Fox and Mr. Pitt (save the mark)', he concluded, 'but alas the spirit of Whig Oligarchical Cliquery, it is too clear, still lives.'[105]

In reply Aberdeen told Newcastle he had perhaps read too much into Russell's last letter:

> I have no doubt that Mr. Pitt called himself a Whig, indeed, I know that he did so [Aberdeen, of course, was Pitt's ward]; but be this as may, there is certainly no public man upon whom the Tory stamp is more indelibly placed. Lord John may do what he pleases; but he will be called a Whig to the end of his life. This is a title of which some persons are proud; but which in the present day really means nothing at all. At all events, whatever it may mean, we do not become Whigs by acting with Lord John; nor does he become a Tory by acting with us.
>
> For my own part, as applicable to myself, I have always repeated the line of Pope
> 'The Tories call me Whig, the Whigs a Tory'.
> On the whole I think that Ld John has shown a good deal of magnanimity in his present position. After the part he has acted it must be humiliating to find himself comparatively set aside by so many of his own friends. You have spoken very plainly, and I have no doubt, told him the truth, which he has taken very well.

He went on to urge Newcastle 'to put the most charitable construction upon all things', since if they were to act with Russell 'it must be upon a footing of mutual confidence and respect'.[106] Newcastle answered in milder tone, admitting that his view of Russell might have been twisted by their correspondence the previous winter. 'I certainly would not willingly be unjust to Lord John Russell or anybody else,' he wrote, 'and am very sensible how great need *every* public man has of charitable construction of his motives.'[107]

Gladstone told Newcastle that he would rather 'keep a position on the Liberal side of the Conservative party, than take one on the Conservative side of the Liberal party', and pointed out that his relations with his constituents made it difficult for him to enter 'into opposition to Lord Derby's Govt. on any grounds I could at present allege'. He continued:

... I believe the real diminution of the Peelites, considered as a middle party, in the present Parlt, as compared with the last, is even greater than the apparent one. The constituencies do not understand or recognise, unless in exceptional cases, any middle or third party. Circumstances therefore, independent of our choice, are bringing on the day when, if we mean to be a party at all, we must look to more extended relations.[108]

Aberdeen's most intimate correspondence remained with Graham who kept him informed of Russell's views, reporting that Lord John was ready to support Aberdeen as prime minister if the Liberals preferred him. Aberdeen expressed incomprehension at the suggestion that the Whigs might prefer him to Lord John as prime minister.[109] He forwarded letters from Newcastle and Gladstone observing:

No doubt, Gladstone is essentially Conservative; but although you have frightened him, as well as the rest of the world, by your ultra liberalism, he cannot really be scared by the bugbear of Democracy. It is clear, that the rallying cry of the Government will not be Protection to Agriculture, but Protection against Democracy. Free Trade is our really strong ground, and it is upon this that the Government should be compelled to fight, when the proper time shall arrive.[110]

Graham characteristically took the darkest view of the correspondence, which Aberdeen had sent him.

There is no hope of reconciling these Gentlemen [he wrote]. They differ on every point. The Duke of Newcastle insists as a sine quâ non, that Ld. J. Russell shall not be the Prime Minister; Ld. John says any other Post would be 'personal degradation'; and Gladstone says 'Ld. John is right in declining any appointment but the First'. Again the title of Whig is Lord John's distinctive Appellation; the Duke of Newcastle demands its renunciation as a preliminary; forgetting that Paley's Maxim in matters of Religion is true also in Politics: 'Men often change their creed, but rarely the name of their Sect'. To un-Whig Ld. John Russell is like the unfrocking of a Parson, or stripping the Buttons from a Soldier's Jacket. Certain things cannot be done without dishonour and to require them is not conciliatory. I, however, am not a fair Judge in this occasion; for my antecedents in this respect are quite different from those of all my colleagues in Peel's Government, with the exception of Lord Derby.[111]

In a subsequent letter Graham asserted that 'the paramount duty, perhaps the sole remaining duty, of Peel's Friends as a Party is the defence of his Financial and Commercial Policy'. When this was settled he assumed that Gladstone would swing back towards the Conservatives.[112] Oddly enough, almost these same words were echoed by Gladstone himself when he wrote to Aberdeen: 'One thing as Peelites we have yet to do, namely to see that the financial measures are kept in harmony with the free trade policy. Till that is done our work is not complete; when it is done we may straightway go about our business. Ardently indeed I hope that those who now keep together may not then separate; but we shall have passed into a new phase of politics.' This may suggest that Graham was too pessimistic in his prognostications about Gladstone.[113]

The correspondence between Russell and Graham became more intimate. In one letter, for instance, Lord John playfully alluded to the local railway line that parted at Barnes and rejoined at Windsor. 'So may our two courses in politics be. You have gone by the loop line, & I have gone by the Richmond line; but we set out together, & may come to the end of our journey together.' In the same letter he accepted Aberdeen's wise advice to keep himself at liberty with respect to the question of who was to head a new government.[114]

Graham responded warmly but with characteristic heavy-handedness to Russell's railway line quip. 'We commenced public life together', he wrote, 'and I feel that I am drawing to my Journey's End. If Windsor be still our Destination, I prefer the Richmond Line, because it is yours: I have no fancy for "Loop" Lines; they are full of Curves and are indirect. As we began the Journey side by side, so let us end it as old Companions and Friends.'[115]

When Graham showed Aberdeen his correspondence with Russell the latter not unnaturally came to the conclusion that the Graham-Russell alliance was an accomplished fact, which had been first forecast in Graham's Carlisle speech. 'I regret to see you removed a step further from union with Peel's friends', he wrote, 'but I still hope that the force of events will bring about such a fusion as cannot be effected by previous stipulation and discussion.' He made his own position clear when he said:

> I am thoroughly convinced of the necessity of a Government of progress, and am prepared to advance more rapidly than probably was ever contemplated by Peel himself; but this progress must be Conservative in principle. You may fall back on Whiggism, in which you were bred; but I was bred at the feet of Gamaliel, and must always regard Mr. Pitt as the first of statesmen.[116]

Graham's answer was defensive. He was strongly opposed to the Derby government and consequently ready to work with Russell, but he did not repudiate Peelism at Carlisle; rather he claimed he was 'drummed out of the Regiment' by all except Cardwell and Aberdeen himself. He accepted, as not unnatural, this breach from his other colleagues in Peel's government, but to Aberdeen he wrote: 'I should be sorry indeed, if I thought that I were removed by one hair's breadth further from you.' Indeed, he suggested that Aberdeen's tone to Lord John had been even 'more confiding and more conciliatory' than his own.[117]

Aberdeen's reply was warm and friendly; he recognised his relationship with Russell might be cordial, but it could never be quite the same as Graham's for 'it must be as a Liberal Conservative, and not as a Whig'. But he was not prepared to say that the rest of Peel's friends were bound to return to Derby when the Free Trade issue was settled.[118] Graham responded characteristically by suggesting that he and Aberdeen were more likely to be 'spectators' than 'active players' and that 'in the Evening of Life when the heat of Passions is abated and when the shadows of Recollection are prolonged', the bond between them would remain strong. 'Our early training and predilections', he wrote, 'were not alike; but our present views and opinions are similar; and our past attachment to the common Friend, whom we have lost was equally ardent and sincere.'[119]

News of the Whigs came from the anti-Russell camp through Herbert, who wrote to Aberdeen after visiting Palmerston at Broadlands in mid-October.[120] Palmerston had confirmed all that they had heard as to his exertions to bring about a Lansdowne administration. 'He said that his confidence in "Johnny" as a *leader* was quite destroyed,' Herbert wrote, 'that his love of popularity wd always lead him into scrapes & that when a man made sudden announcements of new policy without consulting his colleagues one might acquiesce rather than break up a Government, when the actor was a friend, but not otherwise.' Palmerston considered Russell now out of the question and strongly urged Lansdowne as the most likely man to rally conservative Whigs and Peelites. 'He said he had proposed this plan to Lord Lansdowne,' Herbert continued, 'whose answer was "Give me a majority of 100 and I am ready" wh he construed as an acceptance & I construe as a refusal.' Herbert reminded Palmerston that Lansdowne had formally retired from public life, that he was 72 years old and in poor health, and so he argued against the proposal on the grounds that 'the public would look upon it as a mere provisional arrangement with little prospect of permanence or stability'.

Palmerston made a veiled reference to the possibility of a juncture with the Derby ministry. Although he contemptuously referred to it as consisting for the present of only three men and a half, he thought eight ministers were ready to make room for newcomers. (More than a century was to elapse, in fact, before a prime minister would juggle his cabinet on that scale.) Thus Herbert saw Palmerston as having 'two strings to his bow', but was inclined to believe he would eventually 'overcome his dislike [of] Lord John'.

As the opening of Parliament approached Russell issued invitations to a dinner to a select group of eighteen of his close associates. This presented a problem to Graham who was among the invited guests. He did not wish to injure his good relations with Lord John, but was even more unwilling to give such 'an outward and visible sign of "allegiance" '.[121] In the end he managed to excuse himself on the plea of returning to Netherby to welcome his newly married son. To Aberdeen he wrote critically of Russell's action:

> This dinner is an ill-advised Repetition of the premature meeting there [Chesham Place] after the overthrow of the late Government. Those who dine there will be considered as pledged to something more than Opposition: those who are not invited to

dine there, will consider themselves as excluded from the Family Circle. Hume has declared off; Cobden has declared off; Palmerston will never consent to serve under Lord John again; the Peelites have come to the same determination; and the Whigs are divided; yet the little man 'is in high Spirits'! This is a love of hot water and of difficulties which exceeds all belief.[122]

Cornewall Lewis did his best to persuade Graham to attend the dinner, but Graham defended his decision firmly. With a certain Pecksniffian eloquence he wrote: 'I care little for the imputation of false motives [which Lewis had foretold]. Lust of Power and Place has not been my besetting Sin: and I shall endeavour so to act as to defy slander, and to prove that at least the motives of my conduct are irreproachable.'[123] One may wonder whether there was any besetting sin to which Sir James would admit.

In the end Graham told Russell openly his real reason for not attending the dinner. Russell expressed his regrets but still hoped for cordial co-operation. Typically he justified himself by saying that 'not giving a dinner would have been equivalent to that degradation which Mr. Crawford proclaimed was to be my fate'.[124] Graham, perhaps unreasonably, detected reserve in this reply and feared old Whig animosities might be rekindled.[125]

Aberdeen expressed his approbation of Graham's avoidance of the Russell dinner, but he spoke warmly of Lord John whom he described as 'really a wonderful little man'. He hoped some good might come from a rather exclusive little meeting at Bowood of Russell, Lansdowne, Clarendon, Lewis and Macaulay, of which Lewis had given some account to Graham.[126]

Perhaps one reason for Russell's high spirits was the success of a speech he delivered in Perth early in October[127] on which he was congratulated by many of his former colleagues, who were now writing to him in friendly tones.[128] Minto told him that he should continue to act as leader of the Whig party and that he could stand second to none in a purely Whig administration. He warned his son-in-law whatever decision he came to to keep it to himself; 'do not let it go forth', he advised, 'that you may be induced to renounce any of your own pretensions, till the moment of decision has arrived'.[129] In following Russell's devious course in the next two months it will be important to keep this advice of

K

his father-in-law in mind. Having delivered it, Lord Minto departed to Italy for the winter.

In his Perth speech Russell elaborated a policy of 'Conservative Progress', which he suggested was the essence of Whiggism, and he warned against any direct challenge on the address when Parliament opened. This was not likely to encourage the radical wing of the Liberal party, which Lord John seemed little interested in courting at this time. Bright and Cobden commented critically on the speech to each other[130] and old Joe Hume delivered a broadside to the press in which he said that he considered 'Lord John as *not sincere* as a Reformer both *civil* and *religious*'. He hoped that Cobden would agree with him and that all Reformers would 'set the two great oppressing parties at a distance'.[131] But there was no unity in the Radical camp. Bright commented to Cobden that 'our old friend Hume has got quite a Whig phobia upon him', but forecast that he would return to his old modes of action when the house met.[132] Cobden refused to say anything against 'Old Joe' in view of his past service, but regretted that he remained in politics when 'his better powers are declining'.[133]

A little earlier than this another Radical spokesman, J. A. Roebuck, had shown his distrust of Russell by making a personal appeal to Graham to come forward as the new Liberal leader, 'the Great Commoner' as he called it. He even sketched a programme which the Reformers might take up under Graham's leadership, if he would only be more daring.[134] It was the fact that this sort of appeal was possible, of course, that made Graham suspect at this time among the more orthodox Peelites.

It is more difficult to generalise about the Radicals than about any of the other groups into which the Opposition forces were split. They all seemed to have an ingrained suspicion of each other that made effective co-operation on any significant scale impossible. The letters of Cobden and Bright are full of caustic remarks about most of the other so-called Radical leaders of the time,[135] and Roebuck, one of the most outspoken Radicals in Parliament, was contemptuous of most of his associates with the exception of Bright, 'the pugnacious Quaker', as he called him.[136] Dr Maccoby, in discussing the ineffectiveness of the Radicals of this period, points out one obvious weakness, their lack of administrative experience,[137] but the causes of their failure lay deeper than this. In some cases personal deficiencies were a bar to effective leadership and office,[138] but the basic trouble seemed to be that independence of spirit associated with nineteenth-century radicalism. Historically, in the Radical's view, all government had been bad, and while the Radical wanted to improve it he was instinctively against it and not mentally prepared to assist in taking it over.[139]

During the forties the crusade for the repeal of the Corn Laws provided an issue on which all Radicals were agreed, but in the fifties divergences were more pronounced, especially in the field of foreign policy where the views of men like Roebuck were quite opposite to those of Cobden and Bright. Indeed this was one of the reasons for the Manchester men's coolness to other Radicals. They unfurled their colours, however, in a giant Free Trade banquet held in Manchester on the eve of the meeting of Parliament, attended by more than 3,000 persons and over sixty MPs of whom several were Irish independents. The banquet was organised by George Wilson, President of the Free Trade League, to warn the Government of the formidable propaganda machinery that could be brought back into being against it if it dared to ignore the public opinion of the country. Cobden and Bright, although initially dubious of the wisdom of such a meeting at this time, were the major speakers on the platform, but significantly they were followed by the one-time Peelite, Keogh, who avowed the support of the Irish members in the cause of Free Trade. The meeting, as *The Times* observed, was a fair but solemn warning to the ministers to settle the great question once and for all before Christmas.[140]

Four long months had elapsed between the dissolution of the old parliament in July and the meeting of the new one in November, sufficient time for the Government to prepare its programme in view of the election results and for the Opposition to rally its forces. It was clear, however, that these were still too diverse to make any safe prediction as to what would happen when Parliament met. The result of the elections precluded the possibility of the Whigs coming back to office on the same basis as their former administration. Conversations with the Peelites had left the door open to an understanding, but there would be many susceptibilities to satisfy on both sides. Indeed, the Whigs themselves were not entirely united under Russell's banner, let alone the Radicals who remained belligerently independent. And the Irish Liberals, mostly, bound by pledges to the Tenant League, had not forgiven the minister responsible for the Ecclesiastical Titles Act. The Opposition had the advantage in numbers and in talent, but it remained to be seen whether they were capable of working together towards a common end, and whether if they brought the Government down they had a leader under whom they could all unite. Russell's stock was at its lowest in his own party, Lansdowne's age and health seemed to preclude him, Palmerston was still an outsider, popular in some quarters, but not yet possessing a sufficient parliamentary following. Graham as a renegade Whig was scarcely to be trusted, and for all his ability there was a timidity and a querulousness in his character that seemed to rule him out as a prime minister. Could it be that an old Tory nobleman who had never sat in the House of Commons and who had begun his ministerial career under the Duke of Wellington was capable of rallying the forces of Liberalism against a Tory government still suspected of being Protectionist? It seemed unlikely at first sight, and yet no other alternative was really any more likely. Only time would tell. It was up to the House of Commons to perform what the contemporary Bagehot saw as its main function, the choice of a prime minister, even though he might not sit in that House.

*Notes to this chapter are on pages 201–9*

# Chapter 6 THE FALL OF THE DERBY MINISTRY

WITH THE meeting of Parliament on 4 November the anti-ministerial ranks began to close. Interest now centred on the framing of a Free Trade motion to challenge the Government at the beginning of the session, but this in itself did not necessarily mean a united Opposition. Graham told Russell that he believed 'Gladstone's eager desire to carry a free trade amendment' immediately was to remove the barrier which separated him from the Derbyites. Newcastle, however, he regarded as a Reformer 'with strong Liberal tendencies' and with 'no affinity to Lord Derby', leaving Herbert torn between his two friends and 'much perplexed'. Palmerston he suspected would be 'anxious to carry Gladstone and Herbert with him to either camp'. 'Joe Hume and Cobden on the one hand, and the Irish Brigade on the other, render the confusion in the state of parties ludicrously complete,' he concluded. 'The ball will open with a country-dance in which no one has secured a partner.'[1]

Graham's suspicion of Gladstone was not entirely without foundation, for some weeks before the opening of Parliament the latter had come to London for the purpose of communicating with Lord Hardinge, whom he regarded as the one possible intermediary to Lord Derby. He set forth what in his opinion the House of Commons would require:

1. Frank explicit adoption of Free Trade by the Address in answer to the Queen's Speech.
2. The immediate production of the promised financial measures.

Hardinge met Gladstone a second time on 5 November and informed him that Derby agreed to the first of the two points, but apparently the Government was not yet ready for the second. 'The numerous & prolonged Cabinets moreover which took place between the 4th & the 11th of Novr caused us some misgivings,' Gladstone recorded. By 'us' he meant Herbert, Newcastle, Young, Aberdeen and himself who met twice that week at Aberdeen's house.[2] Aberdeen gave some account of the first of these meetings to Graham, who was still excluded. After much discussion it had been decided that there should be an independent resolution on Free Trade rather than an amendment to the speech from the throne, unless it turned out that some part of the speech had to be repudiated. It was agreed that Gladstone was the best man to move the amendment, since he would command more support than Villiers, or even Russell, who would antagonise the Irish. Aberdeen told Graham that there was less hostility to Russell among his friends and that Graham was quite wrong in his opinions as to Gladstone's intentions. 'Gladstone's object', he wrote, 'is precisely the same as your own. He believes that no good can be done until the present government shall be displaced.'[3]

Graham continued to play his lone game, although he kept Aberdeen fully informed of his doings. He avowed his intention of calling on Russell 'for the purpose both of ascertaining his intentions as to the Address', and of marking his 'wish cordially to co-operate . . . as an *Opposition Ally*'.[4] This of course provided a very useful link between the Whigs and the Peelites, although Russell was ready as well to keep a direct line open to Aberdeen.

On 9 November Lord Derby offered to show Russell a copy of the Queen's speech for his parliamentary dinner on the following evening, as Russell had done to him when their roles were reversed. He said that in framing the speech he had sought to avoid provoking an amendment.[5] Russell, in accepting the offer, hoped there would be no occasion for an amendment, but refused to make any promises.[6]

The Peelite chiefs held their second meeting on the same night as Russell's dinner (the 10th) and at about midnight received a copy of the relevant paragraph in the Queen's speech, which had been supplied by Derby. 'We were all much dissatisfied & disappointed,' Gladstone recorded. The wording appeared to them to allow the possibility of the Government falling back on Protection if their remedial measures failed. 'I was especially warm and indignant,' Gladstone added, 'and showed some small portion perhaps of this feeling in speaking on the address.' He was, however, better pleased when he subsequently learned that Disraeli intended to bring in his financial proposals at an early date.[7] Russell told Aberdeen that his party were agreed in thinking the paragraph on Free Trade to be 'inadequate and unsatisfactory', but they did not think an amendment was desirable.[8]

Although Parliament met on 4 November, apart from the unanimous election of the Speaker, Shaw Lefevre, and the swearing in of new members, no business was done until 11 November and another week elapsed before Wellington's funeral obsequies had been completed and mourning speeches made from all sides. The Duke's death damaged the Government in more ways than one. Not only did they lose the prestige of his great name, but they lost credit in making the funeral arrangements, for many people considered it unseemly that the burial should have been postponed so long. (The Government insisted on waiting until Parliament had met so that the Houses could be officially represented.) To cap it all Disraeli made a most unfortunate speech in which he plagiarised a large section of an old essay by Thiers on the qualities of a good general. Although he protested to his friends that he did this inadvertently, it made a bad impression on the public.[9]

The Queen's speech was very brief and on the subject of Free Trade enigmatic. The Queen was made to welcome the 'generally improved condition of the country and especially of the Industrious classes'. As to Government policy, the speech continued:

> If you should be of opinion that recent Legislation in contributing, with other Causes, to this happy Result, has at the same time inflicted unavoidable Injury on certain important Interests, I recommend you dispassionately to consider how far it may be practicable equitably to mitigate that Injury, and to enable the Industry of the Country to meet successfully that unrestricted Competition to which Parliament, in its Wisdom, has decided that it should be subjected.[10]

Needless to say, this Delphic pronouncement was not well received by the Opposition, but the more moderate were mollified by Derby's assertion in the Lords that he was prepared to accept the recent decision of the electorate and that the Government would announce its long-awaited measure in two weeks' time. The Opposition was thus divided between the Simon-pure Free Traders such as Cobden and Hume who were for immediate attack and those such as the Peelites who were content to wait and see. Russell and Graham were rather caught in the middle, but it was Palmerston who was to produce a solution.

The series of complicated movements that went on among the Free Traders between 20 and 24 November is both instructive and entertaining. The fullest account of the affair has been given by Sir James Graham in a lengthy parliamentary explanation[11] that many listeners thought revealed too much of the different shades of opinion within the Free Trade camp. Graham arrived back in London on the very night (the 10th) on which Russell and Aberdeen had held their meetings. The next morning he learned of the outcome of these meetings from Aberdeen, and later he met Bright in the House, who told him that he and his friends were inclined to move an amendment to the address, but that they were refraining from doing so in order to maintain the unity of the Free Traders. Instead it was proposed that Villiers should make a Free Trade motion. Graham endorsed this idea and himself proceeded to draft such a motion, paying particular attention to the wording of the Queen's speech and of the speeches made by Derby and Disraeli in their respective Houses on the first day of the debate on the address. He bore in mind, he later told the House, that this was a resolution to be presented 'in an Assembly of gentlemen' and consequently he was careful to avoid putting in anything unnecessary that might give offence; he was sure that Peel would have approved of what he drafted 'although he would have framed a better Resolution'. He then showed his handiwork to Lord John who approved it and even suggested a third paragraph about readiness to hear Government proposals. Graham next showed his draft with this addition to his former Peelite colleagues, who, after suggesting some changes in wording, expressed their agreement. He was particularly anxious to word the second paragraph so as to avoid suggesting that Free Trade had done any harm to the agricultural interest and thereby to acknowledge the existence of a case for compensation, but he accepted some modification to his wording here, apparently on Gladstone's urging.[12]

Graham then turned his draft motion over to Lord John, who in turn discussed it with some of the leading Free Traders among his followers. Graham could scarcely object when they proposed to insert a direct reference to the beneficial legislation of 1846. When the motion was published in the form eventually proposed by Villiers Graham found it acceptable and much preferable to the amended form which Disraeli proceeded to suggest.

The Radical Free Traders were anxious to make the most of the occasion, and consequently that old parliamentary hand, Joseph Hume, resorted to a device known as a 'call of the House' for the day before the motion was to be presented in order to secure a full attendance. The proposal was passed with Disraeli's acquiescence, but the majority in favour was small because of the lack of notice allowed. Nevertheless the stratagem appeared to serve its purpose since it hastened the process of swearing members in prior to the debate, and once this had been achieved the sponsors of the motion agreed to let it lapse to avoid the lengthy waste of time involved in the formal roll call.[13]

Finally on 23 November Villiers moved his long-awaited motion which contained three resolutions. These dwelt upon the improved conditions of the country and 'particularly of the Industrious Classes', resulting from the recent commercial legislation, especially the Repeal Act of 1846, which was described as 'a wise, just and beneficial measure'. They advocated a further extension of the policy of Free Trade as opposed to Protection and concluded by expressing the House's readiness to consider 'any measure consistent with the principle of these Resolutions' which might be 'laid before it by Her Majesty's Ministers'.[14]

Despite an attack of influenza Disraeli made a vigorous attack, arguing that the resolutions were uncalled-for, since the Government had clearly accepted the *fait accompli* of Free Trade, and objectionable in their attempt to revive the animosities of 1846. It was, he suggested, as if the Whig Opposition in 1835 had tried to make Peel accept a motion praising the Reform Act of 1832, which he had once opposed but now accepted. Disraeli claimed that the Protectionists had done nothing to reverse the great decisions on Free Trade once they had been made, and remarked

that on the matter of compensation they had obtained support
from no less a champion of Peel's policy than the Honourable
Member for Oxford. His argument was rather strained, but on
the evidence of one or two speeches of Gladstone's in 1850 he
proclaimed:

> The followers of Sir Robert Peel, then, who are, we are told,
> banded together against the existence of that Government which
> they are always calling on to produce their measures—the fol-
> lowers of Sir Robert Peel, on the two great questions, first, of
> agricultural distress, and secondly, of the distress of the sugar-
> producing colonies, entirely approved the policy pursued by the
> Protectionist party.[15]

Objecting to the Opposition's tactics of forcing such a motion
on a Government that had honourably accepted the policy, he
managed to touch some tender spots in the Free Trade ranks.
Suppose, he said, a new government was formed but the Opposition refused to accept Lord John as a leader—he, Disraeli, had no
objection to him—and that a follower of Sir Robert Peel became
prime minister. Then would it be fair to make him swallow a
resolution upholding the Ecclesiastical Titles Act of 1851? However, to demonstrate his readiness to abide by the Free Trade
decision he offered an alternative in the form of an amendment
to Villiers' motion to the effect that:

> This House acknowledges, with satisfaction, that the cheapness
> of provisions, occasioned by recent Legislation, has mainly con-
> tributed to improve the condition and increase the comforts of
> the Working Classes; and that unrestricted competition having
> been adopted, after due deliberation, as the principle of our
> Commercial System, this House is of opinion that it is the duty
> of the Government unreservedly to adhere to that policy in those
> measures of Financial and Administrative Reform which, under
> the circumstances of the Country, they may deem it their duty
> to introduce.[16]

More than a century after the event there may not seem to be
any very great difference between these two alternatives, but in
1852 men thought otherwise. Disraeli's form found favour with
few since it was wormwood and gall to many of his Protectionist
followers to make any such formal concession to the hated Free
Trade doctrine, while to the Free Traders the reference to

'burdens' in Disraeli's speech suggested a commitment to the unacceptable idea of compensation.

Bright followed Disraeli and demolished his argument that the Protectionists had never attempted to reverse the decisions on Free Trade once they were made by quoting numerous Protectionist spokesmen in the recent elections.[17] Peel's second son, Frederick, emphasised this point by saying that it was only the Protectionist leaders and not their followers who had given up the cause and hence the need for a public recantation.[18]

It was at this point that Lord Palmerston came forward with his compromise. He said that he had found the Queen's speech evasive and that he agreed in principle with Villiers' motion. He did not really think that there was much difference between it and the proposed amendment and he did recognise that it was asking a lot of the Protectionists to have them 'go down on their knees' and express opinions they did not entertain. He thought there was a danger that the original motion might be converted 'into an opportunity for overturning the Government' and consequently he suggested an alternative form of wording that he hoped might be acceptable to all parties. This attributed the improved condition of the country to recent legislation which had 'established the principle of unrestricted competition, and abolished taxes imposed for purposes of protection', thus reducing the cost of food for the people. The prudent extension of this policy was advocated and the House was asked to consider 'any measures consistent with those principles which, in pursuance of Her Majesty's gracious Speech' might be laid before it.[19]

There are different accounts as to the origin of this compromise. From the time the terms of the Villiers resolutions were settled the Peelites recognised that they would produce trouble and a meeting to discuss the problem was held at Lord Aberdeen's, which was attended by Gladstone, Herbert, Newcastle, Young and the Duke of Buccleuch. In writing to Gladstone about the meeting Young said that some were prepared to vote for the Villiers motion, but that 'many others say—we know we must eat dirt—but why not let us swallow it quietly—why add insult to it?' 'An amendment appears an obvious course,' Young commented, 'but it is not quite so easy as it seems.'[20] On 19 November Graham sent Gladstone a copy of the resolutions, in the form that Villiers proposed to move them. He regretted the changes, but found it impossible to refuse. 'It might have been generous to spare our Adversaries and not to insist on passing them under the Yoke,' he wrote; 'you know I was willing and even anxious so to do; but the great majority of the Free Traders are resolved to record their Triumph; and I must own, that Peel's implacable Enemies, whom Time and Death have not softened, can urge no claim but that of compassion on our forbearance.' Despite its melodramatic phrasing, there was probably much truth in this analysis of the situation.[21]

Gladstone wondered whether it might not be desirable to make an effort to avoid conflict. He thought the Villiers motion went too far and ran the risk of courting defeat; that it also raised the danger of the Government resigning before it had brought in its financial measures, which Gladstone said he would regard 'as a great calamity'. Moreover, he thought it much better to try and settle 'the great controversy of Free Trade' with something approaching unanimity, rather than leave it up in the air with a narrow majority.[22]

In the meantime Palmerston's thoughts had been turning in the same direction. He wrote to Villiers urging a compromise and sent a copy of the letter to Gladstone with the draft of an amendment which he said he had compiled from the Queen's speech, the Villiers resolutions and the Disraeli amendment. Gladstone heartily concurred in Palmerston's action, but suggested that if Palmerston's amendment were considered too close to Disraeli's he might use the form of words that Herbert had sent him that day. This is presumably what he did, for it was observed that the amendment he proposed was almost identical with Graham's original motion. Obviously Herbert had referred to this document when making his proposed wording to Palmerston. In later life Gladstone wrote an account of the incident in which he says that he and Herbert visited Palmerston and made the proposal for an alternative motion to him, but the correspondence between Palmerston and Gladstone indicates that the initiative came from Palmerston. Thus Russell was unfair in criticising Palmerston for bringing forward Graham's wording, when Palmerston apparently did it to meet the suggestions of Herbert and Gladstone. He agreed, however, that an attempt

should be made to persuade both Villiers and Disraeli to withdraw in favour of Palmerston. 'Pray inform Mr. Gladstone of my
opinion', he wrote to Graham, '& if he concurs, our triple opinion
might be conveyed to Villiers.'[23]

On the night of the 24th the Peelite party, according to Lord
Jocelyn who attended,[24] dined at the home of Mr Wortley, one of
its members, and discussed their course of action. Jocelyn told
Derby that they decided to support the Villiers motion if the
Government did not accept Palmerston's amendment, and this
news may well have affected Disraeli's subsequent decision.
Jocelyn also reported that the question of reunion with the Conservative party was discussed and that there was an expression of
willingness to join the Government on certain conditions, one of
which was that Lord Palmerston should lead the House of
Commons, 'Mr. Gladstone refusing to serve under Mr. Disraeli'.[25]

Disraeli told the House that the Government had been prepared to accept the Free Trade motion in its original form as
passed on by Graham to Russell, and a copy of which had come
to their attention. However, they would have nothing to do with
Villiers' wording, which insisted on calling the Act of 1846 'wise,
just and beneficial', words that Disraeli described as 'three odious
epithets'.[26] Likewise, they refused to give any undertaking to
Palmerston when he communicated to them the terms of the
resolutions he proposed.[27] Nevertheless, Palmerston decided to
take his chance and it soon became clear that his motion, which
was duly moved as an amendment on 25 November, would have
wide support. By this time Disraeli had seen which way the wind
was blowing and agreed to withdraw his amendment in favour of
Palmerston's.[28] Graham and Aberdeen in correspondence with
Russell did their best to persuade Villiers and his friends to
accept the Palmerston amendment and Russell made an appeal
in the Commons to this effect, but without success.[29] Villiers
noted that the waverers had originally assented to the terms
of his resolutions, which he thought were much less offensive
to the Protectionists than Herbert had been in his speech, and
said that he saw no reason to conciliate the opponents of Free
Trade.[30]

The debate in the Commons lasted for four nights, including

the better part of one evening of 'explanations' made on a motion of adjournment moved by Sir James Graham to enable him to explain his role in the preparation of the resolutions.[31] Disraeli made great fun of the Free Traders for their amazing revelations, which he said were most instructive to new members as to the way in which the Opposition conducted its business.[32] But speakers on the Government side also showed a division between those ready for a compromise, whether framed by Disraeli or by Palmerston, and those diehard Protectionists who would never support Free Trade resolutions.[33]

Gladstone's interventions in the debate were brief and mainly to explain his position in the light of what others had said. He agreed with Graham's plea to avoid unnecessary antagonism and argued that the Government should be given the chance to produce their financial measures for consideration.[34] Sidney Herbert on the other hand made a surprisingly sharp attack on the Protectionists, not for changing their minds, but for saying one thing and doing another.[35] He accepted, however, the gentler form of Palmerston's resolutions. Making the customary Peelite tribute to Peel he alluded to the calumnies he had suffered, but argued that Peel needed no vindication; 'and I say', he continued in his most cutting passage, 'if ever retribution is wanted—for it is not words that humiliate, but deeds—if a man wants to see humiliation—which, God knows is always a painful sight—he need but look there (*pointing to the Treasury Bench*)'.[36]

Russell made much of the Opposition's forbearance in not pressing an amendment to such an unsatisfactory Queen's speech. He failed to see why the terms 'wise and just' used in Villiers' resolutions were considered as 'odious' by Disraeli; nevertheless to avoid controversy he was prepared to advise Villiers to give way in favour of Palmerston's compromise.[37] Villiers, however, remained adamant and was reinforced in his stand by Cobden, who made a short but effective denunciation of the idea of compromise and particularly of leaving any door open for compensation to the landed interest. He waxed sarcastic at the attempt of the gentlemen of the Carlton and Reform clubs to find a basis of unanimity, and showed some pique at the failure of the Liberals to consult him. He was particularly critical of the Peelites for being 'soft' to the Protectionists.[38]

This brought Gladstone back into the fray, saying that 'the friends of the late Sir Robert Peel' supported Palmerston's amendment because they believed 'that vote to be dictated by a regard to the principles of justice'. He presumed Villiers stood by his motion because of his fear of the possibility of compensation. Gladstone observed that it was possible to combine some compensation with a just reform, as in the case of the abolition of slavery, but in actual fact Palmerston's resolutions made no commitment on this score. Gladstone almost sounded like Disraeli when he suggested that to make the Protectionists swallow the wording of the Villiers resolutions would have been like asking Russell to eat his words on the subject of Appropriation in 1838.[39]

When the vote was taken on the night of 26 November only 256 Free Traders supported the original motion against 336 who supported the amendment. When the vote was taken on the motion as amended, however, it received an overwhelming majority of 468 to 53, the resistant minority being dyed-in-the-wool Protectionists. The majority saw Villiers, Cobden, Russell, Palmerston, Graham, Gladstone, Herbert, and Disraeli all in the same lobby. Six 'liberal-conservatives' supported Villiers on the first vote.[40]

The victorious motion was Palmerston's, but according to Greville it broadened the gap between him and the Liberals. On the other hand, Lord John Russell, in Greville's opinion, increased his stock in the Liberal party by the course he took in the debate.[41]

In the House of Lords there was a pale shadow of the great Free Trade debate in the House of Commons. It was precipitated by Lord Clanricarde, who expressed his surprise that the Lords had failed to endorse the vote in the Commons and gave notice of a Free Trade motion. Derby met this proposal with considerable diplomacy, averted any acceptance of the wording of the Commons motion and indeed turned the occasion to his own advantage by inducing Clanricarde to abandon the wording of his own motion for a less effective statement, which Derby himself suggested. In this way he sought to put himself right with his own party, who were smarting from the meeting in the Commons.[42]

This was too much for Aberdeen who said that he would have been content to forego any motion at all, but that he could not accept one as reactionary as that proposed by Derby, which favoured the continuation of Free Trade merely because it was inexpedient to be constantly changing the nation's commercial policy. In the end a Peelite peer on the cross-benches, Lord Harrowby, suggested a still briefer, more innocuous wording by leaving out the clause explaining why the House favoured Free Trade. The Duke of Newcastle seconded this suggestion in a short speech in which he intimated that he would have liked to say more on the subject had the occasion been opportune, but in which he did manage to attack some of Derby's arguments. In the end Harrowby's compromise resolution was passed without opposition, although several peers expressed regret that the subject had ever been raised.[43]

Graham's views of these events were well expressed in a letter to Cornewall Lewis in which he wrote:

> On the whole I am tolerably well satisfied with the result of last week's operations. The Government has been humiliated without having an excuse for resignation; and there is no escape from the necessity of producing their Budget. The Whigs stood firmly by Lord John; and I have regained some influence with the Peelites, while I have lost no ground, I hope and believe, in Ld John's confidence and esteem.

It was painful to vote on Free Trade with Palmerston and Disraeli against Villiers and Russell (on the first vote Russell had supported Villiers), but, he said, 'I should have destroyed my usefulness, if I had acted otherwise, and it was impossible for me not to stand by my own words'. He suggested that if Bright and Cobden had been consulted earlier they might have agreed to the compromise. He continued:

> But their jealousy is extreme; they are even envious of C. Villiers; and the least appearance of neglect is resented at all hazards. I am afraid that it will be found impossible to amalgamate them with any Liberal Party, into which the aristocratic element is admitted, and on the other hand their pure Democracy is viewed with horror and alarm by the 'Gentlemen' on both sides of the House. It is very much like the dread of the Red Republicans in France.

Anything, even Ld Derby with D'Izzy, is considered better than a Reign of Terror under Manchester Dictation. Cobden's tone was very offensive throughout last week. . . . D'Izzy is or pretends to be very ill.[44]

In face of all these developments the Government was not unnaturally looking for means of strengthening itself. Graham had long supposed that they would seek to win over Lord Palmerston and that he might be so disposed. Disraeli indeed had a private interview with Palmerston on 24 November, but it came to nothing. He told Disraeli that while he sat in the House by Sidney Herbert, who was an old friend, he did not act in concert with him or Gladstone.[45] The Court was hostile to any suggestion of an alliance with Palmerston whom they suspected of seeking 'absolute power' for himself. The Prince expressed particular anxiety at Derby leaving anything to be settled between Disraeli and Palmerston directly, 'considering the *laxity of the political consciences* which both these gentlemen have hitherto exhibited'. He concluded: 'Should Mr. Disraeli have to relinquish the lead, Mr. Gladstone would be a much fitter successor than Lord Palmerston, for, whatever his peculiar crotchets may be, he is a man of the strictest feelings of honour and the purest mind.'[46]

On 25 November Derby informed the Queen and Prince Albert that he had received a letter from Lord Claud Hamilton, 'who had seen Mr. Corry (one of the Peelites),[47] who had given him to understand that they would *not* serve under the leadership of Mr. Disraeli; that they were ready on the other hand, to serve under Lord Palmerston'. Since neither Derby nor the Queen would consider such a possibility, 'this put all further negotiation out of the question'. Prince Albert asked why Gladstone might not lead, but Derby rejected the idea emphatically, saying 'that Mr. Gladstone was, in his opinion, quite unfit for it; he had none of that decision, boldness, readiness, and clearness which was necessary to lead a Party, to inspire it with confidence, and still [more], to take at times a decision on the spur of the moment, which a leader had often to do'. As an afterthought Derby added that 'he could not in honour sacrifice Mr. Disraeli', who 'possessed the confidence of his followers', and who 'had no idea of giving up the lead'.[48] Derby's critical appraisal of Gladstone was not without point in 1852 and yet there is an irony in the fact that

L

one of the least successful of Victoria's prime ministers should have so underestimated the potential of one of her greatest. In perceiving Gladstone's weaknesses he overlooked his strength, but much of this was still hidden at that time.

That very evening Gladstone attended a party given by Lord Derby, where he had a very interesting political conversation with his host. Derby appeared pleased with the outcome of the debate and thanked Gladstone for the tone of his speech. He commented on Herbert's hostility, but seemed to agree when Gladstone attributed it to Disraeli's speech.

Despite what he had said to the Queen, Derby proceeded to sound Gladstone out about the future. He expressed the hope that they could rise above personalities and pressed the possibility of *rapprochement*. Gladstone said that he thought the position of the Peelites remained much the same, 'for although most important progress had been achieved', everything still turned on the nature of the budget proposals. He emphasised the 'difficulties of a personal nature . . . arising from various causes, present & past relations, incompatibilities, peculiar defects of character or failures, in bringing them into harmony'. Derby agreed with him when he observed 'that as to relations of parties circumstances were often stronger than the human will'.[49] And so another Derbyite overture came to nothing.

On 3 December Disraeli at last rose to make his budget proposals. Normally they would not have been submitted for another three or four months, but the Government had been allowed to survive in the previous session on the understanding that it would bring forward its financial proposals in a special pre-Christmas meeting of the new parliament. As we have seen the ministers had accepted the electoral verdict on Free Trade and now they must show where they stood in the matter of taxation, particularly with respect to their promises of compensation to the agricultural interest. Disraeli's budget announcement and the historic debate that ensued have been described by his biographer and by Gladstone's, vividly and at some length. It was the first head-on collision between these two protagonists who were to dominate Victorian politics for the next quarter century or more. Disraeli's initial five-hour speech, delivered while he was still recuperating from an attack of influenza, was undoubtedly a great *tour de force*. It was part of his genius that, despite the short time he had held his office and his lack of training in public finance, he was able to present wide-ranging new proposals with lucidity and ease. There was general admiration for his dexterity of presentation, but less readiness, at any rate on the Opposition benches, to accept the wisdom of his recommendations.[50]

Basically, Disraeli's aims were two-fold, to compensate the interests that had been disturbed by the Free Trade revolution and to revise the national system of taxation on a more equitable basis. The sugar interest was pronounced to be flourishing and given only the minor privilege of refining sugar in bond, while the shipping interest was given equally small concessions in the matter of tolls and light dues. The major compensation was supposedly to the agricultural interest, who were to be relieved of half the malt tax, at the cost of some £2,500,000, and to obtain some improvement in the assessment of highway rates. The poor rate was left untouched because it was admitted that this burden had greatly decreased in recent years. On the side of taxation the big concession to the consumer was the halving of the tax on tea to be spread over six years (a device which someone called 'drawing bills on popularity and discounting them at once'). The income tax, which came to an end that year, was to be renewed, but with lowered exemptions, and with a new differential principle distinguishing between precarious and permanent income. The Chancellor also proposed to extend the income tax to Ireland in the case of income from investment, but not from land. The method of computing farmers' profits for tax purposes was to be adjusted so as to cut their tax in half. Finally the extra revenue required to make up the deficiencies created by the tax concessions was to be found in part from an increase in the house tax. The House went into committee immediately and the debate on the budget as a whole was nominally held on resolutions with respect to the house tax,[51] which began on 10 December and continued for four nights.

A century later these proposals may seem unexceptionable on casual inspection, but at the time they were greeted from all sectors of the Opposition benches with varying degrees of suspicion, distrust and contempt. They were criticised by an imposing range of authorities;[52] by Goulburn and Gladstone, who strongly condemned the principle of differentiation in the assessment of income tax as a betrayal of the public credit because fundholders were discriminated against; by Russell, who disliked the income tax provisions; by Wood, who found the whole thing very amateur and recommended its complete reconstruction; by Graham who, with the usual pious references to Peel, found Disraeli's views on direct taxation quite incongruous; by Cobden, who denounced the whole principle of compensation; and by Robert Lowe, who spoke at length on the inequities of the proposed malt tax. Gladstone, Lowe, Wood and Goulburn, each one a former or future chancellor, all harped on the miscalculations upon which they claimed the budget was based. The only member on the Opposition benches who sounded half-friendly was Joseph Hume, who welcomed Disraeli's radical approach to the income tax and scolded Gladstone for his conservative views on it. Bright remained silent, which may have prompted Disraeli's strange private appeal to him for support.[53] Palmerston excused himself from the debate on account of illness, but there is a suggestion that he was unwilling to contribute to Derby's fall.[54] Support from the Government side of the House was pitifully weak, with the exception of Walpole and Bulwer Lytton.[55]

The debate reached its climax on the fourth and final night, 16 December. The House was crowded, the atmosphere tense and the drama of the occasion heightened by an unseasonal but noisy thunderstorm that raged without. Disraeli began his rebuttal at twenty minutes past ten. For four nights his critics had 'derided and ridiculed him, taunted and twitted him, scoffed and scouted him'.[56] Now he lashed back at them in what Gladstone himself recognised as one of the greatest speeches of his opponent's career.[57] He gave no quarter and in particular he heaped his scorn on his predecessor, reminding the House remorselessly of Wood's past blunders. Next he turned his sarcasm on Graham, 'whom' he said, 'I will not say I greatly respect, but rather whom I greatly regard.' Foreseeing what was to follow he concluded on a prophetic note:

> Yes! I know what I have to face. I have to face a Coalition. The combination may be successful. A Coalition has before this been successful. But Coalitions, although successful, have always found

this, that their triumph has been brief. This, too, I know, that England does not love Coalitions.[58]

Disraeli sat down at one in the morning amidst the cheers of his supporters. The atmosphere of the House had reached a state of high tension and the drama of the occasion was heightened by Gladstone jumping to his feet, determined to answer him despite the lateness of the hour. 'I had a most difficult task to discharge in following him . . .,' Gladstone told Aberdeen. 'The absolute necessity of entering on this personal question with him at the outset greatly encumbered me in laying the ground for an appeal to his supporters as a conservative party, on attempting which I was entirely set.'[59] Normally Disraeli's speech would have marked the end of the debate, but Gladstone had not yet spoken since the House went into committee. For some days, he told his wife, he had had 'a long speech fermenting' within him.[60] It seems unlikely, however, that Gladstone's decision to speak after the Chancellor of the Exchequer was premeditated, but it was greeted with indignation by many of the Government's supporters, who continually interrupted him for the first few minutes that he was on his feet, maddened, Buckle suggests, not only by the apparent breach of propriety,[61] but also by the anticipation of their coming defeat.[62]

Gladstone's attack on the budget was devastating and helped to make this defeat certain. He literally tore Disraeli's handiwork to shreds, demonstrating that what appeared on the surface to be a plausible, indeed an imaginative, programme, was in fact a house without a foundation. Gladstone's arguments were clearly directed at those Liberal Conservatives sympathetic to the fiscal traditions of Peel to turn the scale against the Government they had hitherto supported, or at least tolerated. 'My great object', he wrote to his wife, 'was to show the conservative party how their leader was hoodwinking and bewildering them, and this I have the happiness of believing that in some degree I effected.'[63]

Since the defeat of Disraeli's budget in 1852 was the greatest single turning-point in the history of the Peelites between the fall of the Peel ministry in 1846 and the formation of the Palmerston ministry in 1859, and since Gladstone's masterly case against it was the final blow that led to the Government's fall, we may consider the line of argument that he developed.[64]

He began by sternly reprimanding Disraeli for his personal attacks on his opponents, especially on the Honourable Member for Carlisle, but these remarks were largely drowned by the uproar from the opposite benches. He then turned to a grave and systematic analysis of his opponent's proposals that contrasted noticeably with Disraeli's highly coloured elocution. Noting this contrast, the *Times* correspondent said of this speech:

> It was characterised throughout by the most earnest sincerity. It was pitched in a high tone of moral feeling—now rising to indignation, now sinking to remonstrance—which was sustained throughout without flagging and without effort. The language was less ambitious, less studied, but more natural and flowing than that of Mr. Disraeli; and though commencing in a tone of stern rebuke, it ended in words of almost pathetic expostulation.[65]

Attacking the extension of the house tax and the lowering of the exemption of the income tax, Gladstone pointed out how this would impose two new taxes on low-income householders, including two important groups whom the Government claimed to cherish and who had looked to it for assistance, the bulk of the yeomen farmers and of the lesser clergy! He next proceeded with highly technical arguments to demolish the case for reducing the malt tax. At the price of a great surrender of revenue the cost of beer would be reduced by less than three-eighths of a penny a quart, but it remained to be seen how much of this would go to the agricultural producer, the cultivator of the light lands, who in fact was not the same farmer who had complained of the repeal of the Corn Laws, the cultivator of the heavy wheat lands. Ridiculing Disraeli's claims as an innovator of great tax reforms, Gladstone contrasted his hit-and-miss approach with the carefully worked out programme of Peel, which was based on solid principles. Indeed Disraeli precisely reversed the whole policy of Peel, for he proposed 'to impose a tax on the general body of the community, to make the most ineffectual and worthless attempt at relief, not of a class, but of the portion of a class'. Gladstone denounced in particular the failure of the Government to face up to the difficulties inherent in administering the taxes they proposed to levy and promised his firm opposition to any such financial policy.

Remorselessly he then proceeded to demolish Disraeli's income tax proposals. The Chancellor, he said, boasted that he was adopting entirely new principles on which to base the tax, and yet when his proposals were inspected it was found that, on the plea of lack of time, he had fallen back on the old schedules with resultant anomalies. Gladstone did not so much object to the idea of distinguishing between different types of incomes, provided there was no discrimination against the fundholders, but he did insist that the Government produce a plan. If such changes were to be initiated they must be developed from a rational basis and with careful calculation, of which there was no sign in the present proposals.

Finally, Gladstone exploded Disraeli's claim to a surplus by pointing out that not only were there blatant mistakes in calculation, which he demonstrated, but that in fact it was a fictitious surplus since it was to be found from funds allotted to debt repayment. No minister would have his support who 'departed from the sound policy of supporting a surplus revenue', a policy he found especially deplorable in a Conservative government. He announced that he would vote against the budget because it was one of 'the most subversive in its tendencies and ultimate effects' of any that he had ever known submitted to the House. 'If I vote against the Government', he said, 'I vote in support of those Conservative principles which I thank God are common in a great degree to all parties in the British House of Commons, but of which I thought it was the peculiar pride and glory of the Conservative party to be the champions and the leaders.'

In voting with Sir Charles Wood against the budget he claimed he was voting as any who agreed with Peel's principles of 1842 should vote. 'I look back with regret upon the days when I sat nearer to many of my hon. friends opposite than I now am,' he confessed; but he felt it his duty to warn them that if they supported 'this most unsound and destructive principle' on which the Government based its financial scheme they would some day look back upon their vote 'with bitter, but with late and ineffectual regret'.[66]

We may ask whether Gladstone succeeded in making any impression on any of his listeners across the House after the initial barracking that greeted his lecture to Disraeli. He gave his own impressions in a note to Aberdeen the next day. 'As far as I could see from the countenances and demeanours over against me,' he wrote, 'and as far as I can judge from what I hear today, I do not think that the debate and division have altered materially for the worse our relations with the moderate and steady portion of the Conservative party. Young joins me in this opinion.'[67] An analysis of the division will give a more precise answer to the question.

The Government was defeated by a vote of 305 to 286.[68] 'The Peelites as a body ran admirably true,' Gladstone wrote to his wife, 'they voted in the majority 33: in the minority 5.'[69] Actually 41 Conservatives voted against the Disraeli budget, but evidently Gladstone did not regard them all as Peelites. They included 24 of the 27 whom we have so identified,[70] 5 of the 16 uncertain Liberal Conservatives,[71] 10 new Liberal Conservatives,[72] and 2 Derbyites[73] (of whom one supported the Aberdeen coalition after it was formed). Three Peelites voted for the budget.[74] Of the 41 Conservatives who opposed the budget, 37 regularly supported the Aberdeen coalition after it was formed and these were augmented by 2[75] who did not participate in the division, 4 who did not get into the House until after the new year,[76] and one (Owen) who had voted for the budget, making a total of 44.[77]

But the Peelites were not the only middle group that contributed to the Government's defeat. More numerous, although less important in parliamentary debate and the formation of ministries, were the Irish Brigade, those Irish Liberals who were sympathetic to the claims of the Roman Catholics and of the Irish Tenant League. Some 48 were pledged in one way or another to take an independent course in the new parliament. They had not forgotten the Ecclesiastical Titles Act and would not consider Russell as their leader. Disraeli, with characteristic expediency, had sought to make a deal with the Brigade, but on 10 December Derby ruined his plans when he publicly and emphatically rejected the idea of countenancing a Tenant Leaguers' Bill, and consequently lost all the Irish votes that Disraeli had been cultivating.[78] No doubt the partial extension of the income tax to Ireland further alienated the Irish members. At any rate, 45 of the 48 voted with the Liberals and the Peelites against the budget.[79]

Defeat of the budget resolutions brought about Lord Derby's

resignation later the same day, Friday, 17 December, and the fact was announced in both Houses on the following Monday. Lord Derby did so in rather a querulous speech, that undoubtedly helped the Peelites to abide by their decision. He analysed the results of the summer's elections and pointed out that by far the largest party were the 310 members who supported the Government 'on questions not involving the questions of free trade'. Next there was the main Opposition party of 260 'including in it all the various gradations of opinion, from the high aristocratic and exclusive Whig, down to the wildest theorist and the most extreme Radical'. The third party were the Irish members 'representing the views of the Irish Roman Catholic clergy', whom he did not number; while the fourth party numbering thirty to thirty-five were 'Gentlemen who once professed, and I believe do still profess, Conservative opinions'. Alluding ironically to Graham's 'curious revelations', he noted that the plans initially worked out by the Free Traders had been foiled by Palmerston's resolutions, but the Government had only 'escaped defeat on this occasion by the falling asunder of the different materials of which that discordant combination was composed'. When the ministers were subsequently defeated they had to resign, but he could not refrain from alluding to the character of the combination and the animus displayed in this settled purpose to overthrow the Government.

He went on to announce that Lord Aberdeen had undertaken to form a government, he presumed 'upon strictly Conservative principles, and in a Conservative spirit', and promised the new prime minister that he would have 'more forbearance shown him by the great Conservative party . . . than that Conservative party has experienced at the hands of others'. With some discourtesy, however, he expressed his surprise that Aberdeen had asked for a week's adjournment to give him time to make the necessary arrangements.[80]

In Aberdeen's absence Newcastle defended the Peelites against the unfair charges of combination brought against them, which were indeed disproved, he pointed out, by the very length of time which Derby criticised Aberdeen for taking.[81]

Disraeli's announcement in the House of Commons was more gracefully done, for he took the opportunity to apologise for any feelings he may have inadvertently hurt by remarks made in the heat of the recent debate.[82] This precipitated kind words and apologies all round, from Russell who paid tribute to the 'ability and gallantry' with which Disraeli had conducted the business of the House,[83] from Wood who fully accepted Disraeli's frank statement and apologised for any expressions he might have used beyond the limits of debate,[84] and from Graham who received Disraeli's apology in a rather more stilted manner, but joined Russell in congratulating Disraeli on the 'signal ability' with which he had conducted the business of the House under great difficulties.[85] Colonel Sibthorp, the arch-Tory of the House, characteristically provided some unintentional comic relief by making it clear that he did not hold with all this apologising, and deplored the formation of a government by the conspirators who had ousted Lord Derby. He promised that in future he would be on his guard 'against the man-traps and spring-guns of hon. Gentlemen opposite'.[86] Joseph Hume said he had no apologies to make to anyone, but hoped that the next government would be more successful than the last in meeting the demands of public opinion for progressive improvement.[87]

*Notes to this chapter are on pages 209-13*

# Conclusion

---

IT TOOK Lord Aberdeen ten days of hard bargaining with the Liberals to complete his task, but he succeeded and, on the whole, with good will. Lord John Russell made innumerable difficulties throughout the ten days and for the twenty-five months that the coalition lasted, but that was in his nature and he was in a difficult position, a leader who had lost the confidence of many of his followers, but was expected to bargain on their behalf. Nevertheless the new administration proved to be a perfectly viable instrument of government, despite the forecasts of some critics who did not give it many months of life.[1] The coalition cabinet worked much better together than any of its members are likely to have thought possible before they met, and when there were divisions in it they were never on purely party lines. There were Peelite and Liberal Reformers, Peelite and Liberal anti-Reformers, Peelite and Liberal hawks and Peelite and Liberal doves. Lord John Russell frequently made trouble, but never carried the majority of his Whig colleagues with him and in January resigned from the cabinet alone.

The Peelites secured fifteen places in the new administration, six of them in the cabinet, which, of course, was quite out of proportion to the numbers of their rank and file.[2] This over-representation of the Peelites in proportion to their numbers is to be explained partly by the peculiar circumstances of the situation, partly by the nature of the internal divisions in both the major parties, and partly by the merits of the individuals appointed to office. In the previous decade the Conservative party under Peel had shown itself richer in ministerial talent than the Liberal party of Melbourne and Russell. This situation was doubtless promoted by traditional Whig exclusiveness, which tended to confine candidates for office to a fairly small charmed circle of aristocratic Whigs, occasionally supplemented by a few privileged outsiders. The supply of young Whigs of talent, however, seemed to be drying up, owing in some degree perhaps to the contraction in the number of Whig families during the French Revolution. Indeed, it is a striking fact that in 1852 Lord Granville seemed to be the only Whig of ministerial calibre under the age of fifty. On the other hand, almost all the younger Conservatives to whom Peel had given office remained loyal to him, and after his death to his memory, and were lost to the Conservative party led by Lord Derby. So in a sense the Aberdeen coalition was drawn from two fairly equal elites, although only one of them had a normal party basis. Certainly no Whigs were excluded from the cabinet with superior qualifications to at least five of the six Peelites, and the sixth, the Duke of Argyll, although young and untried, proved his ability and his acceptability to the Whigs with whom he was soon completely at home.

As we have seen, the consideration uppermost in Aberdeen's mind, when insisting on his Peelite appointments with an almost uncharacteristic firmness, was the conviction that his Government would not get the independent Conservative support that he sought if it proved to be predominantly Whig. The history of the Aberdeen coalition proved the wisdom of his judgement. It will be recalled that the votes of 41 Conservatives helped to turn Derby out of office. Of these 37 regularly supported the new administration; they were augmented by two[3] who did not participate in the division and by four[4] who only entered the House in 1853, making a total of 43 Conservatives who had not supported the Disraeli budget. In addition there were at least another 11 Conservatives,[5] who had voted for Disraeli, who generally supported the coalition once it was formed, bringing the total of Conservative supporters to 54. There were also another 26 who gave it frequent if not regular support and about 22 who supported it occasionally, making almost fifty more Conservatives on whom Derby and Disraeli could not depend.[6]

Not all of those Conservatives who supported the Aberdeen coalition were permanently estranged from the Conservative party, but it was undoubtedly a parting of the ways for many of them. No Peelite who took office in 1852 ever subsequently entered a Conservative administration, although the accidental way in which the coalition broke up in 1855 postponed in some cases their eventual juncture with the Liberal party. Writing about the events of 1852 many years later Gladstone observed that there were some Peelites such as Henry Corry, Colonel (later General) Peel and Lord Mahon (later Lord Stanhope), 'who by degrees took their places in the ranks re-baptized as Conservatives', but that there were others 'whose opinions were more akin to those of the Liberals, notwithstanding cherished personal sympathies, and lingering wishes, which made them tardy, perhaps unduly tardy, in drawing towards that party . . .'. Among the latter he included Sidney Herbert and himself.[7]

At first sight the acceptance of the coalition by the Liberals without a share of offices in any way proportionate to their numbers may seem strange. We must, however, recall the extremely divided state of the Liberal party in 1852 and realise that their only other option was opposition. Almost fifty Irish Liberals had been elected as independents, reducing the number of the party for practical purposes to about 270—less than the Protectionists whom they had just defeated—and this figure included an indeterminate number of Radicals, whose loyalty to Whig leadership could not be counted on. The Irish independents were obviously readier to support a ministry containing so many Peelite opponents of the hated Ecclesiastical Titles Act, while the Manchester School Radicals could look to the Peelite component of the ministry to promote the sort of fiscal policies that they professed. The Whig core, from whom most of the Liberal officeholders were drawn, was, as Newcastle had observed, probably not substantially larger than the Peelite party. The more enlightened Whig leaders themselves recognised the need to recruit talent, and they no doubt found the Peelite ministers whom they now met more congenial than many of the abrasive Radical tribunes on their own benches. Indeed the recruitment of Peelite talent might be considered a device (not wholly successful) for bolstering and retaining the Whig leadership of the Liberal party. The Peelite price was high in terms of the share of offices, and this would cause some temporary disquiet on the Liberal back benches, but if the coalition succeeded the Peelites must in time be absorbed into the much larger Liberal mass. This was virtually what happened, although the process was interrupted for some years by the circumstances of the Crimean War and the unfortunate collapse of the Aberdeen administration. In the end, however, the Peelite rump was absorbed into the Liberal party, but it helped to give that party a new complexion, by introducing a new element that a quarter of a century later bore fruit in the unique plant known as Gladstonian Liberalism.

Although the Peelites were richly rewarded in terms of office for their juncture with the Liberals, in a sense they paid a higher price since by their act they severed all connections with the Conservative party to which they had long belonged, and in a political system based on party such a step is not lightly taken. In a two-party system each party inevitably covers a wide political spectrum. Thus while the centres of both parties may be sufficiently far apart to be clearly identified, the left wing of one party may more than overlap the right wing of the other. The left and right wings of any party are bound to look upon each other with some suspicion and misgiving, but normally they are reconciled by the necessity of compromise to obtain political ends and by the recognition of certain common traditions that help to keep them together.

The Peelites were left-of-centre members of the Conservative party whom circumstances had alienated from the main body; in many cases the alienation was mutual, although there was a centre element, not unsympathetic to them, but nevertheless solid in its Conservatism. In 1852 the Peelites still regarded themselves as Conservatives; that name, after all, had been adopted by Peel himself and the older term, Tory, was more applicable to the right wing of the party. Most of the Peelite Conservatives, however, were ready to accept the adjective 'liberal' to indicate that liberal views were compatible with a generally conservative position. By and large, as we have seen, they believed that the *status quo* could only be conserved by an enlightened policy that took fully into consideration the claims of natural justice and of political economy. In the Peelite view, if people were treated fairly and intelligently they would accept the rule of their betters, but to tolerate the perpetuation of abuses was to encourage the growth of democracy. Although opposed to democracy they had no paranoid fear of it, believing that the best antidote lay in a policy of what they called 'Conservative Progress', a concept taken up by Russell, if less effectively. The chief danger in the Peelite view lay in standing still. As Newcastle said, their object was to strike a balance between the extremities of the Manchester School and the impotence of Whig finance. The Peelites had an instinctive contempt for reactionaries, and it was this as much as anything that cut them off from the main body of the old Conservative or Tory party, which was still intolerant in religion and Protectionist by instinct, even though its clever leaders might tell them that Protection was dead. Not all Derbyite Conservatives were reactionaries, but the more sophisticated were ready to live with their backward-looking colleagues and to humour them, even though such a course often left them open to charges of expediency.

In short, the atmosphere of the Derbyite Conservative party was basically uncongenial to many of the Peelites, and they themselves were looked upon with suspicion and dislike by a large section of the Derbyite backbenchers. Their own political tradition had made it difficult for these Liberal Conservatives to effect any formal juncture with the Liberals while the latter were in office, although it had seemed expedient to give them enough support to keep them there until 1852. The Liberals out of office, however, had been more approachable and joint action with them now came more easily, especially after the election campaign that the Derbyites had waged, which had made some of the Peelites particularly bitter. The not unexpected failure of Disraeli to hew to the sound line of Peelite finance, when he eventually brought down his budget in December, settled the matter for the majority of the Peelites, and, having turned the Derby government out of office, they recognised that they had to face up to the consequences. The Peelites' main criticism of the Whigs in office had been their way of doing things rather than what they did, and now, by becoming colleagues, the former could hope to exert influence on the latter, and in their view raise the standard of government.

Gladstone's decision to join the coalition was of especial interest and significance, for he was the Peelite leader who had seemed least inclined to join the Liberals, although eventually he was to become the greatest Liberal leader of the century. He was instinctively a strong party man and, of course, an intensely

devoted member of the Church of England, and his long hesitation is understandable if we bear these two points in mind. There
was nothing in his political views, however, to bar him from
joining the Liberals, and indeed, as we have seen, much to induce
him to do so. He was a strong exponent of Free Trade, a devoted
believer in the need for retrenchment in public finance, and an
ardent administrative reformer. His support of Jewish emancipation and of the Maynooth grant, not to mention his opposition to
the Ecclesiastical Titles Bill, testified to his genuine belief in the
principle of religious toleration, despite his own strong religious
convictions and his earlier writings on Church and State. His
passionate espousal of the case of the imprisoned Italian national-
ists indicated his readiness to apply moral considerations to
foreign policy that found more support on the Radical wing of
the Liberal party than among the more traditionalist Conservatives. Once he was persuaded that religion would not be en-
dangered by his action and that he might hope to achieve goals
not otherwise possible, he was prepared to take the step. Some of
his old friends were more doubtful, but once he had made his
decision he defended his course with characteristic vigour. When
his old friend, Sir William Heathcote, who was his election
committee chairman at Oxford, wrote to express doubts as to the
possibility of his retaining that post, Gladstone replied: '. . . to
tell you the truth all I have done . . . has in my view flowed so
simply and distinctly from the absolute dicates of duty that in the
main I have not felt that I have had an option to exercise'. He
went on to say that he had had no hostility to the late government,
despite the unfair allegations made against him by Derby, but
that even if all obstacles had been removed, he could not have
become a colleague of Disraeli, such was his opinion of the
latter's political character; he claimed, however, that nothing
would have induced him 'to lift a finger' for the purpose of removing Disraeli from the leadership that he had gained. His differences
with the Derbyite government, he avowed, were not about Free
Trade, which he considered settled, but over the budget.

> To you I must frankly state [he continued] that in the [?] parts
> of that Budget, & in the prompt refusal of its framer to consider
> the manner of proceeding, I read on his part (not mark you on
> Lord Derby's) a determined intention that there should be no

union with the Peelites, whose financial principles he knew very well.

If you had a clergyman who was the best preacher and churchman in the world but who failed in the elementary duties of morality, you would not be restrained by his merits, especially after warning him, of complaining to the Bishop. It is just in this same manner that however I might value the existence of Ld Derby's Govt for the sake of religion (had it been so) I could not on that account have refused to resist what I do not scruple to call a dishonest and profligate scheme of finance; & homely as these questions may appear, I believe that nothing can tend so forcefully as this financial dishonesty to the demoralization of government at large.[8]

Gladstone denied that the interests of religion would be any less secure in the hands of Lord Aberdeen (he was presumably thinking of church appointments) and concluded with the argument that having contributed to the fall of the late government it was his duty to help provide one to take its place.

Clearly, whether he fully recognised it or not, Disraeli's position in Derby's Conservative party was a not unimportant factor in Gladstone's decision in 1852, as it would be again in 1859. In a two-party system juncture with the Liberals was in fact the only way in which he could make himself effective in public life. Some said that it was ambition that drove him to his decision, but he would have preferred to think of it in terms of his usefulness. The same problem would recur again later in the decade, but in 1852 he took the long first step that in the end proved decisive.[9]

Heathcote was not fully convinced by his friend's arguments, but promised Gladstone his vote 'in a spirit of trust'.[10] Other Oxford constituents were more suspicious, for example the Reverend P. C. Cloughton, later Bishop of St Albans, who told Roundell Palmer that he thought Gladstone's acceptance of office 'most *dubious*' and his answer to Disraeli in the budget debate a 'most unfair attack'. 'I am afraid ambition is Gladstone's bane,' he wrote, '—I have no confidence in him and it is very hard to vote for a man one does not trust.'[11] It is perhaps surprising that Gladstone kept his seat at Oxford until 1865.

Undoubtedly not all of Sir Robert Peel's old followers fully

M

recognised the path along which they were moving. Do we not all walk into the future looking backwards? But the straws were in the wind during the years 1846–52 and the course was confirmed by the Peelite contribution to the legislative and administrative achievement of the Aberdeen coalition. The determination to see Peel's fiscal system completed by the fullest extension possible of the programme of Free Trade coupled with a rational solution of the problem of the income tax probably preoccupied the leading Peelites more than anything else during their years out of office and certainly formed the essence of Gladstone's achievement at the Exchequer in 1853–4 and 1859–66. The resolute opposition to religious intolerance and sympathetic approach to Irish problems seen in their constant support of Maynooth and of the various measures for Jewish emancipation on the part of the Peelite leaders and a substantial number of their followers distinguished them from the mass of the Derbyite Conservative party and put them alongside the forward ranks of the Liberals. (See Appendix A.) In foreign policy most of the Peelites stood out against the more chauvinistic aspects of Palmerstonianism as seen in the Don Pacifico case. On the other hand Gladstone went rather beyond his friends in his championing of the victims of Neapolitan tyranny, but this approach to foreign policy was to characterise the contribution that he was to make to English Liberalism in the years to come. In the Aberdeen coalition the Peelites joined with the more pacific Whigs to moderate from the start Palmerston's pressure for a more bellicose line towards Russia, but in this they were in the end unsuccessful. Indeed most of them considered the Crimean War justified, but in 1855 those who withdrew from the reorganised administration severely criticised the prolongation of the war under Palmerston's leadership.

In Peelism there was much that might be called utilitarian with a small 'u'. The Peelites showed a Benthamite passion for making institutions work more efficiently. This was reflected in Gladstone's Oxford University Act of 1854, in his proposals for the reform of the Civil Service of the same year, only completed when he became a Liberal prime minister, and in Cardwell's Pilotage and Merchant Shipping Acts of 1853, not to mention his later army reforms. The Peelites had no monopoly of such reforms and not all of them were equally zealous in their promotion, but by and large a juncture of this group with the younger Whigs and the Radicals would help to bring about an important metamorphosis of the old Whig-Liberal party. The misadventure of the Crimean War and Palmerston's consequent acquisition of the leadership of that party postponed the final outcome, but in some form or other it was assured by the formation of the Peelite-Liberal coalition under Lord Aberdeen in December 1852.

*Notes to this chapter are on pages 213–14*

# References

*Chapter 1*  PEEL AND THE PEELITES: OUT OF OFFICE 1846–50
(pages 9–33)

1  British Museum Add MS 44745, fol 173 of an unpublished paper entitled 'Party as it was and as it is', fols 173–222.

2  See N. Gash, 'Peel and the Party System', *Transactions of the Royal Historical Society*, 5th series, I (1951), 47–59.

3  Add MS 44745, fols 181–2.

4  W. O. Aydelotte, 'The Disintegration of the Conservative Party in the Eighteen-Forties: A Study in Political Attitudes', a mimeographed paper read to the American Political Science Association, September 1969.

5  See Robert Stewart, 'Lord Derby and the Protectionist Party, 1845–52', a doctoral dissertation, Bodleian Library, Oxford.

6  W. O. Aydelotte, 'Country Gentlemen and the Repeal of the Corn Laws', *English Historical Review*, LXXXII (1967), 53 and 60.

7  Ellenborough Papers, PRO 30/12/21/1, 29 May 1846 (copy). Ellenborough's hostility to Peel may be seen in letters to Lord Hardinge and Sir Charles Napier written four days later (ibid, PRO 30/12/21/7).

8  Ibid, 30 May 1846.

9  Lord Campbell, *Lives of Lord Lyndhurst and Lord Brougham* (1869), 163–5. Peel and Lyndhurst were never close. According to Campbell, Peel considered Lyndhurst devoid of principles and Lyndhurst laughed at 'Peel's pedantry, affectation of secrecy, constrained manners, and incapacity to pronounce his "h"s'. Graham likewise regarded Lyndhurst's action as an 'intrigue', while Bonham congratulated Peel on his handling of the incident. (Add MSS 40452, fols 153–6, 31 August 1846, and 40597, fols 126–7, 28 August 1846.)

10  Ellenborough's correspondence with Stanley began on 25 July. Lyndhurst took little further part in political activity for several years, but in 1850 he actively joined the Protectionists.

11  Some of what follows in this and the following chapters is taken from my 'Peel and the Peelites, 1846–1850', *EHR*, LXXIII (1958).

12  *Divisions in Session of 1846 (9 & 10 Victoria) House of Commons Division lobby*, 91–4.

13  H. J. Baillie, Lord Francis Egerton, Peter Kirk, Alexander Oswald, W. T. Praed, T. C. Whitmore, J. A. S. Wortley (all paired), J. Atwood, C. B. Baldwin, J. Hornby.

14  W. Mure and Lord William Powlett. I have omitted A. D. R. W. Baillie Cochrane and W. Baird, both of whom took the Chiltern Hundreds after supporting the second reading.

15  *Divisions in Session of 1846*, 143–6. The four were Beckham Estcott, R. M. Milnes, E. M. L. Mostyn, and C. B. Wall.

16  Canning, Dalhousie, Gladstone, Lincoln, and Young, of whom all but Dalhousie went to Eton.

17  W. B. Baring, former Postmaster-General, disappeared from view into the House of Lords on becoming the second Lord Ashburton in 1848, while Lord Jocelyn, who had been a secretary of the Board of Control, appears to have acted with the Protectionists after 1847, although keeping lines of communication open to Peelite friends.

18  Add MS 43065, fols 203–6, 14 August 1846. See also Peel's letters to Lord Hardinge (C. S. Parker, *Sir Robert Peel* (1899), III, 472–4).

19  Add MS 44745, fol 184.

20  Ibid, fol 186.

21  Ibid, fol 190. Gladstone and other Peelites were also most unhappy about Peel's famous eulogy of Cobden in his last speech to the House of Commons as Prime Minister on 29 June.

22  B. Disraeli, *Lord George Bentinck* (London, 1852 ed), 371–2.

23  Add MS 40598, fols 62–5, 28 January 1847.

24  Add MS 40481, fols 400–3, 23 January 1847.

25  Add MS 44745, fol 190.

26  Add MS 40598, fols 34–7, 15 January 1847. Sibthorp appears to have rejoined in 1847 (C. R. Dod, *The Parliamentary Companion* (London, 1847), 234).

27  *Hansard*, 3rd series, LXXXVIII, 93–103.

28  Ibid, 179–84; *Divisions 1846*, 163–5. Four Free Trade Conservatives paired in support of the Government and two against.

29  Add MS 40598, fols 62–5, Young to Peel, 28 January 1847.

30  Ibid, fols 147–8, 30 March 1847.

31  Ellenborough Papers, PRO 30/12/21/3, 3 January 1847 (copy).

32  Ibid, to Lincoln, 3 January 1847 (copy).

33  Ibid, 5 January 1847.

34  Ibid, to Stanley, 21 March 1847.

35  L. J. Jennings (ed), *The Croker Papers* (London, 1884), III, 75–6.

36  'The Close of Sir Robert Peel's Administration', *Quarterly Review*, vol 78. Peel never forgave Croker and coldly rejected his old friend's attempt at personal reconciliation the following year. See Jennings, *Croker Papers*, III, 91–5.

37  Jennings, *Croker Papers*, III, 85–6.

38  Add MS 43196, fols 243–5, 12 December 1846.

39  Add MS 40445, fols 386–7, 19 December 1846.

40  See N. Gash, 'Peel and the Party System, 1830–50', loc cit, 47–69.

41  Parker, *Peel*, III, 474.
42  Surrey Record Office, Goulburn Papers, 11/20, 20 December 1846.
43  Add MS 40445, fols 388–90, 24 December 1846.
44  Add MS 40481, fols 392–7, 1 January 1847.
45  Add MS 40452, fols 188–91, 15 December 1846.
46  Add MS 40598, fols 22–7, 14 January 1847, partly printed in Parker, *Peel*, III, 480–1.
47  Add MS 44777, fols 271–4, Memorandum 65, Session 1847–8.
48  *Hansard*, XC, 65–86. The last half of one sentence in Peel's speech is worth quoting. Urging the merits of private rather than public investment, he said to his Irish listeners:

> ... if you will permit commercial considerations to prevail over political—if you will trust to the energy of private enterprise—if, forgetful of religious and political differences—united by common danger—standing in the awful presence of that desolating calamity under which your country is suffering—you will concentrate all your strength in the mitigation of that calamity and in the improvement of social conditions of the millions who are dependent upon you for their future well being—you will do more to promote the interests of your native land, and to improve your own properties, than if, resigning yourself to sloth, idleness and despair, you place all your confidence in Parliamentary grants, and in Government interference.

49  Ibid, 123–6.
50  Ibid, XCII, 297–9. Fourteen Free Trade Conservatives supported the Bill.
51  Ibid, XC, 175–8. The vote was 195–87.
52  Ibid, XCI, 1199–1234, 1398.
53  Jennings, *Croker Papers*, III, 107–8.
54  Based on a study of all the constituencies in C. R. Dod, *Electoral Facts 1832–1852* (London, 1852).
55  See list of nominations in England and Wales, *The Times*, 26 July 1847.
56  *The Times*, 1, 21, and 30 July 1847.
57  Ibid, 21, and 23 June, 20, 24, 26, 29, and 30 July 1847.
58  See J. B. Conacher, 'Mr Gladstone Seeks a Seat', *C.H.A. Report— 1962*, 55–67.
59  See correspondence and circulars in Add MS 40599, and for the subsequent by-election, 40609. W. Y. Peel took the Chiltern Hundreds before Parliament met on account of ill-health, and the seat was lost to a Liberal at a by-election.
60  Add MS 40599, fols 121–2, 2 August 1847. For the address, see fols 26–43, 15 July 1847.
61  Goulburn Papers 11/20, 15 July 1847. Peel was much relieved when he heard that Goulburn had managed to scrape through in face of stiff opposition (ibid, 3 August 1847).

62 Based on Dod, *Electoral Facts 1832–52* and *Parliamentary Companion* (1847).

63 Lord Ashley, the Marquis of Blandford, F. W. Charteris, and A. D. R. W. Baillie Cochrane.

64 W. Bolding, W. Cripps, D. Godson, and Lord Granville Somerset in 1848, and Sir R. Peel, G. R. Robinson, and C. W. W. Wynn in 1850.

65 F. Baring, E. B. Denison, J. B. B. Estcourt, G. C. Legh, and J. Sandars in 1848, Frederick Peel in 1849, and the third Sir Robert Peel in 1850.

66 Sir T. D. Acland, G. G. V. Harcourt, G. H. W. Heneage, Lord Norreys, and Philip Pusey.

67 The seven who came in at by-elections brought the total list to 120, but, of course, there was never this number at any one time. *The Times*, 3 September 1847, quoting the Leeds *Mercury*, listed 336 Liberals, 201 Protectionists, and 117 Peelites.

68 Lambeth Palace, Selborne Papers, [No.] 1861, fols 150–1, Palmer to Hardy, 6 September 1847.

69 Add MS 40599, fols 45–6, 73–4, 80–1, 99–100, 121–2, 17 July to 2 August, when he wrote: '. . . I hold myself pledged to remain here the whole of this week with reference to the many Elections still pending. And unfortunately there is not a soul here to answer questions or undertake various business contingent on the progress of elections.' This suggests that Bonham was trying to maintain something like a Peelite election headquarters. He joined Peel the following week and consequently his letters contain no overall results.

70 Add MS 40599, fols 1–2, 18–21, 103–4, 144–7, Cardwell, 13, 15, 27 July and 6 August 1847; fols 138–40, S. Herbert, 5 August; fols 189–90, J. Young, 9 August; Add MS 40481, fols 408–16, Lincoln, 16 and 23 July and 3 and 7 August; Add MS 40445, fols 400–3, Goulburn, 4 August.

71 Add MS 44275, fols 309–10, Peel, 24 June 1847, explaining his previous commitment to Cardwell; Add MS 40470, fols 444–5, Gladstone, 24 June, thanking Peel for his support which he called 'generous', 'because it touches matters in which I stand less near to you than, happily for me, I have stood in the region of opinion purely political'!

72 Graham Papers, De Gray, 10 and 12 May 1847; to De Gray (copy), 11 May.

73 Add MS 40599, fols 134–5, 183–6, from C. B. Adderly, 5 and 8 August 1847 and to Adderly (copy), 9 August.

74 Disraeli, *Bentinck*, 450–1.

75 Croker, *Papers*, III, 129–30, 140.

76 Ibid, 132–4.

77 PRO 30/12/21/12, 23 September 1847. Brougham also wrote at

great length about the election to Aberdeen (*Aberdeen Correspondence (1845–48)* (privately printed, B.M. State Paper Room), 524–8).

78   Add MS 40452, fols 226–9, 22 August 1847.

79   Add MS 43065, fols 322–6, 19 August 1847.

80   L. Strachey and R. Fulford (eds), *The Greville Memoirs* (London, 1938 ed), V, 457.

*Chapter 2* PEEL AND THE PEELITES: THE RELATIONSHIP WITH THE WHIG MINISTRY 1847–50 (pages 34–68)

1   C. S. Parker, *Sir James Graham* (London 1907), II, 63.

2   Add MS 44745, fol 194, from the unpublished article entitled 'Party as it was and as it is', written in 1855.

3   PRO 30/12/21/3, Lyndhurst, 7 and 9 February 1848.

4   Add MS 44777, fol 278, from W.E.G. Memorandum No 65 on Political Situation 1847–8, dated 12 December 1948.

5   Add MS 40452, fols 278–83, Graham to Peel, 25 September 1847, partly reproduced in Parker, *Peel*, III, 495–6.

6   Add MS 40452, fols 321–5, Graham to Peel, 21 January 1849 (Parker, *Peel*, III, 502–3); Graham Papers (microfilm), Londonderry to Graham, 18 February 1850; and Parker, *Graham*, II, 95–7, who omits Londonderry's admission that he wrote without Disraeli's direct knowledge but immediately after a conversation with him.

7   Add MS 40452, fols 328–33, Graham to Peel, 10 March 1849.

8   Graham Papers, 4 July 1846.

9   Add MS 40461, fols 480–1 (copy), Peel to Wellington, 4 July 1846. Peel had no objection to Wellington's remaining Commander-in-Chief.

10  Russell Papers, PRO 30/22/5B, fols 349–50, Russell to Dalhousie, Lincoln, and Herbert, 1 July 1846; Dalhousie, Lincoln, and Herbert, fols 372–7, all 2 July. See Lord Stanmore, *Sidney Herbert* (London 1906), 1, 68, and J. Martineau, *Henry Pelham, Fifth Duke of Newcastle* (London 1908), 81.

11  PRO 30/22/5B and C, fols 762–3, 806–7, 30 August and 2 September 1846; Graham Papers, Graham, 31 August, and Peel, 2 September.

12  Goulburn Papers 11/20, Peel, 17 October 1846. Lord Campbell's own irritation may be judged from a note he addressed to Russell, when the arrangements had been completed, in which he remarked that the formation of the council had taken more trouble than that of the cabinet. PRO 30/22/5C, fols 1062–3, 23 September 1846.

13  PRO 30/22/5B, fols 749–50 and 781–2, Dalhousie, 24 August 1846, and Russell, 28 August.

14  Add MS 40559, fols 105–6, Dalhousie, 28 July 1847.

15  There is no correspondence that I can find in the Graham or Peel papers, for the offer was made through Ellice acting as a go-between; see Parker, *Graham*, II, 57–9.

16  Add MS 40559, fols 105–6, 28 July 1847.

17  Ibid, fols 393–8, Cardwell to Peel, 15 November 1847; Add MS 40602, fol 51, Arbuthnot to Peel, 1 August 1849.

18  Add MS 40452, fols 224–5, 1 August 1847.

19  PRO 30/22/6D, fols 1134–5, Hobhouse, 14 July 1847: 'I wish to observe, that, although I think Lord Dalhousie and Lord Elgin are very good men, and would fill the post in question very fairly, yet I see no necessity for going beyond our own political friends for a Governor General of India.'

20  Add MS 40480, fols 552–5, St Germans, 2 October 1847, and Peel, 3 October.

21  Add MS 43065, fol 338, 7 October 1847.

22  G. P. Gooch (ed), *The Later Correspondence of Lord John Russell 1840–1878* (London 1925), I, 180.

23  Ibid, 181.

24  PRO 30/22/7E, fols 1666–7, 2 January 1849.

25  Broadlands MS (Palmerston Papers, H.M.C.), GC/RU/241/1, 4 January 1849.

26  Ibid, 241/2 (copy), 5 January 1849.

27  PRO 30/22/7E, fols 1685–7, 4 January 1849.

28  Ibid, fols 1698–1702, 6 January 1849. There is no written answer from Wood in the Russell Papers, nor have I found any letter from Wood to Peel on the matter in the Peel Papers.

29  Ibid, fols 1712–13, Lansdowne, 9 January.

30  Ibid, fols 1716–18, 9 January.

31  Add MS 40452, fols 315–20, Graham to Peel, 16 January 1849. For other points in this long letter see Parker, *Peel*, III, 500–1, and Parker, *Graham*, II, 73–5; Parker omits the parts quoted above. Graham also reminded Russell of their joint responsibility in strengthening the democratic principle by the passage of the Reform Act and warned that 'the will of the Middle Class in this country cannot be long resisted'. He said they would insist on 'cheap Government' and that 'Royal Government here would not be safe if we were not wise in time . . .'.

32  S. Walpole, *Lord John Russell* (London 1891), II, 96–7; PRO 30/22/7E, fols 1727–8, Graham, 12 January 1849; Add MS 40452, fols 305–8, Graham, 12 January 1849.

33  Add MS 40452, fols 311–14, 12 January 1849.

34  Add MS 40455, fols 466–7, 15 January 1849.

35  Add MS 40481, fols 454–7, 27 January 1849.

36  Add MS 40598, fols 38–42, 16 January 1847.

37  Add MS 40597, fols 350–3, 21 December 1846.

38  Add MS 40598, fols 84–7, Peel's memorandum of interview with Wood, dated 11 February 1847.

39  Goulburn Papers 11/20, Peel, 27 August 1847; Add MS 40445, fols 407–10, Goulburn, 29 August, 411–16, Peel (copy), 31 August; Add MS 40452, fols 232–5, Graham, 10 September.

40    Add MS 40599, fols 293–8, Wood to Peel, 11 October 1847.

41    Ibid, fols 307–15, Peel's memorandum of conversations with Wood, October 1847, an important document in the history of the financial crisis of 1847.

42    Goulburn Papers 11/20, 28 October 1847.

43    Add MS 40599, fols 293–393, correspondence with Wood and Cardwell, 19 October–15 November 1847.

44    Graham Papers, Wood to Peel, 4 December 1847.

45    Add MS 40452, fols 240–5, Graham, 16 November 1847; Add MS 40445, fols 430–5, Goulburn, 6 and 30 October 1847.

46    Add MS 40600, fols 239–41, Wood to Peel, 20 May 1848. On the other hand, Wood often passed on information to Peel. On one occasion he wrote cheerily: 'You will be glad to hear that Mitchell has been sentenced to 14 years transportation' (ibid, fol 259, 28 May 1848).

47    Ibid, fols 380–416, Wood to Peel, 11, 14, 15, 19, and 21 August 1847; Add MS 40445, fols 441–3, Goulburn, 14, 18, and 21 August 1848.

48    Graham Papers, Peel to Graham, 24 August 1848. The motion was negatived without a division (*Hansard*, CI, 432).

49    Ibid, fols 284–7, Wood to Peel (? 6 May 1849); see also fols 277–83 for the other letters.

50    Ibid, fols 288–9, 8 May 1849. 'Nobody but Lord John knows that I have seen you or communicated directly with you,' he wrote on 18 May (fols 290–2).

51    *Hansard*, CV, 117. See text, pp 52–3.

52    Add MS 40601–3.

53    Add MS 40602, fol 363, Wood to Peel, 19 December 1849. In reporting to Russell that he had passed on this message, Wood wrote: 'I have heard from Peel who assures me, in spite of some very strong and plausible stories which have reached him, his faith in the government never wavered for a moment' (PRO 30/22/8C, fol 683, 19 December 1849).

54    Add MS 40603, fols 257–9, 25 May 1850.

55    Goulburn Papers, 11/20, 14 August 1846. Goulburn had been consulted by Russell but had been non-committal in his replies (Add MS 40445, fols 365–6, 13 August 1846 (Parker, *Peel*, III, 461) ).

56    Graham Papers, 2 September 1846 (Parker, *Peel*, III, 462).

57    *Hansard*, CIV, 87–117.

58    Parker, *Peel*, III, 509; *Hansard*, CIV, 114.

59    Add MS 40601, fols 139–44, 6 April 1849.

60    Parker, *Peel*, III, 512.

61    Add MS 40601, fols 91–100, Peel memorandum presented to Clarendon, 2 April 1849 (inaccurately reproduced in Parker).

62    See Add MS 40601 and 40602 and the Graham Papers for 1849 and 1850. Some extracts are printed in Parker, *Peel*, III, chap 18.

63  Add MS 40602, fols 47–9, 30 July 1849.
64  Ibid, fols 308–12, 5 December 1849. Graham, to whom Peel showed the letter, expressed some scepticism, observing that Bedford tended to adopt the opinion of the person he was addressing. 'He is not insincere', Graham added charitably, 'but he is often betrayed into inconsistencies' (Add MS 40452, fol 406, 8 December 1849).
65  Add MS 40602, fols 365–9, 22 December 1849. For Russell's letter to his brother see Gooch, *Later Correspondence of Lord John Russell*, I, 197–9. It appears from the Russell Papers that Russell in turn heard of Peel's good opinion of him from Lord Hatherton who, a few months before Peel's death, visited him at Drayton Manor to inspect the drainage system. 'He spoke in the most respectful tones of Lord John Russell,' Hatherton recorded in his journal. He reported Peel as saying that he had 'great reliance' in Russell and 'an earnest desire to support him'. Peel reiterated his determination never again to return to office (PRO 30/22/8D, fols 1150–8, extract from Lord Hatherton's Journal, 27–8 March 1850).
66  J. Morley, *Life of Gladstone* (London 1903), I, Book iii, chap 2.
67  Their correspondence shows how Lincoln's friends rallied round him on this occasion. Herbert took care of his children while Gladstone set out on that heroic but forlorn mission, 'which', Peel wrote in one of his very few letters to Gladstone in these years, 'with unparalleled kindness and generosity you undertook in the hope of mitigating the affliction of a friend and conducing possibly to the salvation of a wife and a mother' (Add MS 44275, fols 317–20, 26 August 1849).
68  See Stanmore, *Herbert*, I, 110–20. There is correspondence on the subject in the Herbert, Peel, and Graham Papers.
69  Newcastle Papers, University of Nottingham, Cardwell, 15 October 1849.
70  H. R. Fox Bourne, *English Newspapers* (London 1887), 153–6; T. H. S. Escott, *Masters of English Journalism* (London 1911), 231. James Grant in *The Newspaper Press* (London 1871), 310, includes Gladstone among the purchasers and describes the paper as the organ of the Puseyite party in religion as well as of the Peelite party in politics. The biographies of Newcastle, Herbert, and Gladstone are silent on the purchase.
71  The Newcastle Papers contain many such letters from Cooke, all undated except for the day of the week. There is also much correspondence with Hayward.
72  Add MS 44777, fols 281–2. On the question of Jewish disabilities he shows Peel, Graham, Lincoln, Herbert, Wortley, Cardwell, Young, St Germans, Canning, and himself as supporting the Government measure, while Goulburn, Thesiger, Aberdeen, Wellington, Buccleuch, Ellenborough, and Lyndhurst were opposed. Peel, Graham, Young, St Germans, and Wellington, he noted, supported the repeal of the Navigation Acts without reservation, Lyndhurst and

Ellenborough opposed it outright, and Aberdeen, Lincoln, Herbert, Cardwell, Clerk, Wortley, Thesiger, and himself favoured only a conditional acceptance but were 'failing that for the Government'. On the Government's acceptance of the Canadian Rebellion Losses Bill Gladstone listed ten including Peel, Graham, Goulburn, and Cardwell in support and ten including Aberdeen, Lincoln, Herbert, and himself in opposition. Only three out of ten (Peel, Graham, and Young) supported the Government on the West Indian question in 1848 and only two out of eight (Aberdeen and Buccleuch) supported it on the Vancouver Island issue in 1849. Cf Appendix A, below.

73 *Hansard*, XCV, 1030–45, 1126–78.

74 Ibid, 1163–5; *Divisions in Session of 1847–48 (11 & 12 Victoria)*, House of Commons Divisions Lobby, 27–8. In Graham's view, if the Peelites had not stood firm the Government would have yielded and Bentinck would have won 'a dangerous triumph' (Newcastle Papers, 17 December 1847).

75 Of whom Lincoln wrote somewhat vindictively: 'Disraeli's speech was obviously addressed to Rothschild's money bags and was a bad selection from his novels. It formed however a good practical commentary upon the value of the existing test for if it meant anything it meant that he was a Jew' (Newcastle Papers, to Herbert, 19 December 1847).

76 See W. D. Jones, *Lord Derby and Victorian Conservatism* (Oxford 1956), 125–7; Robert Blake, *Disraeli* (London 1966), 261–2.

77 *Annual Register 1848*, 81–93; *Divisions 1847–48*, 43–5. The Bill was supported by Cardwell, Gladstone, Graham, Lincoln, and Peel, and opposed by Goulburn. Gladstone's friends were concerned as to how his vote might affect his position. For instance, on 7 September George Moberly wrote to Roundell Palmer about Gladstone's need to husband his influence at Oxford. 'I am much more interested in his not voting for the Jews admission, than for the exclusion of the Jews,' he observed (Selborne Papers, 1861, fols 152–6). Lincoln counted 18 Peelites and 6 Protectionists supporting the first reading (Newcastle Papers, to Herbert, 19 December 1847).

78 *Hansard*, XCVII, 192–7, 281–96, 406–12, 438–54.

79 PRO 30/22/7B, fols 392–3, 7 March 1848.

80 Ibid, fols 429–32, 10 March 1848; also fols 398–9 and 413–16, 7 and 8 March.

81 *Divisions 1847–48*, 81–3. Tufnell told Russell that his speech had more than counteracted the effect of Peel's, 'which though well meant', he said, 'was very ill-timed' (PRO 30/22/7B, fols 473–6, 15 March 1848).

82 *Annual Register 1848*, 64–80.

83 Ibid, 80.

84 *Divisions 1947–48*, 283–5.

85 *Annual Register 1848*, 11–21.

86 *Hansard*, XCIX, 1242.

87  Ibid, 1014–31.
88  *Divisions 1847–48*, 313–16. The *Morning Chronicle* (1 July 1848) supported Pakington's amendment only because it thought that it might lead to something better.
89  See *Annual Register 1849*, 2–19; *Hansard*, CII, 217–20.
90  *Divisions 1849*, 8–9.
91  See text, pp 45–6, and *Annual Register 1849*, 71–3.
92  *Divisions 1849*, 125–7. The measure was eventually passed by the Lords. The more important Encumbered Estates Bill was enacted without opposition.
93  W. F. Monypenny and G. E. Buckle, *Life of Disraeli* (New York 1929, two vol ed), I, 1014–15; *Hansard*, CIII, 805–9, 824–9; *Divisions 1849*, 96–8.
94  Add MS 44777, fols 286–93, W.E.G. memorandum 69, 1848–9.
95  *Annual Register 1849*, 28–30.
96  Ibid, 32–3.
97  *Hansard*, CIV, 675.
98  Ibid, 690–701.
99  Ibid, 702–5.
100 *Divisions 1849*, 82–4 and 145–7. There were surprising changes in the voting pattern of Free Trade Conservatives between 1848 and 1849 that emphasised the conflicting pressures under which they acted. Of 55 who supported repeal in 1848, 3 reversed their vote and 21 failed to vote in 1849. Only one of the 1848 opponents failed to repeat his vote. Of 27 who had not voted in 1848, 12 now supported and 15 opposed repeal in 1849.
101 The House divided: Content, 173 (including 68 proxies), Non-Content, 163 (including 44 proxies) (*Hansard*, CV, 117–20). The majority included some 35 Conservative lay peers led by the old Duke of Wellington and 6 Conservative bishops (ie peers and bishops identified by Dod as opposing the Government).
102 PRO 30/22/7F, fols 2070–2, 14 April 1849.
103 Broadlands MS, GC/RU/267/2, 16 April 1849.
104 *Annual Register 1849*, 171–80.
105 *Divisions 1849*, 239–41. Disraeli, of course, in this case always loyal to his convictions, voted against his party.
106 *Annual Register 1849*, 109–18; *Divisions 1849*, 253–5.
107 *Hansard*, CVI, 1429.
108 *Divisions 1849*, 315–18. Actually one of the nine, H. Herbert, an Irish member, joined the Peelites in supporting the Aberdeen coalition in 1852.
109 Sir G. F. Lewis (ed), *Letters of the Right Hon. Sir George Cornewall Lewis, Bart. to various Friends* (London 1870), 211.
110 *Annual Register 1850*, 7–13; *Hansard*, CVIII, 253–7; *Divisions 1850*, 5–9.
111 *Annual Register 1850*, 13–20; *Divisions 1850*, 35–8; the vote was 252 to 273.

112   Add MS 40603, fols 92–7, 22 February 1850. Unhappily Young's
      lists are missing, which makes it impossible to know which four
      names on my list of 32 Peelites supporting the Government he does
      not accept. Presumably four of mine he counts as having already
      gone over to the Liberals, although the parliamentary reference
      books do not show it. His list of Peel's friends voting against the
      Government is less than my list of Free Trade Conservatives doing
      so, because actually some of mine had become assimilated with the
      Derbyite party. See text, pp 109–10.

113   *Divisions 1850*, 237–9. The exception was Philip Pusey, an inde-
      pendent Conservative and a friend of Gladstone's, whom Dod calls
      a Liberal after 1846, although he voted against the Corn Laws on
      one division in that year.

114   *Annual Register 1850*, 51–6; *Divisions 1850*, 275–8.

115   PRO 30/22/8D, fols 1017–20, Charles Wood, undated note; fols
      1078–83, Wood, 17 March 1850; fol 1092, printed text of Russell
      speech in Downing Street, 19 March 1850, urging Liberals to vote
      against the motion.

116   *Hansard*, CIX, 1093–1183.

117   Ibid, 1170–1.

118   *Divisions 1850*, 107–9.

119   Ibid, 149–50.

120   Ibid, 187–9. On 12 April 16 out of 48 Free Trade Conservatives had
      supported a hostile Derbyite amendment to a motion for a com-
      mittee on salaries (ibid, 143–5).

121   *Annual Register 1850*, 98–100; *Divisions 1850*, 223–5. The Free
      Trade Conservatives also divided on an Irish supply motion when
      20 supported and 22 opposed a Derbyite amendment registering
      Protestant objections to the system of national education in Ireland
      (ibid, 359–61).

122   Add MS 40455, fol 491, Aberdeen to Peel, 4 April 1850.

123   Add MS 43065, fol 420–7, 2 April 1850.

124   Add MS 40452, fols 438–40, 7 April 1850; see also fols 434–7,
      3 April.

125   Parker, *Graham*, II, 105–7.

126   Stanmore, *Herbert*, I, 124–5.

127   Morley, *Gladstone*, I, 369–70.

128   *Annual Register 1850*, 85–6.

129   *Divisions 1850*, 369–72.

130   Add MS 44745, fol 190.

131   See Appendix A below; cf Morley, *Gladstone*, I, 372, quoting a
      letter from his father, 2 July 1850; Gladstone put the Peelites in the
      majority as 'some twenty rank and file'.

132   Add MS 44745, fol 190; cf Appendix A.

133   Ibid, fols 191–2.

134   Ibid, fol 194. Although Gladstone was critical of Peel's course in

these years he always retained a very high opinion of him as a statesman and remained in many respects his disciple.

135 For a further analysis see text pp 109–10 and Appendix A. Peel himself voted in 19 of the 20 divisions analysed and always with the Government. I have not included the division on the Roebuck motion for obvious reasons.

136 Newcastle Papers, 15 October 1849; likewise Lincoln to Herbert, 4 December 1847, denouncing the Whig Coercion Bill as 'a wretched piece of imbecility', but recognising that they must support it.

137 Roundell Palmer expressed the Peelite attitude well in a letter to a friend on his first election to Parliament. 'With respect to Roman Catholics', he wrote, 'the line I propose, by God's help, is this—to give them and all others whatever is due upon grounds of justice or religious liberty; but to show them no *favour* whatever . . .' (Selborne MSS, 1861, fols 140–3, to S. Waldegrave, 6 August 1847).

138 Newcastle Papers, 14 October 1850. The Peelite *Morning Chronicle* continually harped upon the incompetence of Sir Charles Wood who, for all his amiability in private life, they pronounced to be 'a great public calamity' as Chancellor of the Exchequer (21 June 1848).

139 *Industry and Empire* (Penguin ed 1969), 83.

140 'Country Gentlemen and the Repeal of the Corn Laws', *EHR*, LXXXII, 47–60.

141 These were John Duncuft and James Heald. H. B. Baring, W. B. Baring, and John Walter were the other three with some business involvement, the two Peels, Gladstone, Cardwell, and perhaps E. B. Denison the remaining four or five with a business background.

142 My analysis, based on Dod, *DNB*, and Burke's *Landed Gentry*, is not exhaustive, but bears out Professor Aydelotte's more complete findings for the previous parliament.

143 Cf Robert Blake, *The Conservative Party from Peel to Churchill* (London 1970), 96, who equates Peelites with Liberal Conservatives as listed in McCalmont's *Poll book*. He rightly points out that a high proportion of the Peelite seats were in the west of England. For the categories of English boroughs I have followed Norman Gash, *Politics in the Age of Peel*, 73–7 and 438–9.

*Chapter 3* THE PEELITES WITHOUT PEEL 1850–1 (pages 69–93)

1 Indeed, Aberdeen, whose memory went back to 1806, told his friend Guizot that public opinion was stirred even more deeply than on the former occasion (*Aberdeen Correspondence* (1848–50), 444, 12 July 1850).

2 Monypenny and Buckle, *Disraeli*, I, 1077.

3 *Letters of Sir G. C. Lewis*, 226; 'he will come forward more and take

more part in discussion', Lewis added, but he did not think that he would displace Disraeli as some supposed.

4  *Hansard,* CXII, 856–8, 3 July 1850. For the widespread sense of loss see Greville's impartial testimony in his *Memoirs,* VI, 234.
5  Add MS 44777, fol 331, memo 79, 4 October 1851.
6  Add MS 44778, fols 76–83, memo 95, 29 November 1876.
7  Newcastle Papers, 16 July 1850.
8  *Aberdeen Correspondence* (1848–50), 445–6, 5 August 1850; see also 444–5, 12 July 1850.
9  Monypenny and Buckle, *Disraeli,* I, 1076.
10  Cardwell Papers, PRO 30/48/8/50, fols 19–22, 5 October 1850. Goulburn's basic conservatism is seen in this letter in which he wrote:
> I fear the growing Radicalism of the Whigs on the one side and Protectionists on the other & should desire as far as my wishes go to stem the progress of that march towards Democracy which the Reform Bill originated and which every new political event unless managed with great prudence as well as firmness assists.
11  Add MS 40602, fols 228–31, 16 November 1849.
12  Ibid, fols 242–7, 19 November 1849, from Lincoln's legal adviser; *Hansard,* CXIII, list of Private Acts not printed no 24 (no page number). Gladstone, while praising Lincoln's readiness to forgive his wife, told him that he himself could not admit the dissolubility of marriage, although he considered it a matter of private judgement (Newcastle Papers, 22 September 1849).
13  Newcastle Papers, 16 July 1850.
14  Ibid, 14 October 1850.
15  Ibid, 26 November 1850.
16  Ibid, 12 January 1851.
17  *Aberdeen Correspondence* (1848–50), 397–9.
18  Add MS 43072, fols 162–8, 21 May 1850.
19  Ibid, fol 153, 16 May 1850.
20  Add MS 43199, fols 1–4, 11 June 1850.
21  Add MS 43201, fols 33–40, 3 June 1850.
22  Add MS 44237, fols 188–91, 15 June 1850.
23  Add MS 44088, fols 75–6, 30 May 1850.
24  He announced that during the pleasure of the Holy See he would 'govern . . . the counties of Middlesex, Hertford and Essex'. 'The great work, then, is complete,' he exulted, '. . . Catholic England has been restored to its orbit in the ecclesiastical firmament, from which its light has long vanished.' For these events see Bernard Ward, *The Sequel to Catholic Emancipation* (London 1915), II, which reprints Wiseman's pastoral in Appendix M; Wilfrid Ward, *The Life and Times of Cardinal Wiseman* (London 1912), I; and E. R. Norman, *Anti-Catholicism in Victorian England* (London 1968).
25  Ward, *Cardinal Wiseman,* I, 544. The following few pages are largely based on or taken from my paper, 'The Politics of the

"Papal Aggression" Crisis 1850–1851', published in *The Canadian Catholic Historical Association Report 1959*, 13–27.

26  Walpole, *Russell*, II, 119–20. 'No foreign prince or potentate', he wrote, 'will be at liberty to fasten his fetters upon a nation which has so long and so nobly vindicated its right to freedom of opinion, civil, political and religious.' He denounced 'the late aggression of the pope' as 'insolent and insidious', saying that 'there is an assumption of power in all the documents which have come from Rome; a pretension of supremacy over the realm of England, and a claim to sole and undivided sway, which is inconsistent with the Queen's supremacy . . .'.

27  Ward, *Wiseman*, I, 550–69.

28  A. C. Benson and Viscount Esher (eds), *The Letters of Queen Victoria* (London 1907), II, 326.

29  Stanmore, *Herbert*, I, 133. See also Parker, *Graham*, II, 113–14, for another letter defining Graham's position. Similar views were expressed by other Peelites in their private correspondence.

30  PRO 30/22/9A, fols 257–9, 15 January 1851, from Sir George Grey, noting Clarendon's objections, and nd from Lord Lansdowne. Lincoln told Gladstone that he had had a conversation with Labouchere who agreed with his condemnation of Russell's letter (Newcastle Papers, 2 January 1851).

31  *Letters of Queen Victoria*, II, 331–2, 336.

32  Broadlands MS, GC/RU/373, 2 November 1850.

33  Ibid, GC/RU/1080/2, 16 January 1851.

34  Selborne MSS, No 1861, fols 216–19, 5 December 1850. Later Dr James Yonge, Palmer's leading supporter in Plymouth, told him that his speech on the Ecclesiastical Titles Bill would make it impossible for him to stand again for Plymouth (ibid, no 1862, fols 4–5, 21 March 1851). He was forced to withdraw from Plymouth on the eve of the general election of 1852, but regained the seat in 1853 when his opponent was unseated following an election petition.

35  *Hansard*, CXIV, 187–211.

36  One Liberal supporter of the Bill made an acute analysis of the various points of view that appeared during the debate. Altogether he detected four parties. The first were the Roman Catholics who were naturally irritated, but who, he said, when the storm blew over would remain loyal subjects. He found a second party 'which', he said, 'strangely mixed up Corn and Catholics together; who thought that to repeal the aggression of the Pope was to re-enact the Corn Laws'. The third party in this gentleman's view 'was composed of those who assumed to have taken a high intellectual eminence and who affected to regard with supercilious disdain all legislation on the subject'. (These clearly were the Peelites and perhaps some Radicals.) 'The fourth party', he asserted confidently, 'combined free traders and protectionists, whigs and tories, conservatives and

N

radicals', all of whom mysteriously supported the Bill as a matter of allegiance to the Queen (*Hansard*, CXV, 366–8).

37    For instance, see *Hansard*, CXIV, 242–56, for Bright; ibid, 211–18, for Roebuck; and ibid, CXV, 544–9, for Hume.

38    Ibid, CXV, 164–82. The Peelite *Morning Chronicle* took a very strong line against the Durham Letter and the Ecclesiastical Titles Bill, devoting almost daily leaders to the issue throughout February and March.

39    Morley, *Gladstone*, I, 410–11. For Gladstone's strong condemnation of the Bill in his private correspondence see D. C. Latherbury, *Correspondence on Church and Religion of William Ewart Gladstone* (London 1910), I, 119–24.

40    *Hansard*, CXV, 280–309.

41    *Hansard*, CXV, 618–21; *Divisions 1851*, 51–4. Fifty-seven Liberal Conservatives were in the majority.

42    *Annual Register 1851*, 63.

43    *Hansard*, CXVIII, 1676–9. Most of the signatures on one of these protests came from Peelite peers. The Duke of Argyll regretfully broke with Aberdeen to support the Bill, as did the Duke of Wellington.

44    Parker, *Graham*, II, 121–2.

45    Graham Papers, 30 January 1851.

46    Parker, *Graham*, II, 123–4.

47    *Hansard*, CXIV, 516–37, 558–65, 606–7; *Divisions 1851*, 13–16. Twenty-eight Liberal Conservatives (of those remaining on our revised list) supported Disraeli.

48    *Letters of Queen Victoria*, II, 343–5. Cf *Greville Memoirs*, VI, 272. Greville says of Graham at this time that 'while disapproving of much that they have done, he is now desirous of reconciling himself with his old friends, looks hereafter to coming into power with them, and is excessively pleased at having put himself on amicable terms with J. Russell'.

49    *Divisions 1851*, 26–7. The majority included one Peelite, Sir John Hanmer. There were very few Protectionists or Liberal Conservatives in the House.

50    *Letters of Queen Victoria*, II, 346–52.

51    Ibid, 356; and Walpole, *Russell*, II, 124–6, who publishes most of the documents.

52    *Letters of Queen Victoria*, II, 361–3; *Greville Memoirs*, VI, 277; C. H. Stuart, 'The Formation of the Aberdeen Coalition', *TRHS*, 5th series (1954), IV, 45–68.

53    Newcastle Papers, 23 February 1851. Lincoln had become the Duke of Newcastle in January. See also Add MS 44777, fols 322–9, Memo 23 April 1851.

54    *Letters of Queen Victoria*, II, 369. See also Disraeli's inimitable account in Monypenny and Buckle, *Disraeli*, I, 1104–12.

55    *Letters of Queen Victoria*, II, 376–7.

56 Ibid, 377–9.
57 *Hansard*, CXIV, 1003–26. It is interesting to note that, with some apology, Stanley used the terms Protectionist and Peelite parties in this speech.
58 *Hansard*, CXIV, 1043–51. Gladstone deplored the tacit support given by Graham in his speech to Russell's Reform proposals (Add MS 44777, Memo 78, fol 326).
59 *Greville Memoirs*, VI, 280–1.
60 Add MS 44777, fol 326, 23 April 1851; Morley, *Gladstone*, I, 407.
61 Add MS 43247, fols 184–6, 200–1, 8 March and 5 July 1851. These letters are not printed in the *Aberdeen Correspondence*.
62 Add MS 43070, fols 204–5, ? April 1851.
63 Ibid, fols 208–10.
64 Ibid, fols 216–17.
65 Add MS 44088, fols 97–8, 15 July 1851.
66 Morley, *Gladstone*, I, 396.
67 Add MS 44088, fols 103–6, 26 August 1851.
68 *Aberdeen Correspondence* (1850–60), 131.
69 Ibid, 168, 29 October 1851.
70 Ibid, 152–3, 21 September 1851.
71 Add MS 44088, fols 114–17, 9 October 1851.
72 Ibid, fols 120–1, 29 November 1851.
73 Add MS 43070, fols 246–7, 1 December 1851.
74 Add MS 44088, fol 126, 6 January 1852.
75 *Annual Register 1851*, 77–80; *Hansard*, CXIV, 703–38.
76 Add MS 44777, fols 326–30, Memo 78, 23 April 1851. After the meeting Graham told Greville that Gladstone had a great mind to vote against the Government, in which case 'others of the Peelites would have gone with him, and the Government would have been in a minority' (*Greville Memoirs*, VI, 291).
77 *Hansard*, CXV, 1196–1200; *Divisions 1851*, 81–4.
78 *Hansard*, CXVI, 118–22; *Divisions 1851*, 95–8; Add MS 44237, fols 194–7, Sir John Young, 21 April. He only noted 30 Peelites in the majority, but he credited Gladstone with giving the lead that saved the Government.
79 *Greville Memoirs*, VI, 291–2.
80 Ibid, 284–5.
81 Ibid, 285.
82 *Hansard*, CXVI, 464–9, 496–9; *Divisions 1851*, 113–15. Again some weeks later in a small house the Maynooth grant in the estimates was only saved by the votes of 17 Liberal Conservatives (*Hansard*, CXVII, 831–3).
83 Add MS 43190, fols 205–8, 5 May 1851.
84 Add MS 43247, fols 184–6, 196–201, 8 March, 6 and 7 June, and 5 July 1851.
85 Add MS 43072, fols 180–1, 14 June 1851.
86 Add MS 43070, fols 212–15, Gladstone to Aberdeen, 24 June 1851;

Add MS 44777, fols 313–21, Gladstone to Young, 8 April 1854; *Hansard*, CXVII, 1416–40; *Divisions 1851*, 285–7.

87  *Hansard*, CXVI, 286–7, CXVII, 204–30, 250–3; *Annual Register 1851*, 136. In a motion censuring the Governor of Ceylon he voted against some thirty Liberal Conservatives, including Graham, Herbert, and Cardwell. In the debate on the Kaffir War, Herbert, Cardwell, and a few other Peelites joined him in a vote of censure against the Government.

88  Add MS 43190, fols 213–16, 31 August 1851.

89  Graham Papers, 4 September 1851.

90  Graham Papers, Graham memo to Russell, 20 September 1851 (partly reproduced in Parker, *Graham*, II, 134–5). Palmerston, while not opposing the offer, doubted its expediency. 'There is no denying Graham's talents and acquirements and his power as a speaker', he wrote to Russell, 'but for a person so gifted he is singularly unpopular and destitute of political following either in or out of Parliament' (Broadlands MS, GC/RU/1086/1, 21 August 1851). Russell thought it wiser to have Graham with them than against them. 'It is certainly strange', he replied, 'that agreeing to nearly all you say I should come to the opposite conclusion' (ibid, 421/2, 22 August 1851).

91  *Aberdeen Correspondence* (1850–60), 165, 22 October 1851.

92  Add MS 43190, fols 224–9, 21 October 1851.

93  For instance, on 21 October he concluded a letter to Aberdeen by saying 'I am always gloomy; I am downcast today' (Add MS 43190, fols 224–9). The sun rarely shone on Sir James's world.

94  Graham Papers, copy of a letter to Greville, 23 November 1851.

95  Ibid, 15 December 1851; see also correspondence with Aberdeen in Add MS 43190.

96  Add MS 44262, fols 110–13, 'draft', 22 October 1851. 'In the first draft of such a corps' Gladstone thought to include from the Lords Buccleuch, Harding, St Germans, and Canning, and from the Commons Herbert, Young, Goulburn, Clerk, and Cardwell. 'Out of respect for the past' he was also inclined to include former members of Peel's ministry such as Lords Haddington, Ripon, Heytersbury, Ashburton (W. B. Baring), and even the Duke of Wellington.

97  Stanmore, *Herbert*, I, 145–6.

98  Graham Papers, 20 November 1851.

99  Ibid, 22 December 1851 (Parker, *Graham*, II, 142).

100  Ibid, 23 December 1851.

101  Ibid, 23 December 1851.

102  Ibid, 25 December 1851.

103  Add MS 43190, fols 246–9, 25 December 1851.

104  *Aberdeen Correspondence* (1850–60), 200, 207.

105  Add MS 43190, fols 250–3, 29 December 1851.

106  *Aberdeen Correspondence* (1850–60), 208–11. Palmerston was less charitable in his view of Ellice, whom he regarded as responsible for

the intrigue against him in 1845. 'As for Ellice', Palmerston wrote to his brother on that occasion, 'he is essentially, radically, thoroughly and incorrigibly dishonest' (Broadlands MS GC/TE/311/3, 26 January 1846).

Chapter 4    DERBY AND THE PEELITES 1852 (pages 94–110)

1    PRO 30/22/10A, fols 206–12, Sir George Grey, 12 January 1852; fols 196–7 and 261–6, Lord Grey, 11 and 16 January; fols 186–9, Clarendon, 9 January. PRO 30/22/9J, fols 411–14, 31 December 1851.

2    Martineau, *Newcastle*, 108–10; PRO 30/22/10A, fols 251–5, 277–80, 313–20, and 326–9, 15, 17, 20, and 21 January 1852.

3    PRO 30/22/10A, fols 313–15, 19 January 1852 (copy).

4    Ibid; Graham Papers, Cardwell, 26 January 1852.

5    *Greville Memoirs*, VI, 325.

6    PRO 30/22/10A, fols 245–6, 269–70, 15 and 17 January 1852 (copy); Parker, *Graham*, II, 151.

7    *Aberdeen Correspondence* (1850–60), 6 January 1852, 222.

8    *Letters of Queen Victoria*, II, 434–5. We may surmise that this letter was drafted by Prince Albert if we look at a very different kind of letter which Victoria wrote shortly afterwards to her uncle Leopold in which she said that Albert had become 'a *terrible* man of business', and in which she admitted that she could 'not enjoy these things'. 'I am everyday more convinced', she added, 'that *we women*, if we *are* to be *good* women, *feminine* and *aimiable* and *domestic*, are not fitted to *reign* . . .'! (Ibid, 444.)

9    *Greville Memoirs*, VI, 328–9.

10    Add MS 43190, fols 270–1, 28 January 1852; Graham Papers, Aberdeen, 29 January.

11    PRO 30/22/10C, fols 700–6, Monday (16 March 1852).

12    Graham Papers, Cardwell, 26 January 1852.

13    Add MS 43190, fols 264–6, Graham, 10 January 1852; Parker, *Graham*, II, 152; Newcastle Papers, to Gladstone, 8 December 1851, to Cardwell, 14 January 1852, and to Bonham, 14 January.

14    Cf Jones, *Lord Derby and Victorian Conservatism*, 159; Bell, *Palmerston*, II, 58. Lord Grey in taking leave of the Queen expressed the view that a future accord between the Whigs and the Peelites was unlikely. 'Lord John had never wished it to succeed', he said, 'and it had been unfair that he had not stated to them (the Peelites) that all his colleagues were ready to give up their places' (*Letters of Queen Victoria*, II, 454).

15    17 and 21 February 1852.

16    *Letters of Queen Victoria*, II, 455–6. Palmerston was offered the Exchequer but declined on the grounds that he could not accept any return to a duty on corn, for he did not believe that there could be any turning back of the clock. Cheap bread, he told Derby, had kept

England safe in 1848 (Broadlands MS, GMC/130, Memorandum of
Conversation, 22 February 1852).

17  *Hansard*, CXIX, 889–904.

18  Ibid, 911–13.

19  Add MS 43072, fols 182–4, 'Sunday night' (29 February 1852).

20  *Aberdeen Correspondence* (1850–60), 244–6, 27 February 1852.

21  PRO 30/48/8/49, fols 3–4, 25 February 1852.

22  Add MS 44778, fols 5–20, 25 February to 12 March 1852,
    partly reproduced by Morley (*Gladstone*, I, 417–18), who made
    some changes in the original wording to suit his syntax. The
    following paragraphs (in the text) are based on this memorandum.

23  Gladstone preferred to see the Peelites 'liberal in the sense of Peel,
    working out a liberal policy through the medium of the conservative
    party', a view which Morley described as typical of 'his constant
    adhorrence of premature committal'.

24  Ibid. This is passed over by Morley.

25  Aberdeen, Graham, Gladstone, Newcastle, Canning, Cardwell, and
    Sidney Herbert, who was host.

26  Ibid. Of Newcastle Gladstone wrote (fol 19): 'So all was well as
    possible between us individually but upon the whole recent ex-
    perience has heightened the fears I more or less entertained before
    that his mind is too combative and his temper too little conciliatory
    not to cause uneasy anticipation if he were actively engaged in
    leading a party.' The decision to sit on the opposition side is not
    alluded to in this memorandum but in a later one cited below.

27  Add MS 44237, fols 199–202, 1 March 1852.

28  Ibid, fols 203–4. The letter is misdated 6 May 1847 but the date
    6 March appears in Gladstone's hand. It is filed with the 1852
    correspondence where it clearly belongs.

29  Add MS 44778, fols 76–83, Memo 95, 29 November 1876, quoted
    in part by Morley (*Gladstone*, I, 428). Cf Greville: 'The Peelites sit
    together, all except Graham, who has regularly joined J.R. and sits
    beside him. Nobody knows what they mean to do, nor which party
    they will eventually join' (*Memoirs*, VI, 337).

30  Gladstone concluded Memo 84 (Add MS 44778, fols 5–20), cited
    above, with a list, dated 12 March 1852, of 6 peers and 28 members
    of the House of Commons 'among Sir R. Peel's friends' with whom
    he had communicated within the period of the crisis. The names
    were listed in four columns as follows: (First column) Ld Aberdeen,
    D of Newcastle, Ld Hardinge, Ld Canning, Ld Ellesmere, Ld De
    Tabley. (Second column) Sir J. Graham, Cardwell, H. Fitzroy,
    Norreys, Ph Pusey. (Third column) Goulburn, S. Herbert, Sir
    G. Clerk, J. Wortley, Sir J. Young, E. Bruce, Sir F. L. Lewis,
    Mahon, Greene (ind), Jocelyn, H. Corry, Col Damer, Ld Jermyn
    (ind). (Fourth column) H. Hardinge, H. Currie, Cornwall Legh,
    Wilson Patten, Roundell Palmer, W. Egerton, Sir J. Johnston,
    F. R. Wegg Prosser, F. Charteris, A. Oswald, Wm Beckett. (My

punctuation.) There is little evidence in respect of some of these that they ever showed themselves to be active Peelites and only 16 of the 26 Commoners eventually broke with Derby. (See my *Aberdeen Coalition 1852–1855* (Cambridge, 1968), 555–9, Appendices A and B.) There are also some surprising omissions from the list, such as the Duke of Argyll, Lord St Germans, Sir J. Hogg, etc.

31 Newcastle Papers, 8 March 1852. 'The rot is in the party and no wonder', Newcastle wrote to Gladstone, '—if Easter finds us as we are we had better shut up shop altogether for Derby and Tufnell are agreed on this if on nothing else—"extirpate the Peelites".'

32 Add MS 44778, fols 1–4, Memo 83, 12 March 1852. I have not found any actual report of the meeting.

33 Add MS 44210, fols 47–8, Mrs Herbert, 15 May 1852.

34 *Annual Register 1852*, 41–2; *Hansard*, CXIX, 1039–64.

35 *Hansard*, CXIX, 1097; Monypenny and Buckle, *Disraeli*, I, 1170.

36 *Hansard*, CXIX, 1105.

37 Ibid, 998–1013.

38 Add MS 44778, Memo 85, fols 21–2, 16 March 1852; Memo 87, fols 25–32, 25–6 March.

39 Ibid, Memo 86, fols 23–4, 18 March.

40 Ibid, Memo 87, fols 25–32, 25–6 March. Derby told Disraeli that there was no engagement, merely a private understanding. Monypenny and Buckle, *Disraeli*, I, 1172.

41 *Hansard*, CXIX, 1261–7. See also Add MS 44778, fols 25–32.

42 *Hansard*, CXIX, 1273–80. On 30 March he rather qualified this statement (ibid, CXX, 345–8). According to Professor Jones, Derby was anxious to prolong the session to improve his electoral prospects (*Lord Derby and Victorian Conservatism*, 165).

43 *Hansard*, CXIX, 1291–7.

44 Graham Papers, Cobden to Graham [? 20 March 1852]; see also Graham to Cobden, 20 March 1852, and to Russell, 17 March.

45 Add MS 44778, Memo 87, fols 30–1; cf Morley, *Gladstone*, I, 419.

46 Ibid, Memo 88, fols 33–9, 19 April 1852; cf Morley, *Gladstone*, I, 420–1. Add MS 44163, fols 55–61, Gladstone to Graham, 29 March. Extracts from the correspondence are printed in Parker, *Graham*, II, 157–8.

47 Add MS 44163, fols 57–8, 29 March 1852. Realising that his first letter had been over-stiff, Gladstone replied to Graham more warmly as far as their personal relations were concerned.

48 Add MS 44210, fols 44–6, 30 March 1852.

49 Add MS 44778, Memo 88, fols 33–42 (cf Morley, *Gladstone*, I, 421–2).

50 In a letter of 30 April to his friend Stafford Northcote, Gladstone discussed the future in characteristically obscure terms:

As to myself I am well pleased on the whole with the course of affairs. What I look to and wish for is the speedy total and final settlement of the question of Commercial Policy. When that has been accomplished probably the way of duty will open itself sufficiently at least for the day. But the future combinations of events may be modified by so many causes at home and abroad that it is a duty to rein in the mind from manifold speculation (Add MS 50014, fols 31–4).

51   *Hansard*, CXX, 1185–8.
52   *Greville Memoirs*, VI, 339; *Hansard*, CXXI, 9–36; Monypenny and Buckle, *Disraeli*, I, 1177–81.
53   *Hansard*, CXXI, 51–4.
54   *Hansard*, CXXI, 989–1005.
55   Cf Jones, *Lord Derby and Victorian Conservatism*, 163.
56   Aberdeen, Goulburn, Newcastle, Canning, and Cardwell.
57   Add MS 44778, Memo 89, fols 43–7, 10 May 1852.
58   Add MS 44140, fols 176–8 [9 May 1852].
59   Ibid, fols 180–1, 10 May to Derby (draft).
60   Add MS 44778, fol 78, Memo 95; *Hansard*, CXXI, 463–5.
61   *Hansard*, CXXII, 616–43.
62   Ibid, 694.
63   Add MS 43190, fols 279–80, 14 June 1852.
64   The Government's Bill was welcomed by Gladstone as a step in the right direction, but along with several of the colonial reformers he criticised some of its details as not being sufficiently liberal, and obtained some amendments in a more democratic sense. Newcastle supported these demands in the House of Lords. *Hansard*, CXXI, 951-74; CXXII, 456–64, 1145–55.
65   There were endless debates over R. Spooner's motion for a 'Select Committee to inquire into the system of Education carried on at the College of Maynooth', and also a demand for a judicial inquiry into the appointment of a very High Church clergyman to the vicarage of Frome. Gladstone introduced a 'Colonial Bishops Bill', but on finding little support gave it up, while another High Church reformer brought in an Episcopal and Capitular Revenue Bill that likewise failed for lack of support.
66   *Hansard*, CXXII, 1404–9.
67   Add MS 44778, Memo 95, fols 78–80.
68   See Appendix A. The division on the Don Pacifico debate is not included since most of the Free Trade Conservatives voted the same way as the Protectionists, but 20 of them did go into the Government lobby. On the other hand, the second reading of the Ecclesiastical Titles Bill, which was opposed by most of the ex-ministers, is included since on this occasion the Protectionists voted with the Government; 18 Peelites voted against the Bill.
69   Graham, Cardwell, F. Peel, Fitzroy, and Oswald, to judge from the evidence in the Gladstone Papers.

Chapter 5  THE ELECTION OF 1852 AND ITS SEQUEL (pages 111–48)

1  Commenting on the inordinate length of the election *The Times* (8 July 1852) predicted that in 1952 all the voting would take place on the same day and that the results would be announced on the following day.

2  Cf Norman Gash, *Politics in the Age of Peel* (London 1953), chapters 5, 6 and 7.

3  *The Times*, 23 July 1852.

4  *The Times*, 5 July 1852.

5  Add MS 43247, fols 253–5, 14 May 1852.

6  Ibid, fols 268–73, 30 June and 2 July 1852.

7  Add MS 44262, fols 114–15, 15 July 1852.

8  Add MS 44208, fols 25–8, 24 August 1852.

9  See PRO 30/48/8/48, fols 28–9, 9 July 1852, Aberdeen to Cardwell.

10  See Morley, *Gladstone*, I, 426–7, for a vivid account of this election.

11  Add MS 44088, fols 131–2, 16 July 1852. Graham also sent his congratulations with the observation that the Warden of Merton might now 'return to the quiet enjoyment of his Prejudice and Port' (Add MS 44163, fols 62–3, 15 July 1852).

12  Add MS 44208, fols 21–4, 27 July 1852. Sir R. Inglis, of course, was the old High Tory senior member for Oxford.

13  Walpole, *Russell*, II, 154–5.

14  *Letters of Queen Victoria*, II, 501.

15  PRO 30/22/10C, fols 836–7, undated and without signature; it is presumably later than an analysis by Parkes probably enclosed in his letter of 24 July which lists 48 Ministerial and 46 Opposition gains (fol 838).

16  Ibid, fol 910.

17  Add MS 44110, fols 230–1, 29 July 1852.

18  Add MS 44237, fols 209–10, 4 August 1852.

19  Add MS 43196, fols 253–6, 27 August 1852.

20  PRO 30/22/10C, fols 958–9, Wood to Russell, 27 July 1852. Hayter was the Liberal whip.

21  *Letters of Queen Victoria*, II, 501, memo of Prince Albert, 18 December 1852.

22  PRO 30/22/10C, fols 942–3.

23  Ibid, fols 958–9, 27 July 1852.

24  *Greville Memoirs*, VI, 346.

25  PRO 30/22/10D, fols 1036–9, 8 August 1852.

26  *Aberdeen Correspondence* (1850–60), 307–10.

27  Graham Papers, 17 July 1852 (copy).

28  Ibid, 26 July 1852.

29  See the *Spectator*, 24 and 31 July 1852. Following the *Globe*, it listed at least 36 Conservative Free Traders of liberal leanings, who,

if subtracted from the non-ministerialists, would leave the Government with a majority of 2 and who, if added to the ministerialists, would give it a majority of 38. Many of the names in the list of 36 doubtfuls recur, of course, in Peelite lists.

30   *The Economist*, 24 and 31 July 1852.

31   Edward Cardwell, Thomas Greene, and Lord Norreys were defeated and Roundell Palmer was forced to withdraw, but all four were subsequently returned. Sir G. Clerk, the Marquis of Douro, J. Heald, W. A. Mackinnon, C. W. Martin, A. Oswald, P. Pusey, G. A. Smythe, and F. J. Tollemache were defeated and remained out of Parliament. John Boyd, Sir C. Douglas, and J. B. B. Estcourt did not stand for re-election. See Appendix A.

32   These were C. H. A'Court (a brother-in-law of Sidney Herbert), H. A. Bruce, Lord R. Clinton (a brother of the Duke of Newcastle), G. F. Heneage, Robert Lowe, Lord Monck, G. E. H. Vernon (a former secretary of the Duke of Newcastle), H. A. Wickam, and R. J. Phillimore (a close friend of Gladstone), who was returned on petition in February. Lowe and Monck are listed as Liberals by Dod, but seem to have been regarded by Bonham and Young as Peelite without question. Indeed, Lowe gained his seat through the influence of the Peelite Lord Ward. Johnstone and Tomline proved uncertain. See Appendix A and also Appendix B.

33   See Appendices A and B. One former Derbyite, H. Herbert, also turned Peelite in this Parliament.

34   Add MS 44110, fols 226–7, 21 July 1852. He suggested that Bonham might subdivide the Liberals into: '(a) Whigs (b) Radicals (c) Roman Catholics; and these last into Brigade and non-Brigade men'; the ministerialists into: '(a) the Protectionist rump, and any stray rogues (b) men of sense'; and finally the Liberal Conservatives into: '(a) known Peelites (b) doubtful or unplaced men'.

35   See Gash, *Politics in the Age of Peel*, 413–18.

36   Add MS 44110, fols 230–1 [29 July 1852]. His Irish Peelites were Sir E. Hayes, H. Corry and himself.

37   Ibid, fols 232–3, 30 July 1852. There is no copy of the list to which he refers in the Gladstone papers and I have worked out the numbers from Bonham's reply. H. Herbert, whom Bonham listed as inclined to Derby, and who had so voted in the previous parliament, proved to be a firm Peelite in this one.

38   Sir H. Willoughby, G. Harcourt, Sir E. Dering, W. Beckett, C. R. Colville, and James Johnstone. Actually only Harcourt proved to be a firm Peelite, but Johnstone gave the Aberdeen coalition frequent support, and Beckett and Colville gave it some independent support.

39   Add MS 44110, fols 234–5, 31 July 1852. The three were W. Fitzgerald, John Walter, and W. Cubitt, but of these only Walter proved to be a dependable Peelite, as he had done in the previous parliament, to judge from his voting record. The same was true of

Wortley, but Jocelyn continued to vote consistently with the Derbyites, although often referred to as a Peelite, perhaps because he had social connections with some of them.

40 Add MS 44237, fols 209–10, 4 August 1852. Young included among the doubtfuls W. T. Egerton, A. Smollett, Lord Jocelyn, W. Beckett, and E. Denison, and gave to the Government H. Stuart, J. Masterman, R. Clive, J. Benbow, W. Stirling, J. Cocks, J. Baird, S. Christy, F. Baring, and G. Sanders, all Free Traders; but among the 34 he included Sir R. Ferguson, E. M. Mostyn, Sir J. Hanmer, and R. M. Milnes. Ferguson and Milnes should probably have been classified as Liberals, but he should have included Denison and F. Baring as Peelites.

41 [G. H. W.] Heneage, [Sir H.] Willoughby, [W.] Fitzgerald, [Sir E.] Dering, [Lord] Jocelyn, W. Beckett, Colonel Lindsay, [Lord] Emlyn, A. Lockhart, and H. Corry. In fact Lockhart (and G. F. Heneage) proved to be firm Peelites, while Emlyn, Fitzgerald, W. Beckett, and G. H. W. Heneage gave the Aberdeen coalition some independent support.

42 [W.] Cubitt, H. Stuart, [Sir J.] Hogg, G. Harcourt, Sir R. Peel, [E.] B. Denison, W. B. Hughes, [A.] Smollett, and [Sir E.] Hayes. Hogg, Denison, Harcourt, and, to a lesser extent, Sir R. Peel proved to be dependable Peelites, while Cubitt, Hughes, and Smollett gave the coalition some independent support.

43 Ibid, fols 211–15, 10 August 1852.

44 Add MS 44110, fols 238–9, 5 September 1852. He regretfully admitted that W. Patten and H. Corry must now be classified as Derbyite.

45 Ibid, fols 236–7, 3 September 1852.

46 Add MS 44237, fols 216–19, Young to Gladstone, 21 September 1852.

47 Newcastle Papers, 20 August 1852.

48 Add MS 44110, fols 246–7, 17 October 1852. The names were: Lord A. Hervey, Lord Jermyn, Sir J. Hogg, [R.] Lowe, [H.] Fitzroy, Lord E. Bruce, H. Baring, J. Sutton, [G.] Vernon, Lord R. Clinton, W. Gladstone, Lord Monck, Sir J. Johnstone, [G.] Tomline, Sir R. Peel, F. Peel, [H.] A'Court, S. Herbert, [W.] Wyndham, F. Charteris, Sir J. Young, H. Corry, [T. S.] Cocks. He did not include Peelites whom he considered to have joined the Liberals, such as Graham. Indeed the names of Graham, Cardwell, and F. Peel are to be found in a list of Whig election returns in the Russell Papers (PRO 30/22/10C, fol 839). In fact Cocks, Corry and Tomline proved to be unreliable. Another list (Add MS 44740, fol 184, nd), entitled by Gladstone in 1877 '1852 Memorandum Names (Political)', was later drawn up, probably by Young with some additions by Gladstone on the eve of the Government's defeat. It drops the names of R. and F. Peel, Cox and Wyndham, but adds those of E. Denison, Lord Drumlanrig, H. Goulburn, H. Herbert,

G. C. Legh, Sir T. F. Lewis, A. E. Lockhart, Colonel Peel, G. E. H. Vernon, J. Walter, J. S. Wortley, and, under a line, E. Cardwell (for whom a seat was found at Oxford), Sir J. Graham, G. G. Harcourt, R. M. Milnes, Lord Norreys (who had found a seat) and Lord Jocelyn (in whom Gladstone continued to have false hopes).

49  *Aberdeen Correspondence* (1850–60), 310–12, 30 July 1852.
50  Add MS 44237, fols 205–6, 24 July 1852.
51  Ibid, fols 216–19, 21 September 1852.
52  Ibid, fols 246–7, 17 October 1852.
53  *Aberdeen Correspondence* (1850–60), 310–12, 30 July 1852.
54  Add MS 44088, fols 138–9, 3 August 1852.
55  Add MS 43196, fols 253–6, 27 August 1852.
56  Ibid, fols 257–8 (copy), 2 September 1852.
57  PRO 30/33/10C, fols 879–84, 17 July 1852.
58  See especially Graham to Russell, 27 June 1852 (PRO 30/22/10C, fols 832–3), printed by Walpole, *Russell*, II, 154.
59  Graham Papers, 17 July 1852. Graham's daughter, Helen Baring, made a marginal note requiring the omission of a passage mentioning the abuse of royal influence in the election. Cf Parker, *Graham*, II, 165–6.
60  Graham Papers, 19 July 1852.
61  The break between Graham and Gladstone, however, was narrowed by an amicable exchange of letters over the election results. (See *Greville Memoirs*, VI, 352, and Add MS 44163, fols 62–3, 15 July 1852.)
62  PRO 30/22/10C, fols 927–9, 22 July 1852. Parker (*Graham*, II, 167–8) has deleted several passages including the last two pages of the letter on the instruction of Mrs Baring. They contain uncomplimentary references to Disraeli, the Conjuror, who is to be treated with slow poison. The exchange with Roebuck is printed by Parker, ibid, pp 161–4. Graham did not repeat Roebuck's words: 'to you I look to be the leader of the Liberal party in the coming Parliament. Lord John will never again unite us, take my word for this'. See also p 146.
63  PRO 30/22/10D, fols 1036–40, 8 August 1852
64  PRO 30/22/10C, fols 913–18, 19 July 1852. Later Clarendon had reported to Russell a conversation with Sidney Herbert who told him 'that the whole fury of the Govt. had been directed agst. the Peelites and the gulph that separates them seems now not to be *bridgeable-over*' (PRO 30/22/10C, fols 850–2, 31 July 1852).
65  Add MS 43066, fols 87–90, 21 July 1852; Walpole, *Russell*, II, 155–6.
66  PRO 30/22/10C, fol 938, 23 July 1852.
67  Graham Papers, 23 July 1852, reproduced with omissions by Parker, *Graham*, II, 168.
68  Graham Papers, to Russell, 26 July 1852 (copy).
69  Ibid, 24 July 1852 (copy).

70  Ibid, 28 July 1852.
71  Add MS 43197, fols 7–9 (copy), 25 July 1852.
72  Add MS 43190, fols 295–8, 31 July 1852. Only a few sentences are reproduced by Parker, *Graham*, II, 169–70.
73  Add MS 43197, fols 11–18, 2 August 1852.
74  Add MS 43197, fols 19–22, 3 August 1852. In a separate note (fol 23) he said he had no objection to Aberdeen showing his letters to Russell, since somebody had to say what was disagreeable to him.
75  *Aberdeen Correspondence* (1850–60), 322–5, 5 August 1852.
76  Add MS 44210, fols 49–52, 11 August 1852.
77  PRO 30/22/10D, fols 1034–5, 8 August 1852. This important letter is ignored by Walpole, Gooch and Lord Stanmore.
78  *Aberdeen Correspondence* (1850–60), 307–10.
79  Add MS 43190, fols 299–307, 5 and 6 August 1852, and Parker, *Graham*, II, 172.
80  Add MS 43066, fols 93–5, 11 August 1852. The correspondence was also shown to Wood and Lord Grey and its substance revealed to Lord Clarendon.
81  Ibid, fols 99–104, 13 August 1852 (partly reproduced in Walpole, *Russell*, II, 156–7).
82  PRO 30/22/10D, fols 1163–4, 28 August 1852; copy in Add MS 43066, fols 107–8, dated 16 August. Sentence in square brackets not in the letter as sent to Russell. The last paragraph is reproduced by Walpole, *Russell*, II, 157.
83  Add MS 43066, fols 109–14, 21 August 1852.
84  Add MS 43066, fols 115–16, 23 August 1852.
85  Add MS 43066, fol 117, 14 September 1852.
86  PRO 30/22/10E, fols 1221–2, 16 September 1852. The two paragraphs about Newcastle and the term 'Whig' are printed by Walpole, *Russell*, II, 157, note 1.
87  Add MS 43066, fols 118–20, 18 September 1852.
88  Add MS 43190, fols 339–42, 19 September 1852. Graham's lament may be contrasted with Bright's sardonic comment to Cobden: 'The old Duke is gone, & I hope the old policy & notions, & principles will be buried with him, or at least some of them. . . . The people owe him little. His sentiments were never liberal—he gave them nothing he could retain—he treated them generally with something like contempt—he served the aristocracy, & they only should be his mourners.' (Add MS 43383, fols 251–4, 15 October 1852.)
89  PRO 30/22/10D, fols 1063–70, 11 August 1852. Among the offices vacated by the Duke's death was the Chancellorship of Oxford University. For the candidacy of the Duke of Newcastle, who ultimately withdrew when challenged by Lord Derby as the choice of the Hebdomadal Board, see his correspondence with Gladstone and Bonham in the Newcastle papers; also Add MSS 43190, fol 350, Graham to Aberdeen, 29 September; 43197, fols 135–8, Newcastle

to Aberdeen, 21 September; 44262, fols 116–18, 135–8, Newcastle to Gladstone, 1 August and 19 September 1852.

90  PRO 30/22/10C and D, fols 973–8, 29 July 1852, 1050–3, 10 August.

91  PRO 30/22/10D, fols 1084–91, 13 August 1852. This suggestion of Peelite influence with the Irish Brigade is probably exaggerated, but the Peelites, of course, were well thought of by the Irish because of their opposition to the Ecclesiastical Titles Bill. Newcastle had some contact with Keogh, and Graham's friend, Brewster, had some connection with the Brigade.

92  PRO 30/22/10C, fols 962–3, 28 July 1852.

93  Ibid, 10E, fol 1225, 17 September 1852.

94  Ibid, fols 1184–7, copy of a letter to Bedford, 2 September 1852.

95  Ibid, fols 1246–7, 20 September 1852.

96  PRO 30–22–10D, fols 1168–74, 31 August 1852.

97  Add MS 43757, fols 55–60, 27 and 28 October 1852, describing a meeting of Whig magnates at Bowood. According to Broughton, 'Clarendon talked as if Lansdowne might be premier', saying that Russell 'lived in a fool's paradise & would not listen to any but women who agreed with him—chiefly the *wife*,' whose influence Clarendon deplored (fol 59). According to Graham, Clarendon's personal preference was for Russell, but his fear of an 'efficient Reform Bill' almost disposed him to favour Lansdowne (Parker, *Graham*, II, 173). This helps to explain the apparent conflict in the various expressions of Clarendon's views.

98  Ashley, *Palmerston*, II, 253–4.

99  Broadlands MSS, GC/LA/74/1–2, 9 October 1852.

100  Ibid, GC/LA/75, 22 October 1852.

101  Ibid, 24 October 1852 (copy). The personal reconciliation had begun in September when Russell had written to inquire after the health of Lady Palmerston who had been ill. In his reply Palmerston wrote in his good-humoured way: 'What are you doing, I hope you use your gun as well as your pen.' (PRO 30/22/10E, fols 1188–9, 3 September 1852).

102  Lord Edward Fitzmaurice, *The Life of Earl Granville, 1815–1891* (London, 1905), I, 79–80. There was undoubtedly some truth in this rather tactless statement, but ironically it was the older generation that was mainly responsible for bringing the two parties together. Indeed Granville was the only front-bench Whig under 50!

103  Add MS 43383, fols 239–44, 26 August 1852; partly reproduced in Trevelyan, *Bright*, 203.

104  Add MS 43649, fols 269–74; 30 August 1852. In a later letter, marred by anti-Semitic overtones, Cobden changed his emphasis: 'The funds keep too low to allow of any operation by the Jew in that direction. I think he will find it difficult to get into the quart bottle. You have more toleration than I pretend to for this condottiere of

the oligarchy. In my opinion there is nothing in France or Austria more contemptible than the political conduct of the circumcised scion of a proscribed and downtrodden race binding himself body & soul to the bigots in religion, exclusion in politics, & illiberals in everything, who would if they could perpetuate amongst us the institutions of the middle ages, and send the Jews again upon a continental pilgrimage. He is a self elected galley slave to the aristocracy—rowing one way and looking another. Don't suppose that I want to keep him in office. In my opinion it is a political scandal that he is leading the British House of Commons, & the only consolation I have is that it is a flagrant proof that the old system of government in the country is worn out, and that the men who worked it are used up. But I am still of the opinion that in opposing the present government we must avoid committing ourselves to a Whig restoration.' Ibid, fols 279–82, 9 September 1852.)

105 Add MS 43197, fols 33–4, 27 August 1852.

106 Ibid, fols 35–6 (copy), 31 August 1852. The last sentence is printed in Stanmore, *Aberdeen*, 210.

107 Ibid, fols 37–8, 4 September 1852.

108 Add MS 43070, fols 262–3, 17 August 1852. Earlier Newcastle had reminded Gladstone that he had received more support at Oxford from Liberals from all parts who had 'plumped' for him, than from the official men in the Government, 'who had made a parade of early votes' against him (Add MS 44262, fols 121–2, 10 August 1852).

109 Graham Papers, 28 August 1852.

110 Ibid, 10 September 1852.

111 Add MS 43190, fols 331–6, 12 September 1852. A few sentences from an earlier part of the letter are printed in Stanmore, *Aberdeen*, 211.

112 Add MS 43190, fols 337–8, 15 September 1852.

113 Add MS 43070 [Hawarden], fols 264–5, 6 September 1852.

114 Ibid, 22 September 1852; the railway passage is quoted in Parker, Graham, II, 178.

115 PRO 30/22/10E, fols 1276–9, 24 September 1852.

116 Graham Papers, 27 September 1852, partly reproduced in Parker, *Graham*, II, 179–80.

117 Add MS 43190, fols 347–51, 29 September 1852 (partly printed in Parker, *Graham*, II, 180–1).

118 Graham Papers, 8 October 1852 (corrected to '7' by 'H.B.'). Parker omits the latter part of this letter. In a further letter on the 12th Aberdeen admitted that Graham's separation from the other Peelites was 'now complete', but he did not fully abandon 'the hope of seeing a reunion' (see Parker, *Graham*, II, 181, 182).

119 Graham Papers, 9 October 1852 (partly reproduced in Parker, *Graham*, II, 181–2).

120 Add MS 43197, fols 101–10, 22 October 1852 (printed in Stanmore,

*Herbert*, I, 162–5). Writing on the same theme to Gladstone, Herbert said: 'Palmerston like all the septuagenarians is in a hurry and being of a sanguine disposition he believes in all those castles in the air which he builds' (Add MS 44210, fols 59–64, 21 October 1852, from Broadlands).

121 Add MS 43190, fols 360–4, Graham to Aberdeen, 22 October 1852.

122 Ibid, fols 365–8, 25 October 1852.

123 Graham Papers, 2 November 1852 (Parker, *Graham*, II, 184).

124 Ibid, 3 November 1852 (Parker, *Graham*, II, 184).

125 To Lady Graham (Parker, *Graham*, II, 185).

126 Graham Papers, from Aberdeen, 24 and 28 October 1852; Lewis to Graham, 30 October 1852.

127 See Walpole, *Russell*, II, 159, note 1.

128 See letters from Lansdowne, Clarendon, Wood, Lewis, Francis Baring, and even Lord Grey, in PRO 30/22/10E, October 1852.

129 PRO 30/22/10E, fols 1353–4, 4 October 1852.

130 Add MS 43383, fols 251–4, 15 October 1852; Add MS 43649, fols 283–8, 16 October.

131 PRO 30/22/10E, fol 1433, press clipping 10 October 1852.

132 Add MS 43383, fols 255–6, 19 October 1852.

133 Add MS 43649, fols 283–8, 16 October 1852.

134 Graham Papers, 20 July 1852 (in part in Parker, *Graham*, II 161–3)

135 For example Add MS 43649, fols 283–8, Cobden to Bright, 16 October 1852.

136 S. Maccoby, *English Radicalism, 1832–1852* (London 1935), 435.

137 Ibid, 436.

138 Ibid, 436, quoting *North British Review*, May 1852, 'Prospects of British Statesmanship'.

139 On reading these remarks about Radical disunity Mr J. L. Sturgis, who is engaged upon a study of the Radicals during this period, has pointed out to me that they tended to reflect the situation in the popular constituencies, where members had to be particularly sensitive to public opinion often varying from one part of the country to another. The result was a variety of compromises between the official Whig position and an independent line, but 'they did not all move in the same direction at the same time'. He argues that 'basically the Radicals were divided because they did not place a high priority on unity'; their tactic was to force issues on existing parties by rousing public opinion. They were primarily interested in getting certain things done and were ready to follow different leaders on different issues. In his opinion, however, the main body of the Liberals was more loyal to the Whigs than is generally supposed (a view substantiated by Dr J. R. Bylsma in his University of Iowa doctoral thesis, 'Political Issues and Party Unity in the House of Commons, 1852–1857') and the most independent-minded Liberals rarely numbered more than forty.

140  *The Times*, 3 November 1852, 'by Special Engine', with additional comment on 4 November.

Chapter 6  THE FALL OF THE DERBY MINISTRY (pages 149–70)

1  Parker, *Graham*, II, 176. Of Gladstone's supposed strategy Russell commented tartly '. . . to ask our help to beat the Ministry, then join the Ministry to beat us savours of a morality more Tractarian than Christian' (Graham Papers, 2 November 1852).

2  Add MS 44778, fols 54–9, Memo 91, 'Autumn Session 52'.

3  *Aberdeen Correspondence* (1850–60), 397–9, but missing from Aberdeen and Graham papers.

4  Add MS 43190, fols 371–3, 5 November 1852.

5  PRO 30/22/10F, fols 1453–4, 9 November 1852.

6  Ibid, fols 1455–6, 10 November 1852.

7  Add MS 44778, fols 56–8, Memo 91.

8  Add MS 43066, fols 123–4, 10 November 1852; fols 125–6, 11 November.

9  See Monypenny and Buckle, *Disraeli*, I, 1208–11; Blake, *Disraeli*, 335; Add MS 43757, Broughton Diary, fols 70–1. Graham touched on the subject in his sardonic vein when he wrote to Russell:
   'His voice seems to say,
   I have done my best
   I am weary; let me rest',
and Lord Derby appears to hope that there is a Charm even in the Ashes of the Duke, which while above may seem to prolong the existence of a Minister.' He commended Harding's appointment to succeed Wellington, however, and expressed relief at Prince Albert's decision to press no claims. (PRO 30/22/10E, fols 1276–9, 24 September 1852.)

10  *Hansard*, CXXIII, 17–21.

11  Ibid, CXXIII, 472–83.

12  His wording precluded compensation for future but not for retrospective claims. In the Gladstone Papers, Add MS 44740, fols 167–70, there is a copy of what is called the Graham-Russell resolution 'agreed to by us'.

13  *Hansard*, CXXIII, 266–73, 302–5; ironically Hume himself was unable to attend on the day for which the call was scheduled and it was Walmsley, another Radical, who, as his agent, was persuaded to drop the call.

14  Ibid, 351.

15  *Hansard*, CXXII, 399.

16  Ibid, 411–12.

17  Ibid, 412–36.

18  *Annual Register 1852*, 141.

19  *Hansard*, CXXIII, 458.

20  Add MS 44237, fols 220–1, 18 November 1852.

O

21  Add MS 44163, fols 64–5, 19 November 1852.
22  Graham Papers, 20 November 1852; on the same day Aberdeen wrote to Graham on very similar lines (Add MS 43190, fols 374–5).
23  Add MS 44271, fols 9–10, Palmerston to Gladstone and Gladstone to Palmerston, 21 November 1852; Add MS 44778, fols 76–83, Memo 95 of 29 November 1876; Graham Papers, from Russell, 24 November 1852; *Hansard*, CXXIII, 458, 471, 610; see also Jones, *Derby*, 174. It may be noted that Palmerston left out one phrase of Graham's barring compensation for any alleged *future* damage, which Graham insisted on having reinserted when the motion came before the House of Commons.
24  This is puzzling since, as we have seen, Jocelyn normally voted with the Derbyites and continued to do so; but he obviously maintained his Peelite connections.
25  *Letters of Queen Victoria*, II, 488–9, Derby to the Queen, 25 November 1852. It is not clear whether the Peelite leaders attended this meeting, although Derby appears to presume it.
26  *Hansard*, CXXIII, 498–507.
27  Graham Papers, Aberdeen to Graham, Wed (24 November); but Buckle, printing Palmerston's letter, says that Disraeli encouraged him to proceed (*Disraeli*, I, 1227–8).
28  *Hansard*, CXXIII, 451–61, 531.
29  PRO/30/22/10F, fols 1470–1, Graham to Russell, 24 November 1852; *Hansard*, CXXIII, 507–13 (24 November).
30  *Hansard*, CXXIII, 687–94.
31  Ibid, 471–83.
32  Ibid, 498–507.
33  Ibid, 491–3, 496–8; *Annual Register 1852*, 146.
34  *Hansard*, CXXIII, 484–8 (24 November).
35  Ibid, 602–14.
36  Ibid, 613.
37  Ibid, 507–13.
38  Ibid, 513–17, 521–5, 666–76.
39  Ibid, 680–5.
40  Ibid, 696–704. R. Lowe, Lord Monck, E. M. L. Mostyn, Frederick Peel, G. Tomline, and J. Walter supported Villiers.
41  *Greville Memoirs*, VII, 12.
42  *Greville Memoirs*, VI, 374–5.
43  *Hansard*, CXXIII, 772–5; 816–21; 922–69 (30 November, 2 and 6 December 1852).
44  Graham Papers, 29 November 1852 (copy).
45  Monypenny and Buckle, *Disraeli*, II, 1238–9.
46  Ibid, 1239–40.
47  He was not a Peelite in this parliament, although he had acted with them in the previous one.
48  *Letters of Queen Victoria*, II, 491–2, Memo by Prince Albert, 28 November 1852. 'We could quite understand', the Prince added,

'that the colleagues of Sir Robert Peel could not feel inclined to serve under Mr. Disraeli.'

49  Add MS 44778, fols 48–53, Memo 90, 27 November 1852; Morley, *Gladstone*, I, 434–5.
50  See *Hansard*, CXXIII, 836–911; Monypenny and Buckle, *Disraeli*, I, 1242–53; Morley, *Gladstone*, I, 435–42; and especially Robert Blake's excellent chapter in his *Disraeli*, 328–48.
51  *Hansard*, CXXIII, 1245.
52  For the debate see *Hansard*, CXXIII, and the *Annual Register 1852*.
53  See the long quotation from Bright's Diary in Trevelyan, *Bright*, 205–7.
54  Monypenny and Buckle, *Disraeli*, I, 1253–4.
55  Ibid, 1253.
56  Buckle, quoting a report in *The Tablet and Telegraph*, 25 December 1852, *Disraeli*, I, 1258.
57  'Disraeli made last night, I think on the whole his greatest speech,' Gladstone told Aberdeen the following day. 'Some parts of it I think could hardly have been surpassed. On the other hand one portion of it I can call nothing but *beastly*.' Add MS 43070, fols 273–4, 17 December 1852.
58  Monypenny and Buckle, *Disraeli*, I, 1262–3; *Hansard*, CXXIII, 1629–66.
59  Add MS 43070, fols 273–4, 17 December 1852.
60  Morley, *Gladstone*, I, 438.
61  Buckle's charge of impropriety is questionable. On 14 December, Gladstone had written to his wife: 'It has been arranged that I am not to speak until the close of the debate' (Morley, *Gladstone*, I, 437). It seems likely that Disraeli chose to speak when he did, even though Gladstone had not yet spoken, because of the lateness of the hour and the state of his health.
62  *Disraeli*, I, 1263. Greville says that defeat was not anticipated at this stage, but that Disraeli expected it when Derby alienated the Irish Brigade (*Memoirs*, VI, 377, 394–5).
63  Morley, *Gladstone*, I, 438.
64  Ibid, 438–40. Morley devotes three pages, largely quoting from Gladstone's letters to his wife and the *Times* correspondent's account of the debate, but he does not spare one sentence to the substance of Gladstone's case. The speech has been reprinted in A. Tilney Bassett, *Gladstone's Speeches* (London 1916), 155–81, and makes interesting reading even today. Cf *Hansard*, CXXIII, 1666–93.
65  Morley, *Gladstone*, I, 440.
66  Bassett, *Gladstone's Speeches*, 178–81.
67  Add MS 43070, fols 273–4, 17 December 1852.
68  *Hansard*, CXXIII, 1693–7; *Divisions 1852–3*, 21–4. According to a marked division list in the Royal Archives (RA C28, fol 2), there were 14 pairs.

69    Gladstone MSS (St Deniols, Hawarden), 18 December 1852.
70    H. B. Baring, F. Charteris, E. Denison, H. Fitzroy, W. E. Glad-
      stone, H. Goulburn, Sir J. Graham, Sir J. Hanmer, G. G. Har-
      court, S. Herbert, Lord A. Hervey, Sir J. Hogg, Lord Jermyn, Sir
      J. Johnstone, Sir T. F. Lewis, A. E. Lockhart, E. M. Mostyn, Lord
      Norreys (just returned at a by-election), F. Peel, J. H. M. Sutton,
      C. B. Wall, J. Walter, J. S. Wortley, and Sir J. Young. (Cf above,
      p 118). Gladstone may not have included Graham and Peel and
      perhaps others such as Hanmer and Mostyn if they were sitting
      with the Liberals.
71    Lord E. Bruce, Lord Drumlanrig, G. C. Legh, W. Mure and
      Colonel J. Peel. All but Colonel Peel gave consistent support to the
      Coalition after it was formed.
72    C. A.'Court, H. A. Bruce, Lord R. Clinton, G. F. Heneage, James
      Johnstone, R. Lowe, Lord Monck, G. Tomline, G. E. H. Vernon
      and H. W. Wickham. All but Johnstone and Tomline gave the
      coalition consistent support, and Johnstone frequently did.
73    Henry Herbert thereafter voted with the Peelites in support of the
      coalition, but Vyvyan, the other Derbyite did not.
74    Sir John Owen, who thereafter gave support to the coalition, G. H.
      Heneage, who frequently supported it, and Lord Wellesley, who
      rarely did.
75    F. Baring and Sir R. Peel, on our uncertain list in the previous
      Parliament, but regular supporters of the coalition after it was
      formed.
76    E. Cardwell, T. Greene, Roundell Palmer, all Peelites in the pre-
      vious parliament, and R. J. Phillimore a new Peelite, whose arrival
      was delayed by an election petition.
77    Cf *Aberdeen Coalition*, Appendix A, where I excluded Owen be-
      cause of his budget vote, but included R. M. Milnes on Bonham's
      evidence, although I now recognise him as a Liberal. It may be
      noted that only 24 of the 41 Conservatives who voted against
      Disraeli's budget were survivors of Peel's band of supporters in
      1846.
78    See Whyte, *Independent Irish Party*, 94–6; Buckle (*Disraeli*, I,
      1217–18) rather plays the story down. See also *Greville Memoirs*,
      VI, 394–5.
79    *Hansard*, CXXIII, 1693–7. The Irish Independent Liberals may be
      identified in Whyte, *Independent Irish Party*, Appendix B, 180–1.
80    *Hansard*, CXXIII, 1698–1705. Derby was strongly criticised by
      *The Times* (21 December 1852) for the speech and even admonished
      by the Queen (*Letters of Queen Victoria*, II, 507).
81    *Hansard*, CXXIII, 1705–9.
82    *Hansard*, CXXIII, 1709–10. According to Russell this round of
      apologies resulted from a suggestion he made to Disraeli (Mony-
      penny and Buckle, *Disraeli*, I, 1265).
83    Ibid, 1710, 1711.

84  Ibid, 1711–12.
85  Ibid, 1711.
86  Ibid, 1712–13.
87  Ibid, 1713–15. Gladstone did not participate in the plethora of apologies, presumably because he did not feel that he had anything to apologise for.

## CONCLUSION (pages 171–9)

1   See my *Aberdeen Coalition 1852–1855*.
2   Aberdeen, Argyll, Graham, Gladstone, Herbert, and Newcastle became cabinet ministers; Cardwell, Canning, St Germans, and Young received ministerial appointments outside the cabinet; Charteris, Fitzroy, Hervey, Lowe, and F. Peel were given junior offices, and Lords Drumlanrig and E. Bruce minor household appointments.
3   Francis Baring and Sir R. Peel.
4   E. Cardwell, T. Greene, Roundell Palmer, and P. J. Phillimore. Lord Norreys had been returned in December.
5   Sir T. D. Acland, J. Benbow, Sir C. Coote, Sir W. Heathcote, G. H. W. Heneage, W. B. Hughes, James Johnstone, Sir J. Owen, J. W. Patten, W. Stirling, and W. Wyndham. In my *Aberdeen Coalition*, Appendix B, I identified these as independent Conservatives because of their initial support for the Derby government. In the thirteen divisions that I then analysed for the lifetime of the coalition these eleven gave at least three-quarters of their votes in its support. One of them (Owen) we identified as a Peelite in the previous parliament (Appendix A), four others (Acland, Heneage, Hughes, and Patten) were on our uncertain list, and one (Benbow) we had considered to be a Derbyite. The other names are new, but several of them (James Johnstone, Stirling, and Wyndham) had been discussed in Gladstone's post-election correspondence with Bonham and Young.
6   See my *Aberdeen Coalition*, Appendix B.
7   Add MS 44778, fols 76–83, Memo 95, dated 'Nov.29.76'.
8   Add MS 44208, fols 33–6, 28 December 1852 (copy): '. . . by financial dishonesty in a Minister', he explained, 'I mean such things as these: relieving the present at the expense of the future; promising what he cannot perform; inviting the people to spend what they have not got. . . .'
9   Fifteen years later in a public speech in Scotland Gladstone alluded in a characteristically involved way to the slowness of his conversion to Liberalism. 'Conviction, gentlemen,' he said, 'has placed me—in spite of early association and long cherished prepossessions, very strong conviction and an overpowering sense of the public interest, operating for many years before full effect was given to it—has placed me in the ranks of the Liberal party.' (I am indebted to Miss

Susan Brown for showing me this quotation from *The Times*, 20 December 1867.) This may have had something of a political ring to it, coming from the man who had just become leader of the Liberal party, but it is substantially borne out by Gladstone's course in these years.

10  Add MS 44208, fol 37, 30 December 1852. A year later, on the retirement of Sir Robert Inglis, Heathcote became Gladstone's fellow member for the university and, although a Conservative, gave independent support to the coalition.

11  Selborne MSS, No 1862, fols 28–9, nd. On the day of Gladstone's speech the writer of this letter met Mrs Gladstone, who said to him: 'You know Mr Cloughton, dear William would do anything to support Lord Derby,' a remark, he confessed, that left him speechless!

# Bibliography

Sources and secondary works cited in the references

MANUSCRIPT SOURCES

Aberdeen Papers, British Museum, Add MSS 43039–43358
Bright Papers, British Museum, Correspondence with Cobden, Add MS 43649
Private diaries, 1842–63, of Sir John Cam Hobhouse, first Baron Broughton, British Museum, Add MSS 43744–43765
Cobden Papers, British Museum, Correspondence with Bright, Add MS 43383
Cardwell Papers, Public Record Office, PRO 30/48/8/47–50
Ellenborough Papers, Public Record Office, PRO 30/12/21
Gladstone Papers, British Museum, Add MSS 44086–44835
Goulburn Papers, Surrey Record Office
Graham Papers, Netherby Manor, Longtown, Cumberland; microfilmed copies read at University Library, Cambridge, and Newberry Library, Chicago
Herbert Papers, Wilton House Archives, Wilton, Wiltshire
Newcastle Papers (fifth duke), University of Nottingham Library, Nottingham (used before they were catalogued)
Broadlands MS (Palmerston Papers), Register of National Archives, London
Peel Papers, British Museum, Add MSS 40441–40617 (including some Bonham Papers)
Russell Papers, Public Record Office, PRO 30/22/5–10F
Selborne Papers, Lambeth Palace

PRINTED SOURCES

*Aberdeen Correspondence*, privately printed by Lord Stanmore, State Paper Room, British Museum (subsequently catalogued); there are nine volumes for the years 1846–62, with varying titles or no titles, mostly undated except for one dated Colombo, 1885; they contain a full and accurate selection of all the major correspondence, excluding routine letters re engagements, etc (*Ab Cor*)

*The Annual Register*, 1846–52 (annual volumes)

*Hansard's Parliamentary Debates*, 3rd series, vols LXXXVIII (June 1846) to CXXIII (December 1852)

*Divisions in Session of 1846 House of Commons Division Lobby.* Ibid for 1847, 1847–8, 1849, 1850, 1851, 1852–3

*The Economist*, 1846–52

*The Morning Chronicle*, 1848–52

*The Spectator*, 1846–52

*The Times*, 1847–52

BIOGRAPHIES, LETTERS, MEMOIRS, ETC

*The earl of Aberdeen.* By Sir Arthur Gordon (Lord Stanmore). New York, 1893

*George Douglas, eighth duke of Argyll*, autobiography and memoirs, edited by the dowager duchess of Argyll. 2 vols. London, 1906

*Lord George Bentinck, a political biography.* By Benjamin Disraeli. Rev ed. London, 1852

*The life of John Bright.* By George Macaulay Trevelyan. London, 1913

*Lives of Lord Lyndhurst and Lord Brougham.* By Lord Campbell. London, 1869

*The Croker Papers.* Ed by L. J. Jennings. 3 vols. London, 1884

*Lord Derby and Victorian Conservatism.* By Wilbur Devereux Jones. Oxford, 1956

*The Life of Benjamin Disraeli, earl of Beaconsfield.* By William Flavelle Monypenny and George Earle Buckle. Rev ed. 2 vols. New York, 1929

*Disraeli.* By Robert Blake. London, 1966

*Gladstone's speeches: descriptive index and bibliography.* By Arthur Tilney Bassett. London, 1916

*Correspondence on church and religion of William Ewart Gladstone.* 2 vols. London, 1910

*The life of William Ewart Gladstone.* By John Morley. 3 vols. London and Toronto, 1903

*Life and letters of Sir James Graham, second baronet of Netherby, P.C., G.C.B., 1792–1861.* By Charles Stuart Parker. 2 vols. London, 1907

*The life of Granville George Leveson Gower second earl of Granville K.G., 1815–1891.* By Lord Edmond Fitzmaurice. 2 vols. London, 1905

*The Greville Memoirs.* Ed by Lytton Strachey and Roger Fulford. 7 vols. London, 1938

*Sidney Herbert: Lord Herbert of Lea—a memoir.* By Lord Stanmore. 2 vols. London, 1906

*Letters of the Right Hon Sir George Cornewall Lewis, Bart, to various friends.* By Sir G. F. Lewis. London, 1870

*The life of Henry Pelham fifth duke of Newcastle, 1811–1864.* By John Martineau. London, 1908

*The life and correspondence of Henry John Temple Viscount Palmerston.* By Hon Evelyn Ashley. 2 vols. London, 1879

*Lord Palmerston.* By H. C. F. Bell. London, 1936

*Sir Robert Peel from his private papers,* ed by Charles Stuart Parker. 3 vols. London, 1891–9

*The later correspondence of Lord John Russell 1840–1878,* ed by G. P. Gooch. 2 vols. London, 1925

*The life of Lord John Russell.* By Spencer Walpole. 2 vols. London, 1891

*Letters of Queen Victoria,* ed by A. C. Benson and Viscount Esher. First series, 3 vols. London, 1907

*The life and times of Cardinal Wiseman.* By Wilfrid Ward. 2 vols. London, 1899

MONOGRAPHS, ARTICLES, THESES, REFERENCE WORKS, ETC

Aydelotte, W. O. 'Country gentlemen and the repeal of the Corn Laws', *E.H.R.,* LXXXII (1967), 47–60

—— 'The disintegration of the Conservative party in the eighteen-forties: a study in political attitudes', a mimeographed paper read at the Political Science Association, September 1969

Blake, Robert. *The Conservative party from Peel to Churchill.* London, 1970

Bourne, H. R. Fox. *English Newspapers: Chapters in the history of Journalism.* 2 vols. London, 1887

Conacher, J. B. *The Aberdeen Coalition 1852–1855: a study in mid nineteenth century party politics.* Cambridge, 1968

—— 'Mr. Gladstone seeks a seat', *Canadian Historical Association Report—1962*, 55–67

—— 'Peel and the Peelites, 1846–1850', *E.H.R.*, LXXIII (1958), 431–52

—— 'The politics of the papal aggression crisis, 1850–1851', *Canadian Catholic Historical Association Report 1959*, 13–27

[Croker, J. W.] 'The close of Sir Robert Peel's administration', *Quarterly Review*, LXXVIII (1847)

Dod, C. R. *Electoral Facts 1832–1852.* London, 1853

—— *Parliamentary Companion.* London, 1846–53 (annual volumes)

Dryer, F. 'The Russell Administration, 1846–1852', unpublished doctoral thesis, St Andrew's University, Scotland

Escott, T. H. S. *Masters of English journalism.* London, 1911

Gash, Norman. 'Peel and the party system', *T.R.H.S.*, 5th series, I (1951), 47–69

—— *Politics in the Age of Peel.* London, 1953

Grant, James. *The Newspaper Press: Its origins, progress and present position.* 3 vols. London, 1887

Hobsbawm, E. J. *Industry and Empire.* Penguin ed. London, 1969

Lee, Sir Sidney (ed). *The Dictionary of National Biography.* 64 vols. London, 1920

—— *The Concise Dictionary of National Biography from the beginnings to 1911.* London, 1920

MacCalmont, F. H. *Parliamentary poll book.* London, 1879

Maccoby, S. *English Radicalism, 1832–1852.* London, 1935

Norman, E. R. *Anti-Catholicism in Victorian England.* London, 1968

Southgate, Donald. *The Passing of the Whigs 1832–1886.* London, 1962

Stewart, Robert. 'Lord Derby and the Protectionist Party, 1845–1852', a doctoral dissertation, Bodleian Library, Oxford. Published as *The Politics of Protection* (Cambridge, 1971)

Stuart, C. H. 'The formation of the coalition cabinet of 1852',
  *T.R.H.S.*, 5th series, IV (1954), 45–68
Ward, Bernard. *The sequel to Catholic emancipation.* 2 vols.
  London, 1915
Whyte, H. H. *The Independent Irish party 1850–9.* Oxford, 1958

# Appendix A
## An analysis of the voting of Free Trade Conservatives in the parliament of 1847–52

---

*List of divisions analysed*

### 1847–8

1. Nomination of E. Cardwell to the Committee on Commercial Distress, 15 December (1847), passed 167–101
2. Jewish Disabilities Bill, second reading, 11 February, passed 277–204
3. Income Tax resolutions, Hume amendment, defeated 13 March, 363–138
4. Repeal of the Navigation Acts, second reading, Herries amendment, 9 June, defeated 294–177
5. West Indies Relief Bill, Pakington amendment, 29 June, defeated 260–245

### 1849

1. Motion to adjourn address debate, 2 February, defeated 221–80
2. Disraeli resolution on local taxation, 15 March, defeated 280–189
3. Poor Law (Ireland) Rates Aid Bill, second reading, 3 April, passed 193–138
4. Repeal of the Navigation Acts, third reading, 23 April, passed 275–214 (brackets indicate another reading)
5. Oaths Bill, third reading, 11 June, passed 272–206
6. Supply, Canada, Herries motion, 15 June, defeated 291–150
7. Disraeli motion on state of the nation, 6 July, defeated 296–156

1850
1. Amendment to the address, 1 February, defeated 311–192
2. Disraeli motion on agricultural distress, 21 February, defeated 273–252
3. Hutt motion on the slave trade, 19 March, defeated 232–154
4. Henley motion on official salaries, 30 April, defeated 269–173
5. Irish Franchise Bill, Walsh amendment, 10 May, defeated 254–186
6. Berkley motion for a committee on the importation of corn, 14 May, defeated 101–97
7. Buxton motion on free-grown sugar, 31 May, defeated 232–154
8. Committee on Supply (Ireland), amendment, 21 June, defeated 225–142
9. Roebuck motion of confidence in Government's foreign policy, 28 June, passed 310–264*

1851 and 1852
1. Disraeli motion on agricultural distress, 13 February 1851, defeated 267–81
2. Ecclesiastical Titles Bill, second reading, 25 March, passed 438–95
3. Herries amendment to the Budget resolutions, 7 April, defeated 278–230
4. Disraeli amendment on agricultural distress, 11 April, defeated 263–250
5. Hume amendment on income tax resolution, 2 May, defeated 244–230
6. Disraeli's financial resolutions, 30 June, defeated 242–129
7. Redistribution of Seats Bill, 10 May 1852, defeated 234–148

The votes of those members who were in the previous Parliament on the repeal of the Corn Laws are shown for information but not included in the totals (brackets indicate another reading).

P: Peelite                    D: Derbyite

* The Roebuck Motion is included for information but not in the totals since it was the one occasion on which the Peelites and Derbyites joined forces; supporters marked Y, opponents N.

DIVISIONS

| | 1847-8 | | | | | 1849 | | | | | | |
|---|---|---|---|---|---|---|---|---|---|---|---|---|
| | 1 | 2 | 3 | 4 | 5 | 1 | 2 | 3 | 4 | 5 | 6 | 7 |
| Acland, Sir T. D. | D | P | P | | D | P | D | P | | D | P | P |
| Ashley, Ld (to 1851) | D | P | | | | P | | D | | | | |
| | | | | | | | | | | | | |
| Baillie, H. J. | | | | D | D | D | | | D | D | D | D |
| Baldwin, C. B. | | | | | D | | D | | | | D | |
| Baring, F. (el 1848) | | | | | | | | D | P | P | | |
| Baring, H. B. | P | | P | P | P | | | | | | | |
| Baring, W. B. (to 1848) | | | P | | | | | | | | | |
| Barkly, H. (to 1849) | | | P | P | D | | | | | | | |
| Beckett, W. | | | | | | | | | (D) | | | P |
| Benbow J. | | | D | D | D | | | | | | | |
| Blandford, Marq of | | | | | | | D | | D | D | | D |
| Bolling, W. (d 1848) | | D | P | P | P | | | | | | | |
| Bowles, Adm W. | | D | P | D | D | P | | D | D | D | P | |
| Boyd, J. | P | | | P | P | P | | | | | | |
| Brackley, Ld (to 1851) | | D | P | D | | | | | | D | D | P |
| Bruce, Ld E. | | D | P | | D | | | P | (P) | | | P |
| | | | | | | | | | | | | |
| Cardwell, E. | | P | P | P | D | | P | P | P | P | P | P |
| Charteris, F. W. | | P | P | P | D | P | P | | P | | P | P |
| Chichester, Ld J. | | D | P | D | D | D | D | D | D | D | | D |
| Christy, S. | | D | P | | D | | | D | | D | D | |
| Clerk, Sir G. | P | P | P | P | D | P | P | P | P | P | | P |
| Clive, R. H. | | | | | D | | | D | | D | D | P |
| Cochrane, A. D. R. W. B. | P | D | P | P | D | | | | | | | D |
| Cocks, T. S. | P | D | P | P | D | | | D | D | | D | D |
| Copeland, W. T. | | | | | D | P | | P | | | | |
| Corry, H. T. L. | P | | P | | D | P | | | (P) | D | | P |
| Cripps, W. (d 1848) | | D | P | | | | | | | | | |
| Cubitt, W. | | P | P | D | P | D | | | D | P | | |
| Currie, H. | | | P | P | D | D | | | | | | |
| | | | | | | | | | | | | |
| Damer, G. L. | | | P | | D | | | D | P | | D | |
| Denison, E. B. (el 1848) | | | | | | | | | | | P | P |
| Douglas, Sir C. | | | | P | P | P | P | | P | | P | P |
| Douro, Marq of | | D | P | | P | P | | | | | | P |
| Drumlanrig, Ld | | D | P | | D | | | | (P) | | P | |
| Drummond, H. | P | D | P | | | | | D | P | D | P | |
| Drummond, H. H. | | | P | P | D | | | | | | | P |
| Duncuft, J. | P | D | P | | | P | | | P | D | | P |
| Dundas, G. | P | D | P | D | D | | | | D | D | D | D |
| | | | | | | | | | | | | |
| Edwards, H. | D | D | | D | D | D | | | D | | D | |
| Egerton, W. T. | D | | | | D | | | | D | D | | |
| Estcourt, J. B. B. (el 1848) | | | P | P | P | | D | D | P | D | P | P |

| | 1847–8 | | | | | 1849 | | | | | | |
|---|---|---|---|---|---|---|---|---|---|---|---|---|
| | 1 | 2 | 3 | 4 | 5 | 1 | 2 | 3 | 4 | 5 | 6 | 7 |
| Fitzroy, H. | P | P | P | P | D | | | | P | P | | P |
| Gladstone, W. E. | P | P | P | P | D | P | P | | P | P | D | P |
| Godson, R. (d 1849) | P | D | | | D | D | | | D | D | D | |
| Goulburn, H. | P | D | P | | D | P | P | D | P | D | P | P |
| Graham, Sir J. | | P | P | P | P | P | P | P | P | P | P | P |
| Greene, T. | P | D | P | P | D | | | P | P | D | | P |
| Haggit, F. R., see | | | | | | | | | | | | |
| Prosser, F. R. Wegg | | | | | | | | | | | | |
| Hamilton, Ld C. | | | P | P | D | | | D | D | | | P |
| Hanmer, Sir J. | | | P | P | | | | P | | | | |
| Harcourt, G. G. V. | | | | | P | P | P | | P | P | P | |
| Heald, J. | D | D | P | P | | P | P | | P | D | P | |
| Heneage, G. H. W. | | D | P | P | P | | D | | P | D | | |
| Herbert, H. | P | P | | P | | P | D | D | D | P | D | D |
| Herbert, S. | | | | P | D | P | P | | P | | D | |
| Hervey, Ld A. | | D | P | P | D | P | P | D | P | D | D | P |
| Hogg, Sir J. | | | P | P | | P | P | P | (P) | P | P | P |
| Hope, H. T. | | | D | P | D | P | P | | D | | | |
| Hornby, J. | P | D | D | | D | D | | | D | D | D | D |
| Hughes, W. B. | | | P | | P | | | | D | | P | P |
| Jermyn, Ld | P | P | P | | | P | P | | P | P | | P |
| Jocelyn, Ltd | | | | | D | | | D | D | | | |
| Johnstone, Sir J. | | | P | D | D | P | | P | D | P | P | P |
| Keogh, W. | P | P | P | P | D | | | | D | | P | |
| Kerr, R. | | P | P | P | | | D | D | | P | D | |
| Legh, G. C. (el 1848) | | | | | D | P | | | D | D | P | P |
| Lewis, Sir T. F. | P | P | P | P | P | | | P | P | | P | |
| Lincoln, Ld (to 1850) | P | P | P | P | D | P | P | D | P | P | | P |
| Lindsay, Col J. | P | D | P | P | D | P | | | | D | P | P |
| Lockhart, A. E. | P | D | P | P | D | | | | P | D | P | |
| Mackinnon, W. A. | | | P | | P | P | P | | | | | |
| McNeill, D. (to 1851) | | | | | | | | | | | | |
| Mahon, Ld | P | D | P | | D | P | P | D | | D | D | P |
| Martin, C. W. | | D | P | P | P | P | P | | (P) | | P | P |
| Masterman, J. | D | D | P | D | D | P | | | D | D | | |
| Mostyn, E. M. | | P | P | P | P | P | P | P | (P) | P | P | P |
| Mure, W. | | P | P | D | D | | | P | D | | | |
| Newry & Morne, Ld (d 1851) | D | P | | | | P | | | (D) | | | |
| Norreys, Ltd | | P | P | P | | P | P | P | P | P | P | P |
| Northland, Ld (to 1851) | | | | | | | | | | | | |

| | 1847–8 | | | | | 1849 | | | | | | |
|---|---|---|---|---|---|---|---|---|---|---|---|---|
| | *1* | *2* | *3* | *4* | *5* | *1* | *2* | *3* | *4* | *5* | *6* | *7* |
| Oswald, A. | P | P | P | D | | | | | | P | P | P |
| Owen, Sir J. | P | P | | | P | P | | P | P | P | | P |
| | | | | | | | | | | | | |
| Palmer, Roundell | P | P | D | P | | P | P | | D | | D | P |
| Patten, J. W. | D | P | P | | | | | P | | | D | P |
| Peel, F. (el 1849) | | | | | | | P | P | P | P | P | P |
| Peel, Col J. | P | D | P | | D | | | (P)D | | | | P |
| Peel, Sir R. (d 1850) | P | P | P | P | P | | P | P | P | P | P | P |
| Peel, Sir R. (el 1850) | | | | | | | D | | | | | |
| Pennant, E. G. D. | | D | P | | D | | D | | | | | |
| Powlett, Ld W. | | P | P | D | D | | | | | | | |
| Prosser, F. R. Wegg* | | | P | P | D | | D | D | | D | | |
| Pugh, D. | | | | P | P | P | D | | | | | P |
| Pusey, P. | | | P | P | P | | P | P | P | P | P | P |
| | | | | | | | | | | | | |
| Reid, G. A. | P | D | D | D | D | P | P | P | D | D | P | P |
| Robinson, G. R. (d 1850) | D | P | D | D | D | D | D | | D | | | |
| | | | | | | | | | | | | |
| Sandars, G. | P | | P | D | | | | D | P | P | | P |
| Sandars, J. (el 1848) | | | | D | D | | P | | D | D | | P |
| Seaham, Ld | | | D | D | | P | | D | | | | |
| Seymour, Sir H. B. (d 1851) | | | | | P | | | | | | P | P |
| Sidney, T. A. | P | P | D | | D | D | | D | D | | | |
| Smollett, A. | D | | P | D | D | | | P | (D)D | | | |
| Smythe, G. A. | P | | P | D | | P | | | | | P | |
| Somerset, Ld G. (d 1848) | P | | | | | | | | | | | |
| Somerton, Ld | D | D | | D | | | | | | | D | D |
| Stuart, H. | D | D | P | D | D | P | D | | D | D | D | P |
| Sutton, J. H. M. | P | | P | D | | P | D | D | P | P | P | |
| | | | | | | | | | | | | |
| Thesiger, Sir F. | P | | P | P | D | P | D | | D | | | P |
| Tollemache, F. J. | P | P | P | | D | | | | P | P | P | P |
| Turner, E. (d 1849) | P | P | P | P | P | | | | | | | |
| Turner, G. J. (to 1851) | | D | D | P | D | P | P | P | (P)D | D | | |
| | | | | | | | | | | | | |
| Urquhart, D. | D | | | | D | D | | D | | | | |
| | | | | | | | | | | | | |
| Villiers, Ld | | | P | P | D | | | | (P)D | | P | |
| | | | | | | | | | | | | |
| Wall, C. B. | P | P | P | P | P | P | P | P | P | P | P | P |
| Walter, J. | | P | D | P | D | P | P | P | | P | | |
| Wellesley, Ld C. | | | D | P | P | | P | | D | | | P |
| West, F. R. | | | | P | | D | P | | | | | |
| Whitmore, T. C. H. | | D | | P | | | | | P | D | D | |
| Willoughby, Sir H. | D | D | | | | | D | D | D | D | D | D |
| Wortley, J. A. S. | P | | | P | D | P | D | | | | P | P |

|  | 1847–8 | | | | | 1849 | | | | | | |
|---|---|---|---|---|---|---|---|---|---|---|---|---|
|  | 1 | 2 | 3 | 4 | 5 | 1 | 2 | 3 | 4 | 5 | 6 | 7 |
| Wynn, C. W. (d 1850) | | | | | | | | | | | | |
| Young, Sir J. | P | | P | P | | P | P | D | P | | P | P |
| Total Peelite votes (P) | 33 | 29 | 74 | 53 | 26 | 34 | 37 | 28 | 45 | 26 | 41 | 52 |
| Total Derbyite votes (D) | 9 | 41 | 8 | 18 | 66 | 7 | 19 | 25 | 34 | 38 | 25 | 8 |

* F. R. Haggit prior to 1850.

DIVISIONS

| | 1850 | | | | | | | | | 1851–2 | | | | | | |
|---|---|---|---|---|---|---|---|---|---|---|---|---|---|---|---|---|
| | 1 | 2 | 3 | 4 | 5 | 6 | 7 | 8 | 9* | 1 | 2 | 3 | 4 | 5 | 6 | 7 |
| Acland, Sir T. D. | P | D | P | P | | P | D | P | Y | D | D | | D | D | | D |
| Ashley, Ld (to 1851) | | | P | P | | | | D | Y | | D | P | P | | | |
| Baillie, H. J. | D | D | D | D | | | D | | N | D | D | D | D | D | D | |
| Baldwin, C. B. | D | | D | D | D | | D | D | N | D | D | D | D | D | | |
| Baring, F. (el 1848) | D | | | | D | | | | | | | | | | D | |
| Baring, H. B. | | | | P | | | | | N | P | D | | | P | | P |
| Baring, W. B. (to 1848) | | | | | | | | | | | | | | | | |
| Barkly, H. (to 1849) | | | | | | | | | | | | | | | | |
| Beckett, W. | P | D | | | P | | | | N | | D | P | P | | P | |
| Benbow, J. | | | | | | D | D | | | | | | D | | | D |
| Blandford, Marq of | D | D | P | | D | D | D | | | D | D | | D | D | | |
| Bolling, W. (d 1848) | | | | | | | | | | | | | | | | |
| Bowles, Adm W. | | P | P | P | | | D | | Y | P | D | P | P | P | | D |
| Boyd, J. | | | | P | | P | D | | | P | | | | | P | |
| Brackley, Ld (to 1851) | | | | | | | | | | | | | | | | |
| Bruce, Ld E. | | | | | | | | | N | P | | | | | | |
| Cardwell, E. | P | P | P | P | P | P | D | P | N | P | P | P | P | P | P | P |
| Charteris, F. W. | P | D | D | | | P | P | | | | P | P | P | P | | P |
| Chichester, Ld J. | | D | P | D | D | | D | D | N | D | D | D | D | D | | |
| Christy, S. | | D | P | D | D | | D | | N | D | D | P | | | P | |
| Clerk, Sir G. | P | P | P | P | | P | | P | N | P | D | P | P | P | P | P |
| Clive, R. H. | | D | | | | | D | | Y | D | D | D | D | | | D |
| Cochrane, A. D. R. W. B. | | | | | | | | | N | D | D | D | D | D | | D |
| Cocks, T. S. | P | D | D | P | D | P | D | | N | D | D | D | D | D | | D |
| Copeland, W. T. | P | P | | D | | | | | N | P | D | | P | D | | |
| Corry, H. T. L. | | D | P | P | D | P | D | | N | D | D | P | D | | | P |
| Cripps, W. (d 1848) | | | | | | | | | | | | | | | | |
| Cubitt, W. | P | D | | | | | P | D | Y | D | D | P | D | D | | |
| Currie, H. | P | D | P | D | | | | | | D | P | | D | | | P |
| Damer, G. L. | | | D | P | D | P | D | P | N | D | D | D | D | D | | |
| Denison, E. B. (el 1848) | P | | | | | | | | | | D | P | P | P | | P |
| Douglas, Sir C. | P | P | P | P | P | P | P | P | | P | D | P | P | P | P | P |
| Douro, Marq of | P | P | | P | | P | | | N | P | D | P | P | | | |
| Drumlanrig, Ld | P | D | | P | P | | D | | Y | D | D | | | | | |
| Drummond, H. | D | D | | D | | D | D | | Y | D | D | | | | | P |
| Drummond, H. H. | | P | | | D | P | D | | N | | | | | | | |
| Duncuft, J. | P | P | P | D | D | P | | D | N | P | D | P | P | | P | |
| Dundas, G. | | | D | | D | D | D | | | D | D | D | D | D | D | |
| Edwards, H. | | | P | D | D | | D | D | N | D | D | D | D | D | | D |
| Egerton, W. T. | | D | | P | D | | | D | N | D | D | D | D | D | | P |
| Estcourt, J. B. B. (el 1848) | P | D | D | P | D | P | P | | N | P | D | P | P | | P | P |

| | 1850 | | | | | | | | | 1851–2 | | | | | | |
|---|---|---|---|---|---|---|---|---|---|---|---|---|---|---|---|---|
| | 1 | 2 | 3 | 4 | 5 | 6 | 7 | 8 | 9 | 1 | 2 | 3 | 4 | 5 | 6 | 7 |
| Fitzroy, H. | P | P | D | | P | | | | N | P | D | P | P | P | P | P |
| Gladstone, W. E. | P | D | D | | D | P | D | | N | | P | P | P | | D | P |
| Godson, R. (d 1849) | | | | | | | | | | | | | | | | |
| Goulburn, H. | P | P | | | P | D | | | N | P | D | P | P | | | P |
| Graham, Sir J. | P | P | | | P | P | P | P | N | P | P | P | P | | P | P |
| Greene, T. | | | P | | P | P | P | D | | | D | P | P | P | | P |
| Haggit, *see* Prosser, F. R. Wegg | | | | | | | | | | | | | | | | |
| Hamilton, Ld C. | D | D | | D | D | | D | D | N | D | D | D | D | | D | D |
| Hanmer, Sir J. | P | P | P | P | | | | P | Y | P | D | P | P | | P | P |
| Harcourt, G. G. V. | D | D | P | P | | D | | | Y | | D | P | D | D | | P |
| Heald, J. | P | | P | | | P | D | D | N | P | D | P | P | P | | |
| Heneage, G. H. W. | P | D | D | P | | P | P | P | N | D | D | P | D | | P | D |
| Herbert, H. | D | D | D | D | | D | D | | N | | P | D | | D | D | |
| Herbert, S. | P | | P | P | | P | D | P | N | P | P | P | P | P | D | P |
| Hervey, Ld A. | P | P | D | P | | | | D | N | P | D | P | P | D | P | P |
| Hogg, Sir J. | P | P | P | P | P | P | P | | N | P | | P | P | P | P | P |
| Hope, H. T. | | P | | D | | | D | | N | D | D | D | | | | |
| Hornby, J. | D | D | D | D | | D | D | | N | D | D | D | D | | D | |
| Hughes, W. B. | | | | P | P | P | | D | N | D | | | D | | | |
| Jermyn, Ld | P | P | P | P | | | | | | P | D | P | P | P | | P |
| Jocelyn, Ld | | D | D | | D | P | | | Y | D | D | D | D | | | |
| Johnstone, Sir J. | P | D | P | | | P | D | P | N | D | D | P | | P | | P |
| Keogh, W. | | P | | P | P | P | P | | Y | D | P | D | D | | | P |
| Kerr, R. | | D | D | | | P | | D | Y | | D | P | | | | |
| Legh, G. C. (el 1848) | P | D | | D | | P | | | N | D | D | P | | D | P | P |
| Lewis, Sir T. F. | P | P | P | P | | P | P | P | | P | D | P | | P | | |
| Lincoln, Ld (to 1850) | | | | | | | | | | | | | | | | |
| Lindsay, Col J. | P | D | P | P | D | P | D | D | N | | P | D | D | D | P | |
| Lockhart, A. E. | P | | | | | | D | | N | P | P | P | P | D | | |
| Mackinnon, W. A. | P | P | P | | | | | D | Y | P | D | P | P | P | P | |
| McNeill, D. (to 1851) | | | | | | | | | | | | | | | | |
| Mahon, Ld | P | D | P | | P | D | P | | N | | | P | | | | |
| Martin, C. W. | P | P | P | P | | P | P | | Y | P | D | P | P | P | P | P |
| Masterman, J. | P | P | D | P | | P | D | D | N | P | D | P | P | P | P | D |
| Mostyn, E. M. | P | P | P | P | P | P | P | P | Y | P | D | P | P | | P | |
| Mure, W. | P | D | | | | P | D | | N | D | P | P | | | | |
| Newry & Morne, Ld (d 1851) | | D | | | D | | | D | N | | | | | | | |
| Norreys, Ld | P | P | P | P | P | P | P | P | Y | P | P | P | P | P | | P |

| | 1850 | | | | | | | | | 1851–2 | | | | | | |
|---|---|---|---|---|---|---|---|---|---|---|---|---|---|---|---|---|
| | 1 | 2 | 3 | 4 | 5 | 6 | 7 | 8 | 9 | 1 | 2 | 3 | 4 | 5 | 6 | 7 |
| Northland, Ld (to 1851) | | | | | | | | | | | | | | | | |
| Oswald, A. | P | | | D | | D | | | N | D | | P | P | P | | |
| Owen, Sir J. | P | | P | P | | | P | | Y | P | D | P | P | P | P | |
| Palmer, Roundell | P | | P | P | | P | P | | N | P | P | P | P | P | P | |
| Patten, J. W. | | D | | P | | P | | P | N | | D | P | D | D | | P |
| Peel, F. (el 1849) | P | P | P | P | P | P | P | P | N | P | P | P | P | P | P | P |
| Peel, Col J. | P | | | | | | D | | N | D | D | | D | | | D |
| Peel, Sir R. (d 1850) | P | P | P | P | P | P | P | P | N | | | | | | | |
| Peel, Sir R. (el 1850) | | | | | | | | | | P | D | | D | P | | |
| Pennant, E. G. D. | | D | | | D | | D | | N | | D | | | | | P |
| Powlett, Ld W. | D | | | | D | | D | | | D | D | | | P | D | |
| Prosser, F. R. Wegg | | D | D | | D | P | D | | N | D | P | P | | P | P | P |
| Pugh, D. | P | P | | D | | | D | P | Y | D | D | D | D | D | | |
| Pusey, P. | D | D | P | P | P | D | P | P | Y | D | | | | P | P | P |
| Reid, G. A. | P | D | P | P | | P | D | | N | D | D | D | D | D | P | |
| Robinson, G. R. (d 1850) | | | | | | | | | | | | | | | | |
| Sandars, G. | P | D | D | D | | | D | | N | D | D | P | D | D | | D |
| Sandars, J. (el 1848) | P | P | D | P | | | D | P | N | P | D | | P | | P | |
| Seaham, Ld | | | | | | | | | N | D | D | | | | D | |
| Seymour, Sir H. B. (d 1851) | | | | | | | | | | | | | | | | |
| Sidney, T. A. | | D | | D | | | D | | Y | D | D | D | D | D | | D |
| Smollett, A. | | P | D | | D | P | D | D | N | D | | | | | P | |
| Smythe, G. A. | P | P | | P | P | | D | | N | P | | | P | | D | P |
| Somerset, Ld G. (d 1848) | | | | | | | | | | | | | | | | |
| Somerton, Ld | D | | | | | | D | | | | | | | | | |
| Stuart, H. | P | D | D | | D | | D | D | N | D | P | P | D | D | | D |
| Sutton, J. H. M. | | | | | | P | P | P | | | D | P | P | D | P | |
| Thesiger, Sir F. | P | D | D | P | D | | D | | N | D | D | D | D | D | D | D |
| Tollemache, F. J. | | P | | P | P | P | P | | Y | | P | P | P | P | P | P |
| Turner, E. (d 1849) | | | | | | | | | | | | | | | | |
| Turner, G. J. (to 1851) | P | D | P | | D | P | P | D | N | D | D | | | | | |
| Urquhart, D. | | | | | | | | | | | | | | | | |
| Villiers, Ld | P | D | | | | | D | | N | | D | P | D | | P | D |
| Wall, C. B. | P | P | P | | P | | P | | Y | P | P | P | P | P | | |
| Walter, J. | P | | D | P | | P | | | N | P | D | P | P | D | | P |
| Wellesley, Ld C. | P | | P | P | | P | P | P | N | P | D | P | P | P | P | |
| West, F. R. | D | D | | | | | D | | | D | D | | D | | | |

| | 1850 | | | | | | | | | 1851–2 | | | | | | |
|---|---|---|---|---|---|---|---|---|---|---|---|---|---|---|---|---|
| | 1 | 2 | 3 | 4 | 5 | 6 | 7 | 8 | 9 | 1 | 2 | 3 | 4 | 5 | 6 | 7 |
| Whitmore, T. C. H. | | | | | | | | | N | | | | | D | D | |
| Willoughby, Sir H. | D | D | | D | D | | D | | N | D | D | D | D | D | | |
| Wortley, J. A. S. | P | P | D | P | D | P | | | N | P | D | P | P | P | | |
| Wynn, C. W. (d 1850) | | | | | | | | | | | | | | | | |
| Young, Sir J. | P | D | | | P | P | P | | N | P | P | P | P | | D | |
| Total Peelites (P) | 58 | 33 | 35 | 45 | 18 | 50 | 23 | 22 | | 37 | 20 | 55 | 42 | 31 | 32 | 34 |
| Total Derbyites (D) | 14 | 44 | 23 | 18 | 29 | 8 | 51 | 20 | | 43 | 71 | 22 | 37 | 31 | 12 | 16 |

\* See note p 221

| | 1846† Repeal | Total 1847–50 P | 1847–50 D | Total 1851–52 P | 1851–52 D | Total 1847–52 P | 1847–52 D | Classification |
|---|---|---|---|---|---|---|---|---|
| Acland, Sir T. D. | D | 11 | 6 | – | 5 | 11 | 11 | Uncertain |
| Ashley, Ld | | 4 | 3 | 2 | 1 | 6 | 4 | Uncertain |
| Baillie, H. J. | (P) | – | 12 | – | 6 | – | 18 | Derbyite |
| Baldwin, C. B. | (P) | – | 9 | – | 5 | – | 14 | Derbyite |
| Baring, F. | | 2 | 3 | – | 1 | 2 | 4 | Uncertain |
| *Baring, H. B. (Marlborough) | P | 5 | – | 3 | 1 | 8 | 1 | Peelite |
| *Baring, W. B. (Thetford) | P | 1 | – | – | – | 1 | – | Peelite |
| Barkly, H. (to 1849) | P | 2 | 1 | – | – | 2 | 1 | Uncertain |
| Beckett, W. | P | 3 | 2 | 3 | 1 | 6 | 3 | Uncertain |
| Benbow, J. | P | – | 5 | – | 2 | – | 7 | Derbyite |
| Blandford, Marq of | | 1 | 9 | – | 4 | 1 | 13 | Derbyite |
| Bolling, W. | | 3 | 1 | – | – | 3 | 1 | Uncertain |
| Bowles, Adm W. | P | 7 | 6 | 4 | 2 | 11 | 8 | Uncertain |
| Boyd, J. (Coleraine) | P | 6 | 1 | 2 | – | 8 | 1 | Peelite |
| Brackley, Ld | | 2 | 4 | – | – | 2 | 4 | Uncertain |
| *Bruce, Ld E. | P | 4 | 2 | 1 | – | 5 | 2 | Uncertain |
| *Cardwell, E. (Liverpool) | P | 16 | 2 | 7 | – | 23 | 2 | Peelite |
| Charteris, F. W. (Haddingtonsh) | | 11 | 3 | 5 | – | 16 | 3 | Peelite |
| Chichester, Ld J. | P | 2 | 14 | – | 5 | 2 | 19 | Derbyite |
| Christy, S. | | 2 | 9 | 2 | 2 | 4 | 11 | Derbyite |
| *Clerk, Sir G. (Dover) | P | 16 | 1 | 5 | 1 | 21 | 2 | Peelite |
| Clive, R. H. | P | 1 | 6 | – | 5 | 1 | 11 | Derbyite |
| Cochrane, A. D. R. W. B. | (P) | 3 | 3 | – | 6 | 3 | 9 | Derbyite |
| Cocks, T. S. | | 6 | 10 | – | 6 | 6 | 16 | Derbyite |
| Copeland, W. T. | P | 4 | 2 | 2 | 2 | 6 | 4 | Uncertain |
| Corry, H. T. L. | P | 8 | 5 | 2 | 3 | 10 | 8 | Uncertain |
| Cripps, W. | P | 1 | 1 | – | – | 1 | 1 | Uncertain |
| Cubitt, W. | | 6 | 5 | 1 | 4 | 7 | 9 | Uncertain |
| Currie, H. | | 4 | 4 | 2 | 2 | 6 | 6 | Uncertain |
| Damer, G. L. | P | 5 | 6 | – | 5 | 5 | 11 | Derbyite |
| Denison, E. B. (Yorksh WR) | | 3 | – | 4 | 1 | 7 | 1 | Peelite |
| Douglas, Sir C. (Warwick) | P | 15 | – | 6 | 1 | 21 | 1 | Peelite |
| Douro, Marq of (Warwick) | P | 8 | 1 | 3 | 1 | 11 | 2 | Peelite |
| Drumlanrig, Ld | | 6 | 4 | – | 2 | 6 | 6 | Uncertain |
| Drummond, H. | | 4 | 8 | 1 | 2 | 5 | 10 | Derbyite |
| Drummond, H. H. | P | 5 | 3 | – | – | 5 | 3 | Uncertain |
| Duncuft, J. (Oldham) | | 9 | 5 | 4 | 1 | 13 | 6 | Peelite |
| Dundas, G. | | 2 | 11 | – | 6 | 2 | 17 | Derbyite |
| Edwards, H. | | 1 | 11 | – | 6 | 1 | 17 | Derbyite |
| Egerton, W. T. | P | 1 | 7 | 1 | 5 | 2 | 12 | Derbyite |
| Estcourt, J. B. B. (Devizes) | | 10 | 6 | 5 | 1 | 15 | 7 | Peelite |
| *Fitzroy, H. (Lewes) | P | 10 | 2 | 6 | 1 | 16 | 3 | Peelite |

\* Held office or household appointment (Bruce) under Peel.

† Not included in the totals; brackets indicate other than the third reading.

Names of members who identified themselves as Peelite in the 1847 Parliament are italicised, and their constituencies indicated in brackets.

| | 1846† | Total 1847–50 | | Total 1851–52 | | Total 1847–52 | | Classification |
|---|---|---|---|---|---|---|---|---|
| | Repeal | P | D | P | D | P | D | |
| *Gladstone, W. E. (Oxford U) | | 11 | 6 | 4 | 1 | 15 | 7 | Peelite |
| Godson, R. | P | 1 | 6 | – | – | 1 | 6 | Derbyite |
| *Goulburn, H. (Cambridge U) | P | 10 | 5 | 4 | 1 | 14 | 6 | Peelite |
| *Graham, Sir J. (Ripon) | P | 17 | – | 6 | – | 23 | – | Peelite |
| Greene, T. (Lancaster) | P | 10 | 4 | 4 | 1 | 14 | 5 | Peelite |
| Hamilton, Ld C. | P | 3 | 9 | – | 6 | 3 | 15 | Derbyite |
| Hanmer, Sir J. (Flint d) | P | 8 | – | 5 | 1 | 13 | 1 | Peelite |
| Harcourt, G. G. V. (Oxfordsh) | D | 8 | 3 | 2 | 3 | 10 | 6 | Peelite |
| Heald, J. (Stockport) | | 10 | 5 | 4 | 1 | 14 | 6 | Peelite |
| Heneage, G. H. W. | D | 9 | 5 | 2 | 4 | 11 | 9 | Uncertain |
| Herbert, H. | | 3 | 12 | 1 | 3 | 4 | 15 | Derbyite |
| *Herbert, S. (Wilts S) | P | 9 | 3 | 6 | 1 | 15 | 4 | Peelite |
| Hervey, Ld A. (Brighton) | P | 9 | 7 | 5 | 2 | 14 | 9 | Peelite |
| Hogg, Sir J. (Honiton) | P | 16 | | 6 | – | 22 | – | Peelite |
| Hope, H. T. | P | 4 | 5 | – | 3 | 4 | 8 | Derbyite |
| Hornby, J. | (P) | 1 | 14 | – | 5 | 1 | 19 | Derbyite |
| Hughes, W. B. | P | 7 | 2 | – | 2 | 7 | 4 | Uncertain |
| Jermyn, Ld (Bury St Edmunds) | P | 12 | – | 5 | 1 | 17 | 1 | Peelite |
| *Jocelyn, Ld | P | 1 | 6 | – | 4 | 1 | 10 | Derbyite |
| Johnstone, Sir J. (Scarborough) | P | 10 | 5 | 3 | 2 | 13 | 7 | Peelite |
| Keogh, W. (Athlone) | | 10 | 2 | 2 | 3 | 12 | 5 | Peelite |
| Kerr, R. | | 5 | 6 | 1 | 1 | 6 | 7 | Uncertain |
| Legh, G. C. | P | 5 | 5 | 3 | 3 | 8 | 8 | Uncertain |
| Lewis, Sir T. F. (Radnor d) | | 15 | – | 3 | 1 | 18 | 1 | Peelite |
| *Lincoln, Ld (Falkirk) | P | 9 | 2 | – | – | 9 | 2 | Peelite |
| Lindsay, Col J. | P | 10 | 7 | 2 | 3 | 12 | 10 | Uncertain |
| Lockhart, A. E. (Selkirksh) | P | 6 | 4 | 4 | 1 | 10 | 5 | Peelite |
| Mackinnon, W. A. (Lymington) | P | 7 | 1 | 5 | 1 | 12 | 2 | Peelite |
| *McNeill, D. | P | – | – | – | – | – | – | Uncertain |
| Mahon, Ld | P | 9 | 7 | 1 | – | 10 | 7 | Uncertain |
| Martin, C. W. (Newport) | P | 14 | 1 | 6 | 1 | 20 | 2 | Peelite |
| Masterman, J. | P | 6 | 9 | 5 | 2 | 11 | 11 | Uncertain |
| Mostyn, E. M. (Flintsh) | P | 19 | – | 4 | 1 | 23 | 1 | Peelite |
| Mure, W. | | 4 | 5 | 2 | 1 | 6 | 6 | Uncertain |
| Newry & Morne, Ld | P | 2 | 5 | – | – | 2 | 5 | Uncertain |
| Norreys, Ld (Oxfordsh) | D | 18 | – | 6 | – | 24 | – | Peelite |
| Northland, Ld | P | – | – | – | – | – | – | Uncertain |
| Oswald, A. (Ayresh) | (P) | 7 | 3 | 3 | 1 | 10 | 4 | Peelite |
| Owen, Sir J. (Pembroke) | P | 12 | – | 5 | 1 | 17 | 1 | Peelite |

\* Held office under Peel.
† Not included in the totals; brackets indicate other than third reading.
Names of members who identified themselves as Peelite in the 1847 Parliament are italicised, and their constituencies indicated in brackets.

| | 1846† Repeal | Total 1847–50 P | D | Total 1851–52 P | D | Total 1847–52 P | D | Classification |
|---|---|---|---|---|---|---|---|---|
| Palmer, Roundell (Plymouth) | | 11 | 3 | 6 | – | 17 | 3 | Peelite |
| Patten, J. W. | P | 7 | 3 | 2 | 3 | 9 | 6 | Uncertain |
| Peel, F. (Leominster) | | 14 | – | 7 | – | 21 | – | Peelite |
| Peel, Col J. | P | 5 | 4 | – | 4 | 5 | 8 | Uncertain |
| *Peel, Sir R. (Tamworth) | P | 19 | – | – | – | 19 | – | Peelite |
| Peel, Sir R. | | – | – | 2 | 2 | 2 | 2 | Uncertain |
| Pennant, E. G. D. | P | 1 | 6 | 1 | 1 | 2 | 7 | Derbyite |
| Powlett, Ld W. | | 2 | 5 | 1 | 3 | 3 | 8 | Derbyite |
| Prosser, F. R. Wegg | | 3 | 8 | 5 | 1 | 8 | 9 | Uncertain |
| Pugh, D. | | 6 | 3 | – | 5 | 6 | 8 | Uncertain |
| Pusey, P. (Berkshire) | (D) | 14 | 2 | 3 | 1 | 17 | 3 | Peelite |
| | | | | | | | | |
| Reid, G. A. | P | 10 | 8 | 1 | 5 | 11 | 13 | Uncertain |
| Robinson, G. R. | | 1 | 7 | – | – | 1 | 7 | Derbyite |
| | | | | | | | | |
| Sandars, G. | | 6 | 6 | 1 | 5 | 7 | 11 | Uncertain |
| Sandars, J. | | 6 | 4 | 3 | 1 | 9 | 5 | Uncertain |
| Seaham, Ld | | 1 | 3 | – | 3 | 1 | 6 | Derbyite |
| Seymour, Sir H. B. | P | 3 | – | – | – | 3 | – | Uncertain |
| Sidney, T. A. | | 2 | 8 | – | 6 | 2 | 14 | Derbyite |
| Smollett, A. | P | 4 | 9 | 1 | 1 | 5 | 10 | Derbyite |
| *Smythe, G. A. (Canterbury) | P | 8 | 2 | 3 | 1 | 11 | 3 | Peelite |
| *Somerset, Ld G. (Monmouthsh) | P | 1 | – | – | – | 1 | – | Peelite |
| Somerton, Ld | P | – | 7 | – | – | – | 7 | Derbyite |
| Stuart, H. | P | 4 | 13 | 2 | 4 | 6 | 17 | Derbyite |
| *Sutton, J. H. M. (Newark) | P | 9 | 3 | 3 | 2 | 12 | 5 | Peelite |
| | | | | | | | | |
| *Thesiger, Sir F. | P | 7 | 6 | – | 7 | 7 | 13 | Derbyite |
| Tollemache, F. J. (Grantham) | P | 13 | – | 6 | – | 19 | – | Peelite |
| Turner, E. (Truro) | | 5 | – | – | – | 5 | – | Peelite |
| Turner, G. J. | | 9 | 8 | – | 2 | 9 | 10 | Uncertain |
| | | | | | | | | |
| Urquhart, D. | | – | 4 | – | – | – | 4 | Derbyite |
| | | | | | | | | |
| Villiers, Ld | P | 5 | 4 | 2 | 3 | 7 | 7 | Uncertain |
| | | | | | | | | |
| Wall, C. B. (Salisbury) | P | 17 | – | 5 | – | 22 | – | Peelite |
| Walter, J. (Nottingham) | | 9 | 3 | 4 | 2 | 13 | 5 | Peelite |
| *Wellesley, Ld C. (Hampsh S) | P | 10 | 2 | 5 | 1 | 15 | 3 | Peelite |
| West, F. R. | | 2 | 4 | – | 3 | 2 | 7 | Derbyite |
| Whitmore, T. C. H. | (P) | 2 | 3 | – | 2 | 2 | 5 | Uncertain |
| Willoughby, Sir H. | | – | 13 | – | 5 | – | 18 | Derbyite |
| *Wortley, J. A. S. (Buteshire) | (P) | 9 | 4 | 4 | 1 | 13 | 5 | Peelite |
| Wynn, C. W. | P | – | – | – | – | – | – | Uncertain |
| | | | | | | | | |
| *Young, Sir J. (Cavan) | P | 12 | 2 | 4 | 1 | 16 | 3 | Peelite |
| | | | | | | | | |
| Total Peelite | 74 | | | | | | | 48 |
| Total Derbyite | 5 | | | | | | | 32 |

* Held office or household appointment (Wellesley) under Peel.
† Not included in the totals; brackets indicate other than third reading.
Names of members who identified themselves as Peelite in the 1847 Parliament are italicised, and their constituencies indicated in brackets.

# Appendix B
## Free Trade Conservatives elected to the parliament of 1852

THIS APPENDIX indicates the course taken in the parliament of
1852 (following my *Aberdeen Coalition 1852–1855*) by all the
Liberal Conservatives mentioned in the present book. The names
of those whom I finally identify as Peelites are italicised, although
I have to make a reservation about Sir J. Owen since he supported
the Disraeli Budget.

| | Disraeli Budget | Aberdeen Coalition | Classification |
|---|---|---|---|
| Peelites in the previous parliament | | | |
| *Baring, H. B.* | Opposed | Supported | Peelite |
| *Cardwell, E. | — | ,, | ,, |
| *Charteris, F. W.* | Opposed | ,, | ,, |
| *Denison, E. B.* | ,, | ,, | ,, |
| Duncuft, J. (d July 1852) | | | |
| *Fitzroy, H.* | ,, | ,, | ,, |
| *Gladstone, W. E.* | ,, | ,, | ,, |
| *Goulburn, H.* | ,, | ,, | ,, |
| *Graham, Sir J.* | ,, | ,, | ,, |
| *Greene, T. | — | ,, | ,, |
| *Hanmer, Sir J.* | Opposed | ,, | ,, |
| *Harcourt, G. V. V.* | ,, | ,, | ,, |
| *Herbert, S.* | ,, | ,, | ,, |
| *Hervey, Lord A.* | ,, | ,, | ,, |
| *Hogg, Sir J.* | ,, | ,, | ,, |
| *Jermyn, Lord* | ,, | ,, | ,, |
| *Johnstone, Sir J.* | ,, | ,, | ,, |
| Keogh, W. | | | Irish Independent |
| *Lewis, Sir T. F.* | Opposed | Supported | Peelite |
| *Lockhart, A. E.* | ,, | ,, | ,, |
| *Mostyn, E. M.* | ,, | ,, | ,, |
| *Norreys, Lord | ,, | ,, | ,, |
| Owen, Sir J. | Supported | ,, | ,, |
| *Palmer, Roundell | — | ,, | ,, |

Q

233

| | *Disraeli* *Budget* | *Aberdeen* *Coalition* | *Classification* |
|---|---|---|---|
| Peelites in the previous parliament | | | |
| Peel, F. | Opposed | Supported | Peelite |
| *Sutton, J. H. M.* | ,, | ,, | ,, |
| *Wall, C. B.* | ,, | ,, | ,, |
| *Walter, J.* | ,, | ,, | ,, |
| Wellesley, Lord C. | Supported | Some support | Independent Conservative |
| *Wortley, J. S.* | Opposed | Supported | Peelite |
| *Young, Sir J.* | ,, | ,, | ,, |
| | | | |
| Uncertain LCs in the previous parliament | | | |
| Acland, Sir T. D. | Supported | Some support | Independent Conservative |
| *Baring, F.* | — | Supported | Peelite |
| Beckett, W. | Supported | Some support | Independent Conservative |
| *Bruce, Lord E.* | Opposed | Supported | Peelite |
| Corry, H. L. | Supported | Opposed | Derbyite |
| Cubitt, W. | Supported | Some support | Independent Conservative |
| *Drumlanrig, Lord* | Opposed | Supported | Peelite |
| Heneage, G. H. W. | Supported | Some support | Independent Conservative |
| Hughes, W. B. | ,, | ,, ,, | ,, ,, |
| *Legh, G. C.* | Opposed | Supported | Peelite |
| Lindsay, Colonel | Supported | Some support | Independent Conservative |
| *Mure, Colonel W.* | Opposed | Supported | Peelite |
| Patten, J. W. | — | Some support | Independent Conservative |
| Peel, Colonel J. | Opposed | ,, ,, | ,, ,, |
| *Peel, Sir R.* | — | Supported | Peelite |
| Pugh, D. | Supported | Opposed | Derbyite |
| Sandars, G. | ,, | Some support | Independent Conservative |
| Smollett, A. | ,, | ,, ,, | ,, ,, |
| * Returned at by-elections. | | | |
| | | | |
| New LCs elected 1852† | | | |
| *A'Court, H. W.* | Opposed | Supported | Peelite |
| Baird, J. | Supported | Opposed | Derbyite |
| Benbow, J. | ,, | Some support | Independent Conservative |
| *Bruce, H. A.* | Opposed | Supported | Peelite |
| Christy, S. | Supported | Some support | Independent Conservative |
| *Clinton, Lord R.* | Opposed | Supported | Peelite |
| Colville, C. R. | — | Some support | Independent Conservative |
| Dering, Sir E. | Supported | ,, ,, | ,, ,, |
| Emlyn, Lord | — | ,, ,, | ,, ,, |
| Fitzgerald, W. R. S. | Supported | ,, ,, | ,, ,, |
| Hardinge, C. S. | ,, | ,, ,, | ,, ,, |
| Hayes, Sir E. S. | ,, | Opposed | Derbyite |
| *Heneage, G. F.* | Opposed | Supported | Peelite |
| Johnstone, James | ,, | Some support | Independent Conservative |
| *Lowe, R.* | ,, | Supported | Peelite |
| Masterman, J. | Supported | Some support | Independent Conservative |
| *Monck, Lord* | Opposed | Supported | Peelite |
| *Phillimore, R. J. | — | ,, | ,, |
| Stirling, W. | Supported | Some support | Independent Conservative |
| Tomline, G. | Opposed | ,, ,, | ,, ,, |

|  | Disraeli Budget | Aberdeen Coalition | Classification |
|---|---|---|---|
| Vernon, G. E. H. | Opposed | Supported | Peelite |
| Wickham, H. | ,, | ,, | ,, |
| Wyndham, W. | Supported | Some support | Independent Conservative |

Derbyites in previous parliament

|  | Disraeli Budget | Aberdeen Coalition | Classification |
|---|---|---|---|
| Cocks, T. S. | Supported | Some support | Independent Conservative |
| Egerton, W. T. | ,, | ,,    ,, | ,,    ,, |
| Herbert, H. A. | Opposed | Supported | Peelite |
| Pennant, E. G. D. | — | Some support | Independent Conservative |
| Stuart, H. | — | ,,    ,, | ,,    ,, |
| Vyvyan, Sir R. | Opposed | ,,    ,, | ,,    ,, |

Total Peelites    44
Total Independent Conservatives    28

\* Returned following petition.

† All these names, except H. A. Bruce and Sir R. Vyvyan, appear in the Gladstone election correspondence, as do the names of Sir R. Fergusson and R. M. Milnes, whom I have classified as Liberal, and R. H. Clive, Lord Jocelyn, R. M. Laffan and Sir H. Willoughby, who were clearly Derbyites from their record in the 1852 parliament.

# Acknowledgements

I WISH to thank the Macmillan Company of Canada and Messrs Macmillan, London and Basingstoke, for permission to quote from the *Greville Memoirs* (1938) edited by L. Strachey and R. Fulford; also the editor of the *English Historical Review* for permission to reprint parts of my own article, 'Peel and the Peelites', *EHR*, lxxiii (1958).

I should like to thank the owners or trustees of all the private collections of papers listed in the bibliography and the custodians of the various archives and libraries in which they are deposited for their kindness in making them available. I should also like to thank the Canada Council for a Research Fellowship that made it possible to complete this book and the Nuffield Foundation for other assistance. Finally I must thank the editor of this series, Mr Michael Hurst, the editorial staff of the publisher for their kind encouragement and assistance, and Mr Francis Nicholson for compiling the index.

J.B.C.

# Index

237